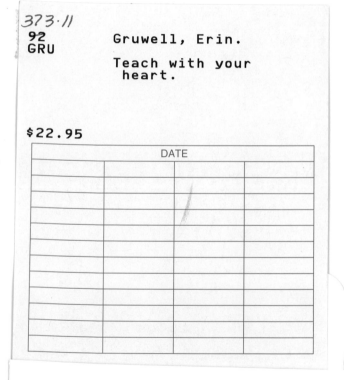

DATE			

TEACH WITH YOUR HEART

Also by Erin Gruwell

THE FREEDOM WRITERS DIARY:

*How a Teacher and 150 Teens Used Writing to
Change Themselves and the World Around Them*

TEACH WITH YOUR HEART

LESSONS I LEARNED FROM THE FREEDOM WRITERS

A Memoir

ERIN GRUWELL

BROADWAY BOOKS   *New York*

PUBLISHED BY BROADWAY BOOKS

Published in the United States by Broadway Books, an imprint
of The Doubleday Broadway Publishing Group, a division of
Random House, Inc., New York.
www.broadwaybooks.com

BROADWAY BOOKS and its logo, a letter B bisected on the diagonal,
are trademarks of Random House, Inc.

Book design by Tina Henderson

Library of Congress Cataloging-in-Publication Data
Gruwell, Erin.
Teach with your heart : lessons I learned from the Freedom
Writers / by Erin Gruwell.
p. cm.
1. High school teaching—California. 2. High school teachers—
California. 3. Teenagers—California. 4. Freedom Writers. I. Title.

LB1737.U6G78 2007
373.110209794—dc22

2006032435

978-0-7679-1583-0

PRINTED IN THE UNITED STATES OF AMERICA

10 9 8 7 6 5 4 3 2 1

First Edition

This book is dedicated to:
My greatest teacher
&
most challenging student,
My father, Steve Gruwell

Chapter 1

W hy do we have to read books by dead white guys in tights?" asked Sharaud, a foulmouthed sixteen-year-old, after he took one look at my syllabus.

Sharaud had entered my class at Woodrow Wilson High School in Long Beach, California, wearing a football jersey from Polytechnic High School. He must have known that donning *the* rival jersey was bound to get a rise out of the other students. He arrogantly strutted around my class, taunting the other players that he was going to take their places on the field, then leisurely strolled to the back of the classroom and took a seat.

As I started to discuss the curriculum, my students rocked in their seats and played percussion with their pencils. Some checked their pagers, while others reapplied their eyeliner. Some slouched, some laid their heads on the desks, and some actually took a nap. This was not the reception I was hoping for on my first day as a student teacher.

I dodged a paper airplane—made out of my syllabus, I quickly realized—and tried to make myself heard over a string of "yo mama" jokes.

I fidgeted with my pearls. I glanced at the polka-dot dress I was wearing—it was similar to the one that Julia Roberts wore in *Pretty Woman*—and wondered if I had chosen the wrong profession.

Why hadn't I gone to law school like I'd originally planned? In a courtroom, unlike this chaotic classroom, a judge would bang his gavel with gusto after the first projectile had flown across the room, and any innuendo about his mother's integrity would bring instant charges of contempt of court. I needed a daunting authority figure in a black robe to tell these kids that they were "out of order." I looked around the room, but an authority figure was nowhere to be found. Then came a panicked realization—I was the authority figure, armed only with a broken piece of chalk.

As a student teacher, I should have been able to rely on my supervising teacher, but he had stepped out of the classroom. When I met with him over the summer, he suggested that it would be a good idea for me to begin teaching on the first day of school, rather than easing my way into it. "If you dive right in," he said, "you'll establish your authority from the get-go." From the comfort of his living room, this suggestion sounded great. I had visions of passing out my syllabus and having students stick out their hands like Oliver Twist and ask for "more." In reality, the only person requesting "more" was my supervising teacher, who conveniently snuck out to get "more" coffee and never returned.

After nearly forty years of teaching, my supervising teacher planned to retire at the end of the school year. He had emotionally checked out and was now simply coasting on autopilot. I'd assumed student teachers were to be handled like timid student drivers, with someone ready to grab the wheel when changing lanes or parallel parking went awry. Since my so-called mentor wasn't there to put on the brakes or take control, I didn't know which direction to go except forward.

To gain my composure, I tried to sound authoritative while reading my supervising teacher's "Guidelines for Student Behavior." I heard some students snickering. I stopped reading to see what they were laughing about.

"You got chalk on your ass," yelled a student from the back.

"Daaamn, girl! Can I have some fries with that shake?" said another.

Somehow the "Guidelines" weren't sticking, because the class was completely out of control. Even though I had studied classroom management, it was obvious that my students were the ones managing me. I just wanted to make it to the end of the hour.

Right before the bell rang, one of my students, Melvin, leaned back in his seat and announced, "I give her five days!"

"You're on," said Manny.

"I'm gonna make this lady cry in front of the whole class," Sharaud bragged as he walked out the door.

At that moment, I could hear my father's smug "I told you so" echo in my mind. A little less foreboding than "Beware the Ides of March," but accurate nevertheless.

I felt like a failure. It was obvious that I didn't know what I was doing. I had no idea how to engage these apathetic teenagers who hated reading, hated writing, and apparently hated me. And to make matters worse, student teachers did not receive salaries—we actually paid for the privilege! I was holding down two part-time jobs after school and on weekends to help pay for my semester's tuition at the university. I worked at Nordstrom department store as a salesclerk in the lingerie department and at a Marriott Hotel as a concierge. Paying to teach in the trenches was like putting my face through a cutout hole at a carnival while a quarterback threw pies at me. At least with a carnival, I'd see it coming.

Once the students left, I picked up the paper airplane off the floor. I circled the room, collecting handouts that had been left behind, and saw *ESL* scribbled in black marker on several desks on the left side of the room. In educational jargon, ESL stands for English as a Second Language. Earlier, when I'd seen *ESL* etched on my door, I'd foolishly thought some Spanish-speaker was paying homage to my classroom. I soon realized this ESL had nothing to do with education—it was the acronym for East Side Longos—the largest Latino gang in Long Beach.

Similar gang insignias were on other desks. These defaced desks marked my students' territory. The Asian students hit up the desks with the name of their respective gang affiliation, as did the African Americans. My multicultural classes in college had conveniently left out the chapter on gangs and turf warfare.

In lieu of a seating chart, I naively let the students pick their own seats. What struck me now was that they chose comfort zones determined by race. This realization gave me pause. I had imagined my students filing into my class and forming a melting pot of colors as they chose their seats, but the pot must have been pretty cold, because there was absolutely no melting. The Latinos had staked out the left side, while the Asian students occupied the right. The back row was occupied by all the African American students, and a couple of Caucasians sheepishly huddled together in the front.

My classroom wasn't the only place where the students segregated themselves. It was worse out on the school quad. During lunch, the students again separated themselves based on racial identity. The students even had nicknamed their distinct areas: "Beverly Hills 90210," "Chinatown" (even though most of the students were immigrants from Cambodia), the "Ghetto," and "South of the Border."

The transparent segregation of the school shocked me, especially since I was expecting Wilson to be a model of integration. On paper, it was one of the most culturally diverse schools in the country, and I'd chosen to student-teach at Wilson for exactly that reason. Clearly, there was a disparity between what I'd read about Wilson High and its reality.

My dad used to share stories about seeing segregation firsthand. In the early sixties, when he was drafted to play minor league baseball for the Washington Senators, some of his teammates were forced to drink out of separate fountains, eat at different sections in restaurants, and stay at separate motels whenever his team traveled through the South. As a catcher, my dad said "he judged a batter by his swing, not the color of his skin." So when Hank Aaron started hitting balls out of the park, my father hailed him as his new hero and named his daughter Erin in honor of the legendary batter.

I was fascinated by my namesake for challenging the status quo and thus helping to change the face of America's favorite pastime. I hoped Hammerin' Hank's influence would make its way out of the stadiums and into the classrooms. Disappointingly, it didn't.

After lunch, all the kids from the "Beverly Hills 90210" section trotted to class together. Among them were students whose apparel and matching school sweatshirts identified them as water polo players, cheerleaders, and student council members. Their classrooms had banners that read "Home of the Distinguished Scholars," along with freshly published textbooks and new computers. In contrast, my room was pretty barren. It didn't have any banners, much less a computer. All I had to work with were hand-me-down textbooks riddled with graffiti.

In the Distinguished Scholars classrooms, the desks were neatly lined up and filled primarily with Caucasians. Nestled between the rows may have been an occasional African American or Asian student, but it was clear that a tracking system was in place.

The few Caucasians in my class were stigmatized as outcasts by their friends in the Distinguished Scholars program. The general assumption was that they had failed out of the Distinguished Scholars program, had a learning disability, or had just returned from rehab. By the look of things, some were probably on their way back in.

There was a perception in the affluent neighborhood south of the school that the caliber of students attending Wilson had plummeted in recent years. At one point, Wilson High was considered a highly desirable public high school, but there had been noticeable "white flight" after the school district implemented an intradistrict busing program. By the early nineties, the Caucasian population had decreased to less than twenty-five percent. Some speculated that the Distinguished Scholars program was an attempt to rescue the school's declining reputation and keep neighborhood kids from transferring out. My hope was that I could find something "distinguished" in all of my students.

At the end of my first day, the security guard popped his head into my class. Earlier that morning, he had stopped me in the hallway. He had a walkie-talkie in one hand and a metal-detector wand in the other. "We have zero tolerance for weapons on campus," he'd warned me. Then he asked to see my ID. I handed him my student ID card from the university.

"I'm a student teacher," I stammered. "I will be teaching junior English."

"Sorry," he said with a shrug, "you look like one of the students."

Now the security guard was here to tell me, "There's a police officer looking for you."

"Why?" I asked. "Did somebody steal my car?"

"No," he laughed, "he said he knows you."

I went to the office and was surprised to see my old neighbor, Mark, in full police uniform.

"Mark, what are you doing here?" I asked.

"Your brother asked me to check up on you," he said. Mark had been checking up on me since I was seven. He even threatened to beat up neighborhood boys with his nunchucks simply for flirting with me when we were in the sixth grade.

Mark and I had grown up in the same gated community, but I always suspected that he wanted to keep people out of those gates, whereas I wanted to bring them in. Our paths diverged after high school. I went on to college, and Mark entered the police academy. Coincidentally, we both ended up in Long Beach. It was obvious that Mark had not come to Long Beach out of moral obligation. He came to Long Beach because that's where the action was.

"I don't see any bullet holes, so I assume you survived your first day," he said.

"Barely!" I laughed. "My family's a little paranoid," I offered. "My father called me this morning and said, 'Erin, no matter what you do, please don't eat the apples!' He's convinced they're laced with strychnine or razor blades."

"He's probably right!" he said, and chuckled.

"Oh, come on. It's not that bad!" I said.

"Don't tell me it's not that bad. I'm a cop, remember? I'm the one arresting these kids. There are parts of Long Beach that are like a war zone. Especially after the Rodney King riots. There have been about a hundred gang-related murders in Long Beach already this year."

Growing up, my only exposure to "gangs" had been through the media or movies. My "hip" high school English teacher made us watch *West Side Story* to understand how the Montagues and the Capulets in *Romeo and Juliet* were like modern gangs. "Gangs" like the Jets and Sharks had staged rumbles. In real life, Jerome Robbins wasn't choreographing Friday-night fights in Long Beach.

"I'd hate to see you get caught in the cross fire," Mark said. "Just be careful."

"I will," I said, hugging him good-bye.

The security guard, who had been eavesdropping on my entire conversation, said, "He's right, you know. Long Beach has changed a lot."

At that moment, I just wanted to escape. I'd had enough negativity for one day, so I ducked into the teachers' lounge to seek solace. The moment I walked in, conversation stopped. They looked me up and down and said nothing. They didn't offer me a chair, a cup of coffee, or a word of encouragement. I looked down and noticed their open-toed Birkenstocks, in earthy contrast to my pumps. I must have looked like I had just stepped out of a Talbot's catalog. I was definitely overdressed.

Their disapproving glances brought out insecurities that had never surfaced before. Obviously, I hadn't made a good first impression. Maybe it was the polka dots. Or maybe it was my Tiffany pearls that pushed it over the top. Even though I craved their acceptance, it was pretty obvious that these particular teachers didn't want me in their clique—or their lounge, for that matter. Maybe I was too young, too preppy, or maybe they assumed I'd been born with a silver spoon in my mouth. Their uncomfortable silence made it pretty obvious that they felt I didn't belong.

I stood against the wall and listened to disgruntled banter about the new crop of students dubbed as "rejects." Apparently, my class was not the only place where things had gone awry. The teachers, many of whom had taught at Wilson since the "good old days," were discussing how the school was "going to hell in a handbasket."

"This place has gone downhill ever since *those* kids started getting bussed in from the projects," one teacher said.

"*They* don't even care about school," said another.

"*They* don't care about anything!" said another.

Their casual banter about *those* kids was startling. I was troubled by how nonchalant they were with their pejorative comments. After a string of generalizations about *those* kids, the teachers moved on to something more specific.

"Did you hear about the latest disciplinary transfer from Poly?" one of the teachers asked.

I instantly suspected that they were talking about Sharaud, because he had sauntered into my class wearing his Poly jersey.

"I heard he brought a gun to Poly last year and was planning to shoot everyone in the teachers' lounge."

"No, I heard he was planning to shoot his English teacher," said another teacher.

"They only let him in here because they couldn't find the gun. It's just a matter of time before that boy blows someone away," said another.

After being sufficiently ignored and hearing tales of how Sharaud would single-handedly destroy the institution, I decided I couldn't handle it anymore. I grabbed my bag and headed for the door. No one said good-bye. Why would they? They hadn't even bothered to say hello.

I fumbled for my keys as I dashed to my car. The lingering conversation about Sharaud had struck fear into me. What if I was the next teacher who triggered him?

CHAPTER 2

I left my first day of school on the verge of tears. The security guard thought I was too young, the students thought I was too white, and the teachers thought I was too tailored. My age, my color, and my clothing had all stood in the way of my merits.

Maybe my father had been right about teaching after all.

His stint as a teacher had left him cynical about the profession. When my father's career as a baseball player ended, he took a job as a history teacher at a high school so he could coach the baseball team. Although his heart was really on the field with his players, he was a dynamic historian in the classroom. He had a charismatic storytelling ability and brought historical events to life. He described the tumultuous sixties as if he had been on the steps of the Lincoln Memorial during Dr. Martin Luther King Jr.'s "I Have a Dream" speech, and with just as much authenticity he talked about holding up signs saying "Make Love Not War" with student protesters at Berkeley.

Yet when he took a scouting position for the Cincinnati Reds in the early seventies, his opinions about the teaching profession changed. At the high school, he faced apathetic students and red tape; with the "Big Red Machine," he scouted talented players and won national championships.

In 1976, my dad's team won the World Series. As a child, whenever I saw him wearing his World Series ring, I believed it gave him super powers. To an impressionable seven-year-old girl, he was larger than life—a knight in shining armor. I imagined he could slay any of the dragons in those fairy tales he used to read to me at bedtime. But as I got older, I realized that the only things my dad was actually slaying were golf balls at the country club. Although he'd argue that shooting birdies was a noble feat, I'd rather have pictured him fighting something more substantial than a sand trap. Perhaps it was the passage of time, perhaps the comforts of success, but it seemed to me that my father's youthful idealism had waned.

Meanwhile, I was full of idealism, but my college experience—University of California, Irvine, in the 1980s—was the antithesis of Berkeley in the sixties. At UCI, no one was staging protests, carrying signs, or burning bras. Irvine was an idyllic, master-planned community in the heart of Orange County and was not synonymous with "causes" or social revolutions. As a student who'd grown up fantasizing about college activism, I felt cheated.

While I was in college, a young Chinese student stood in front of a tank in Tiananmen Square. Not only did he stop the advancement of the tanks, but he captured my imagination as well. I was amazed that one person could stop the forces of evil dead in its tracks.

This young man's convictions made me question myself. What did I believe in? Did I have convictions of my own? When I took inventory of my life, it seemed kind of superficial. I had moved from motivating crowds with my megaphone in high school to singing silly sorority songs in college. In my sorority rush application, there were no questions about my convictions or beliefs. The sorority sisters simply wanted to know my "accomplishments." But besides perfecting the cartwheel, had I really accomplished anything?

I'd spent my life studying other people's beliefs, never really formulating my own. I had found my niche in mastering the art of regurgitation, telling professors what they wanted to hear and writing what they wanted to read. I could BS my way through any course and crank out any paper before sunrise, even if I didn't start until after the fraternity party had ended.

Yet the image of someone my age standing up for what was right and not BSing anyone truly inspired me. Although I wasn't brave enough to stand in front of a moving vehicle like the young man in Tiananmen Square—and had not yet identified a worthy cause to do so—maybe I could stand before a judge and fight injustice in a courtroom.

That's when I decided to become a lawyer. My father couldn't have been more proud.

But my plans to go to law school got derailed when I met a budding architect from Texas just before I graduated from college. I fell in love with him when he gave me a used copy of *Siddhartha* and promised we would change the world together.

There was something so romantic about dating an architect, but his plans of one day designing us a dream home were short-lived: He decided to take a job in the computer industry.

A month after graduation, I moved in with him and his four best friends in a house in Newport Beach. Much to my father's chagrin, rather than studying for the LSAT, I was baking cookies for five men in a beach house that overlooked the ocean.

I spent the better part of the summer learning Texas colloquialisms and coordinating weddings at the Marriott. With its gorgeous gazebo and ocean view, the hotel was a destination site for weddings. After helping several brides prepare for their special day, I suppose that I'd been bitten by the wedding bug too. Witnessing dozens of weddings and having a closet full of colorful bridesmaid dresses with dyed-to-match shoes, I had convinced myself that I was ready to walk down the aisle. So instead of studying legal briefs, I scoured bridal magazines and planned the ultimate wedding.

My father did not want me to play den mother to a house full of men, nor did he want me to be married at the age of twenty-three. He tried to discourage me by suggesting that "I was in love with the idea of being in love."

"No, Dad, we really are in love," I tried to assure him.

The reality was that I had already put down a nonrefundable deposit at the Marriott and picked out sleek bridesmaid dresses, so the idea of postponing my wedding was out of the question.

Although my father had given his blessing and agreed to help pay for the elaborate affair, he did not want me to get married without having established my career. He continued to suggest that if I were smart, I'd wait until I was thirty-five to get married.

My friends and colleagues at the Marriott were determined to make my wedding the event of the season. The head chef was going to specially prepare a five-course menu, the maître d' had picked out the perfect linens, and the manager offered me a sizable employee discount. With the prospect of a free ice sculpture, champagne fountain, and other perks, law school would have to wait.

While I was conjuring my fantasy wedding, the world came crashing in when the verdict in the Rodney King trial was announced on April 29, 1992. I watched the turbulent aftermath during my shift at the Marriott that afternoon. We all gathered around the grainy television set in the employee cafeteria to watch people's reactions. When a brick was thrown at Reginald Denny's head, we all gasped. As the riots escalated, the dinner we were about to cater was canceled, so my boss sent me home.

At home, my roommates were glued to our television set. We watched as people looted, torched cars, and burned buildings. Not knowing the geography of Southern California, their friends and family from Texas kept calling my roommates to check on them. They had seen the horrific images on television and were worried. Once they learned that Newport Beach was about an hour from the epicenter of the riots, the discussion inevitably turned from safety to stereotypes.

"*They* just take, take, take."

"How stupid can *they* be?"

"Can you believe *they're* burning their own liquor stores? Where are *they* going to get their malt liquor tomorrow?"

The racial innuendos that swirled around made me very uncomfortable. I looked at my fiancé, hoping he'd interject. I wanted him to say something, anything—but he said nothing.

I tried to block out the stereotypes that I kept hearing by focusing on the nonstop news coverage. I fixated on an image of a disgruntled man throwing a Molotov cocktail at a Circuit City building. The television crews immediately panned down and showed a little boy looking up at him. The boy had stars in his eyes. I recognized that look—it was the same reverence I had for my father when I was a child. Together, the two of them ran into the burning building and quickly emerged with television sets, stereos, and other electronic equipment.

If I had wanted to follow in the footsteps of my father when I was a child—how would this child respond to his father's actions? What if his father told tales of Florence and Normandie, rather than Haight and Ashbury? What if his tales were not about burning bras, but about burning buildings? I wondered: If a kid could be taught to pick up a Molotov cocktail, could he be taught to pick up a pen instead?

Maybe the best way to equalize the playing field wasn't in a courtroom but in a classroom. When I made the announcement to my father that I wanted to be a teacher, he did not take the news so well.

"Erin, teachers don't make any money," he said.

"Dad, that's not my motivation," I said.

"Well, I hope your fiancé leaves the computer industry to become a successful architect, or else you'll never afford a home in Newport Beach."

"Dad, there are plenty of other places we can live," I said.

"Where do you want to teach?" he asked rather gruffly.

"I want to teach in an urban school district," I said.

"What? Do you have a death wish or something? Haven't you been watching the news? Why can't you choose a school closer to home?"

"Because I want to make a difference."

"Can't you make a difference in Newport Beach?"

"Yes, but . . ." I didn't get to finish my explanation, because my father was on a roll.

"Erin, you have no idea what you're getting yourself into."

"That's why I'm going back to school!" I said.

Since I wasn't expecting my dad to help pay for my wedding and graduate school, I had already researched student loans before I shared my revelation with him.

"I'm going to get a student loan. I'll pick up a few more shifts at the Marriott. I'll make it work," I said, desperately craving his approval.

"Okay," he capitulated. "Just be careful."

In the midst of planning my wedding, I enrolled in education classes at California State University, Long Beach. Luckily, my fiancé was supportive of my decision to get a master's degree and teaching credential simultaneously. We decided that after our European honeymoon, we would forgo furniture for a while to pay for my tuition.

When I enrolled in education courses at the university, my first professor was in the twilight of her career. With her bright white hair, I was convinced that she hadn't stepped foot in a contemporary classroom since the decade of *Leave It to Beaver*.

Her message that "modern-day classrooms are more like a 'salad bowl' than a 'melting pot'" sounded like a refrain from "We Are the World." She described students in terms of "lettuce," "cucumbers," and "radishes"—and to coexist in harmony, all teachers had to do was "toss the salad."

She painted a multicultural scenario similar to a Michael Jackson video, where students moonwalked across the classroom to turn in their homework assignments. It sounded very simple.

CHAPTER 3

Even though I was feeling frustrated from my disastrous first day, I was determined to find a way to reach my students. If I was going to survive the semester, I knew that I'd have to learn to speak their language. My plan was to start with the kids who seemed to be my two toughest students—Sharaud and Melvin. They were the most outspoken—natural leaders—and if I could win them over, the rest were bound to follow.

Since both had worn football jerseys, maybe using sports analogies would be a way to engage them. Even though I'd been a cheerleader years before, I realized it was going to be difficult to talk shop with these boys; all I remembered were silly slogans like "push 'em back, push 'em back, waaaaay back." My football knowledge was limited to chants, and I had no idea what they translated into. If I was going to talk their game, I needed to do my homework. So I called my dad.

I was sure that my dad would be waiting by the phone with bated breath to find out how my first day of school went. When I called, I kept my cards close to the vest, as he'd taught me.

"Dad, could you give me a crash course in football?" I asked. He was a walking encyclopedia when it came to sports trivia, and the perfect Cliffs Notes for my research. "I need to know the latest stats, who's hot, who's not, and some of the damn rules." This was music to my dad's ears—he loved talking about sports.

We used to play catch when I was a kid; now we'd have to play over the phone. He'd throw out a question about my day, and I'd pitch him a question about a sports statistic, an athlete, or a football highlight, all the while scribbling down facts furiously.

Once I was totally saturated with information about running backs and defensive linemen, I gave him a bone: "I hit it out of the park today, Dad. You would have been proud." He must have known I was lying, but at least I made it through the phone call without a lecture.

I felt a little more prepared on the second day. I tried to weave football trivia into casual conversation with Melvin and Sharaud. I had to be subtle and sprinkle in a couple references to the *Monday Night Football* game, without seeming too rehearsed or contrived.

"Did you happen to catch Jerry Rice's touchdown last night?" The posse in the back stopped scribbling on their desks and actually sat up. Then I subtly asked Melvin how fast he ran the forty-yard dash. Score! He had no idea that his coach had helped me out of a xeroxing crisis before class, but it gave me a couple minutes to get some vital stats on his players to accompany my newfound knowledge of football.

At the end of the day, I noticed that fewer handouts had been thrown about and even fewer desks needed scrubbing. I felt more confident than I had the day before, and I decided to walk straight to my car without even stopping by the teachers' lounge.

If I could get my students' attention from a few football references, I thought, what if I brought up what they were watching, what they were listening to, and most important, what were they reading?

I needed to learn everything about what my students did between the hours of 3 P.M. and 7 A.M. To do so, I decided to take a different tack than calling my dad or my college professor, who had a Ph.D. in education. Instead of searching for the answers through traditional authority figures, I would treat my students as if they were the ones with the Ph.D. A Ph.D. of the streets.

I would need to go directly to the source. Maybe they could teach me a thing or two. At least it was worth a try. Thus, my professors in pop culture would become Melvin, the self-proclaimed big man on campus, and Sharaud, the gun-toting wiseass.

Melvin was a little easier to win over than Sharaud. He was a natural-born leader, cultivating his star status both on and off the field. He could navigate his way through an entire defensive line on the football field and charm girls into doing his homework in the classroom. He was a true chameleon, though, because he was also a "gangsta" in training. By day, he ruled the halls and by night he ruled the streets. He had already been kicked out of Wilson twice before he strolled into my class. Bets were on that there would be a third.

The first time he was kicked out of Wilson, he set off an M80 in the quad. When it went off, everyone ducked—everyone except for him, that is. He was the only one running, so it was obvious that he was the one who set it off. His fancy footwork ran him right out of school.

Since Melvin could score touchdowns, he came back to Wilson the next year at the request of his football coach, who had his eye on beating Poly. But once football season was over, so was his good behavior. He had to figure out other ways to "score." One afternoon, he paid a homeless woman outside the local liquor store to buy him and his crew some beer before a school dance show. The liquor store was just two blocks from the campus, which didn't give him much time to down the beer before he ducked into his seat in the auditorium.

"I bet you can't take that forty to the head," they dared, egging him on to drink the whole bottle at once.

Because Melvin was a gambling man, he pounded two bottles during the span of two blocks. With eighty ounces of beer in his fifteen-year-old belly, it didn't take long before his head was whirling like the spin cycle of a washing machine. He proceeded to throw up in the back of the auditorium—minutes before intermission.

The auditorium had a slight tilt to it, and all eighty ounces and his lunch began to ooze its way slowly down toward the front. Like the wave at a ballgame, disgusted parents jumped from their seats just in time to watch Melvin throw up again—this time, all over the principal's pants. Melvin was escorted out of the show—and out of school—again.

In the midst of fall football, Melvin was back at Wilson. "Third time's a charm," he said to me with a wink.

I think Melvin could tell that I was really trying to win him over. My antics must have amused him. I fumbled up references to players and their prospective teams, but since I was going the extra yard for him, Melvin reciprocated the favor. He seemed to pay more attention in class, turned in his homework, and helped to keep unruly students in line.

He told me that no one had ever tried so hard to reach him before. Most teachers gave up too soon or didn't even bother to begin. He told me that when he met with his freshman counselor to see if he could take an advanced math class, she said, "No, that wouldn't be a good idea. Why don't you try something more realistic, like football or auto mechanics?" Since she was the so-called expert, that's exactly what he did.

Once he was placed in those classes, a cycle of complacency began, followed by destructive behavior. It was my mission to motivate him to break that cycle.

Once I had earned my stripes with Melvin and proved I was "down," he became fiercely loyal. He began to call me "Ms. G."

I was used to getting my last name butchered by people. Ever since I was a kid, people had arbitrarily added or subtracted vowels and consonants. Grunwell, Gruel—I had heard it all.

"It ain't nothin' but a G thang, baby!" Melvin would sing more patriotically than the national anthem as he walked into class each day. It was a line from his favorite Snoop Dogg song.

"Thang? You mean thing," I corrected him.

"No, thang. It's a 'G' thang."

I didn't realize till much later that the "G" was for "gangsta," but by the time I figured it out, my new nickname was etched into that classroom as much as their insignias were on the desks.

Calvin Broadus, aka Snoop Doggy Dogg, and other West Coast rappers were Melvin's idols, just like Steinbeck and Salinger were mine. Snoop was a phenomenon, especially since he was from Long Beach. Melvin and his friends all claimed to know Snoop, the skinny little kid who attended Poly before his album *Doggy Style* went platinum. Snoop filmed his videos on the streets of Long Beach, sang songs about their "kick-it spots," and even went on MTV flashing Long Beach gang signs. To Melvin and other boys from Long Beach, Snoop was the heir to the budding rap royalty.

Since I had been using football references ad nauseam, I quickly exhausted my knowledge of the game. I needed something new. Maybe rap could be just the hook I was looking for. I elected Melvin to become my rap aficionado. I was counting on him to supply me with fresh material to weave into my lessons.

When Melvin wasn't singing rap ballads, he was glaring at Sharaud. Melvin had no tolerance for Sharaud's arrogance. Neither did I. Sharaud didn't know when to stop, and I wondered how long his antics would last. His constant confrontational demeanor drove me crazy. It drove everyone crazy.

Sharaud was antagonistic—to the students, his teammates, and his teachers. He was constantly talking back, interrupting, muttering under his breath, and vying for attention—any attention (especially if it was negative, which it generally was). He was loud, he was crass, and he was obnoxious. His "notice me" mentality was exasperating, and it was wearing me down.

As I was leaving class one day, looking particularly haggard, the security guard stopped me in the hallway and said, "Sharaud is a pain in the ass. He won't last more than a month. If he gets too difficult, just send him to in-school detention."

Apparently, that's what some of his other teachers did, with reckless abandon. One teacher bragged that he wouldn't even let Sharaud come to class. He had a stack of detention slips sitting on his desk with Sharaud's name neatly written on each one. Most of the time, Sharaud wouldn't even reach his seat before he was handed the detention slip and sent away.

Even though Sharaud talked a lot of smack in the back row, I did not want to send him to detention. I wanted to try another tactic. I moved Sharaud and Melvin to the front of my classroom to assert more control. I put Melvin on the left side, and Sharaud front and center.

"This is bullshit!" Sharaud said as he reluctantly made his way to the front of the room. "I'm not sitting here," he said, kicking the desk.

I hoped that getting Sharaud out of his comfort zone would calm him down, but he continued to cut up. He became more aggressive and defiant. During one of my lectures, Sharaud was being excessively disruptive. In retaliation, and in an attempt to defend me, Melvin took out a pen and drew a distorted profile of Sharaud. On the ripped piece of notebook paper was a caricature with huge, exaggerated lips. Across the side of the note he wrote "Pass Me," and off it went.

The note made its way down the left row, with raucous laughter in its wake. It quickly made its way up the second row, then down the third. Finally, it came to Sharaud. He took one look at it and, after a moment of silence, his lips quivered and his eyes welled up. His tough veneer was beginning to crack.

I snatched the note from Sharaud and watched Melvin exchange approving looks with another student. Melvin couldn't have been prouder of his stab at modern art.

I looked at the note. Then I looked at Sharaud.

Even though I was at my wit's end with Sharaud, I found myself feeling sorry for him. For the first time, he was speechless. Was all his trash talking simply a defense mechanism? Maybe Sharaud tried to get others to laugh with him so they wouldn't laugh at him. Telling jokes was his way of diverting attention. But this time there was no joke he could tell to deflect the other students' laughter.

Something inside me snapped. I felt like Medusa, with snakes hissing in my hair; I must have had an expression on my face that would turn any student to stone. I felt an urge to protect Sharaud, probably in the same way Melvin had wanted to protect me earlier.

I looked at the note again. The protruding lips reminded me of pictures I'd seen in a museum depicting Jews looking like rats, with long, exaggerated noses. The caricatures were drawn by Nazi propaganda artists during World War II. Joseph Goebbels, who was Hitler's minister of propaganda, believed that if you dehumanized Jews to look like rodents, then it would be much easier to exterminate them.

What if the note led to a battle after the bell? I feared Sharaud's public humiliation would fuel retaliation and the cycle of violence would continue. After all, Sharaud had once brought a gun to school. My gut instinct was that this situation could escalate if Sharaud tried to save face. An altercation in the hall could lead to a brawl on the quad or a fight at football practice. Soon, they'd bring in their friends—fellow "gangstas" in training—and someone might get seriously hurt, or worse.

To regain a semblance of order, I waved the note in the air and said dramatically, "This note reminds me of the Holocaust."

I was met with sullen stares.

From the back of the classroom, DeWahn innocently asked, "What's the Holocaust?"

I felt my stomach drop.

As several students shrugged their shoulders, I asked, "Have any of you ever heard of the Holocaust?"

No one responded. I was aghast. At sixteen years old, how could these students have missed that part of world history? I had always heard that if you don't learn from history, you're doomed to repeat it. As a means of connection, I asked, "How many of you have been shot at?"

Nearly every hand went up in the air.

This was my first teachable moment. An opportunity seemed to be presenting itself if only I could seize it. Perhaps I could use the example of the Holocaust and other examples of intolerance to help my students look in the mirror and evaluate their own lives.

At once, students started pulling up their shirts and showing off their war wounds. It was like show-and-tell. "This is where I almost got hit." Or "this is where I got shanked." I saw scars, I saw bullet wounds, and I saw stitches. One kid even admitted that he had been to "more funerals than birthday parties."

My anger turned to empathy.

Melvin shared a story of how he and a friend were held up at gunpoint by a rival gang. He told the tale with the same enthusiasm that my father used when recounting how the Cincinnati Reds won the World Series. Whereas my father would show off his World Series ring to a captive audience, Melvin showed his scars. Melvin's story prompted others to share similar stories about gang-related violence. I stood at the front of the classroom in disbelief. How could they be so numb to such brutality?

Their war stories went on until the end of the period.

The bell rang, and Sharaud stood up and started puffing out his chest and making threats. Melvin had been defending me, and now Sharaud was defending his pride.

They were cussing at each other and showing off to the crowd gathering in the hall. Word was starting to get out that there was going to be a fight, and spectators were muttering, "Sharaud had it coming" or "Melvin's gonna get his ass whooped."

Foolishly, I tried to separate them, hoping that they would think twice before striking each other with me sandwiched between them. As they got closer, I could feel the tension in their bodies. I made them promise not to fight. "Promise me!" I demanded. They turned away from each other and, without much conviction, grumbled bogus apologies.

I knew I had only defused the problem temporarily. I had merely put a Band-Aid on a shotgun wound.

CHAPTER 4

W hen I told my dad about the note and the fight that followed, he yelled, "Are you crazy? Why didn't you call the security guard or one of the coaches for help?"

"I know, Dad. It was stupid."

"You're getting too close to these kids, Erin. You need to remember that you're just a student teacher who's not getting a dime for this nonsense. Leave your heroic antics at the door and just teach them how to write a five-paragraph essay."

I couldn't explain to my overprotective father that writing an essay was the furthest thing from their minds at that moment. I also couldn't rationalize why I had stood between them. All I knew was that I wasn't ready to detach myself. Merely sending them away or bringing in the football coach probably wouldn't have solved the problem either. Melvin would have gotten a slap on the wrist—on Friday night, the football team was playing the big crosstown rival, Poly, so nobody in their right mind was going to suspend him. In Sharaud's case, this may have been just the excuse the administrators were looking for to get rid of him. But I wasn't ready to get rid of him.

This note was just the beginning.

The next day, when I walked into my classroom, I saw everything through a new set of eyes. The walls, the bookshelves, the books, even my handouts, seemed more dingy and dilapidated than they had the day before. No wonder kids dozed off or doodled on their folders. This was not an environment conducive to stimulating minds and sparking creativity. Most of the students were tuned out.

Since I had discovered that they weren't reading any of the chapters I assigned for homework, I had resorted to reading the chapters aloud. Obviously, reading aloud the entire period was not stimulating. And for the kids with ADD, it must have been torture. I must have sounded like the annoying teacher in a Charlie Brown special: "Waa waa waa waa waa."

I needed to mix things up a bit and bring books to life. In their world of instant gratification, if they got bored, they could simply change the channel, skip to the next song on a CD, or put in a new video game. Maybe a substantive field trip outside of the confines of my stale classroom would make them realize the inappropriateness of the note, and how it could multiply with tragic results.

"There's a museum in L.A. that's about the Holocaust, if anyone's interested," I casually mentioned.

DeWahn stopped doodling. "Can we go there on a field trip?" he asked.

"Um, I don't know, can we?" I looked around to find my supervising teacher to get the expected "no"—but he was nowhere to be found. "I don't know how to do stuff like that yet," I said.

I probably should have done a little more research before I waved the field-trip carrot in front of them. What was I thinking? How was I supposed to take them on a field trip when I couldn't even figure out how to work the copy machine?

"You guys can go there on your own," I recommended.

"You're the one who brought it up, so you should take us," Sharaud said, putting me on the spot.

His comment was followed by a lot of head-nodding and a few "uh-huh"s.

"Okay," I said hesitantly. "I'll look into it."

After class, I went to the teachers' lounge to find out what the procedure was on taking field trips. I was told, "Students like yours don't go on field trips." Another teacher said, "Your students are too much of a liability." I was inundated with potential problems: My students might destroy something or use the field trip as an excuse to ditch school. Plus, there was lots of paperwork that needed to be done; bus requisitions needed to be submitted in advance, and there was no money in the budget. I walked out of the lounge disheartened. It appeared that a trip to the museum was out of the question.

As the bearer of bad news, I hoped my students would not be upset with me. I was just the messenger. When I broke the news to them, I expected them to scream, "This isn't fair!" Instead, they weren't surprised. In fact, they expected it.

"Kids like us don't go on field trips," Melvin said.

"What do you mean, 'kids like us'?" I asked incredulously.

"There are 'kids' like you, Ms. G, and then there are 'kids' like us," Manny interjected rather matter-of-factly.

Unfortunately, Manny was right: "kids like me" seemed to have everything, while others had nothing at all. It didn't seem fair. But for some, fairness is a fallacy. Since I'd been anointed an "honors student" from the moment I came out of the womb, I was entitled to the new books and fancy field trips that the "basic" students didn't get. With high expectations came even higher labels: "Gifted," "Honors," "Advanced Placement," "Accelerated." I never thought twice about them. I just took them for granted and reaped the rewards.

The "best" students naturally got the "best" teachers, who prepared them for the "best" colleges. The best colleges, in turn, prepared them for the best jobs and the best addresses in suburbia. Maybe that was why my dad was disappointed with my decision to be a teacher. He had lived up to his end of the bargain by sending me to the best schools, and he'd probably assumed that I would choose the best profession. In his mind, a teacher's salary wasn't going to afford all the perks bestowed upon me during my childhood. How could I afford a house behind a gate? Maybe my dad, like so many of his golf buddies, equated "best" with professions that had a higher salary than teaching.

I had never thought about the labels given to the kids who weren't vying for the valedictorian slot or trying to get accepted into prestigious colleges. If kids who were thought to be inherently smarter were "gifted," what did the system call kids who didn't have the gift? Worse yet, what did they call themselves?

My students were labeled "basic," "remedial," and "at risk." I wondered when such negative labels started. Were they pigeonholed as early as kindergarten? In some cases, they were. Many of my students didn't know their ABCs efficiently by the first day of kindergarten, so they were scooped up and put in the lowest academic track—where they were to remain until they either dropped out or got kicked out.

I was determined that my students deserved some of the perks I got in school, so I decided I would take them to the museum—even if I had to pay for the trip myself. I would pick up a couple extra shifts a week at the Marriott to help with the expenses. Since I was adept at making arrangements for CEOs and presidents of Fortune 500 companies, I wondered how hard it could be to make field-trip arrangements for a bunch of students. All I really needed were tickets to the museum, a bus, and some food, right?

Logistically, planning a field trip turned out to be much more challenging than booking a romantic harbor cruise for a VIP guest at my hotel. Fundamentally, the guests who stayed at the Marriott had something my students and I didn't—the resources to back it up.

As a concierge, I was able to make calls about the field trip in between booking dinner reservations for guests. I called the Museum of Tolerance to see if they gave teacher discounts, but their quota for the year had already been filled. I then called several bus companies, but they were all too expensive.

I told my students that I was running into a few financial problems and that we might have to postpone the trip. Although a few of them groaned, most were not emotionally invested. They'd never really expected to go anyway.

A Native American student living in abject poverty approached me after class and offered, "Hey, Ms. G, it isn't much, but I'd like to give a little something for the field-trip fund. I've never been to a museum before, so I sure hope you can pull it off." He handed me a quarter and smiled. I wanted to burst into tears.

His generosity inspired others. When another student, who received free meal tickets, donated to the cause, I mustered up the courage to ask for help from my friends and family. It was oddly liberating. In lieu of down payments or holding reservations on a credit card, I appealed to people's sense of philanthropy. I wrote a note to the parents asking for their help, and several responded. One parent even offered to help coordinate the buses. My stepmom, Karen, offered to help serve lunch, while my old cheerleading buddy agreed to be a chaperone. Considering that my girlfriend was beautiful, I was sure she would be able to woo Sharaud into submission.

Since so many people had donated their time and money, my students were able to see how many people truly supported them. The night before the trip, I told my dad that the collaborative approach seemed to make the process more meaningful.

"That's because they've got some skin in the game," he said.

"What does that mean?" I asked. Occasionally, my dad's sports analogies needed clarification.

"It means your players, I mean your students, are invested in the process."

He was right. On the day of the trip, my students' excitement was palpable. Once they got on the bus, they regressed to being giddy kindergarteners.

We got to the Museum of Tolerance, and there was a dramatic pause when my students saw the thick metal detectors at the entrance. LaKeisha, one of our track stars, came up to me in a panic. "Ms. G, what am I going to do with this?" She opened up her purse and showed me an eight-inch switchblade.

"LaKeisha, what are you doing with that?" I said, shocked.

"My mom wants me to carry it, since track practice runs so late. You'd carry one, too, if you lived in my neighborhood," she said. LaKeisha lived in an area of Compton synonymous with gang activity. Since Wilson had a nationally ranked track team, she lied about her address and took several buses to get to school each day, in hopes that she might get a track scholarship to college. Even though she could sprint faster than almost anyone in the country, her mother thought that a knife gave her a little extra security.

The Museum of Tolerance does not mess around when it comes to weapons. They constantly get threats from neo-Nazi groups and religious extremists. I assumed other students might be carrying weapons or even pepper spray for self-protection. I knew they were not planning to deface the museum, but the security officer looked pretty daunting.

"Okay, everybody," I whispered, "huddle up. You have exactly one minute of amnesty. Go discard whatever you need to discard and I'll meet you on the other side of the metal detectors."

I patiently talked to the officer while the students hid their contraband in the bushes outside.

Once inside, we were introduced to our tour guide. Her name was Renee Firestone and she was a Holocaust survivor. She told us that the museum focuses on two themes, "the dynamics of prejudice and the history of the Holocaust."

At the entrance of the Holocaust section, each student was given a passport with a photo of a child and a story about how his or her life was affected. Throughout the tour, the passport was updated. Somberly, we made our way through each passage, listening to Renee's description of each artifact, photo, and memory. When we were done, each student discovered the ultimate fate of the child on their passport.

Renee asked, "Does anyone have Klara Weinfeld's card?"

"I do," one of my students replied, "but she died at the age of fourteen."

"I know," Renee said. "She was my sister."

We were all still in shock when Renee escorted us into a room to tell us her story. Renee was eighteen when she was imprisoned at Auschwitz for thirteen months. She pulled back her sleeve and read the faint tattoo. "A-12307. That was the number they gave me when I got off the cattle car," she said.

The students' eyes were glued to the grim reminder.

"Why haven't you had it removed?" DeWahn asked.

"This is part of me," she said, rubbing it. "That is why I will never have it removed."

She vividly recalled the smell of the camp, and the human skeletons dressed in black-and-white-striped pajamas, and the human ash spewing out of the tall smokestacks. When she asked a female commandant where her parents were, the commandant said snidely, "There go your parents," pointing to the smokestacks, "and when you go through those chimneys, you'll be reunited with your parents."

I was sitting next to Manny. He wiped away a tear.

"I was a slave in my lifetime," she continued, "but I survived. I have come to realize that there are no excuses in life!" By tempering her tragic story with an element of tough love, she not only earned my students' respect, but she profoundly moved them. When Renee finished her testimonial, they all wanted to touch the numbers on her arm or hug her.

As she was walking with us to the bus, she said, "I try to connect the past to what is happening today, so please learn a lesson from the Holocaust so you're not doomed to repeat it."

On the bus ride home, I realized that my tough students suddenly weren't so tough. When we got back to school, I asked Sharaud, "How are you getting home?"

"I'll probably walk or take the city bus."

Without thinking, I asked, "Do you want a ride home?"

"Can some of the guys come too?"

Although my car wasn't very big, I said, "Sure."

Sharaud called out, "Shotgun," and he and three other students, Manny, Khari, and James, crammed into the backseat of my convertible VW Rabbit.

Sharaud coaxed me into putting the top down, even though it was cool outside.

"Hey, Ms. G, have you ever seen Long Beach?" Manny asked. To which I quickly replied, "Yes."

"No, Ms. G, have you seen 'our' Long Beach?" he asked.

I hadn't. Every morning, I would get into my car in Newport Beach and drive forty-five minutes to school in Long Beach. After work, I would get back in my car and simply drive home with little thought as to what was around the corner.

"This should be good," Sharaud said, and motioned to his buddies. "Let's take *her* on a field trip!"

As we got farther away from the school, the landscape started to change drastically.

"Let's take her to the cut," said Sharaud.

The "cut" was close to Martin Luther King Jr. Park, a much grittier part of town. Unfortunately, the park honoring the great man was an urban nightmare. Unlike the parks where I grew up, filled with soccer moms who handed out slices of oranges at halftime, my students claimed that MLK Park was filled with homeless people and gang members. Some were throwing dice; others were discreetly taking hits from a pipe. There were no kids in sight.

"Welcome to my childhood," Sharaud said. Like Renee, the child survivor we'd seen earlier at the museum, he had been deprived of his innocence.

I think Sharaud wanted to show me firsthand a world that didn't exist in museums, textbooks, or in the literary canon. He wanted me to learn about his life not from a book or from TV—but live, in 3D.

As I drove through his neighborhood, the boys popped in a Snoop CD and sang at the top of their lungs. As we got deeper into the "cut," I got a little scared. Grown men were sipping out of paper bags, perched on run-down stoops. Sharaud nodded his head as people drove by, or threw out gang signs when necessary. In my nervousness, I turned the music down, as if that would make us less conspicuous.

When a car backfired in the distance, I thought someone was shooting at us. I hit the gas. Sharaud said, "You're scared, aren't you?" I was. I was terrified. I'd seen *Boyz n the Hood* and I envisioned being a headline on the nightly news.

"Okay, you've probably seen enough for one day," Sharaud said.

I had. I was exhausted. The museum, the music, the mayhem in and outside of my car was sensory overload. I needed to process everything I had just experienced.

Just as Renee wasn't able to wash away her tattoo from Auschwitz or her childhood memories, neither was Sharaud. Maybe that's why he wanted me to see where he was from—to understand that there were different kinds of wars and that he was a survivor, too.

When I pulled up to Sharaud's apartment, he said, "I had a really good time today, Ms. G."

"I did too!" I said eagerly.

"It was tight," he said as he hopped out of my car.

Finally, a connection.

CHAPTER 5

E verything changed after the field trip—everything: the way my students treated each other, the way they treated me, and even the way
they treated education. When we were at the museum, nobody got bored,
nobody doodled, and nobody's attention wandered.

To keep my students engrossed, I needed to stimulate their senses in the
same way the museum did—with photos, videos, and hands-on technology.
Simply reading or writing for the entire period was a recipe for disaster. If I
wanted them to read a book from cover to cover or to write that perfect
essay, I would have to be a little tricky, like a parent when they're trying to get
a kid to eat something that's "good for them."

My best friend, Nikki, had just had a baby and I loved watching her try
to feed him. To get him to open up his mouth, she'd make all kinds of silly
airplane noises and would fly the spoon full of some kind of green goop
through the air. Eventually, after enough noises and loop-the-loops, some of
the green goop made its way into his mouth.

Even though it was bound to get a bit messy, I needed to do some loop-
the-loops too. Maybe Mary Poppins was onto something with her "spoonful
of sugar" technique. If reading and writing was "medicine," it was worth a
shot. With a little bit of sugar or airplane tricks of my own, maybe I could
make an essay or two go down before the end of the semester.

As I became familiar with my students' idiosyncrasies, I began to subtly
infuse them into my lessons. The more creative I was, the faster those fifty-five
minutes went by, and more important, the more I was able to engage my stu-

dents. Finally, my years as a cheerleader and a sorority sister paid off. I had cos-
tumes for everything; hippie gear, tiaras—you name it, I had it all stashed away
in boxes in my garage. The campier the activity, the more they responded.

My goofiness rubbed off and I began to pull my students into my act.
My graffiti artists became my Picassos, my hams became my actors, and the
ones who were painfully shy were sent on missions to bring in video clips,
songs, or the perfect prop. Collectively, we could make any costume, draw
any picture, and find any song to illustrate my English lessons.

Even though many of them had missed out on show-and-tell as kids, they
were making up for lost time. They were constantly scheming about how to
snatch toys from their siblings' closets—dolls, stuffed animals, or even Dis-
ney movies—to make my lessons more relevant. Before I knew it, the bell
would ring and they were still engrossed.

Melvin was shameless. He would sing just about any tune and wear just
about any costume without its being an affront to his masculinity. He even
graciously volunteered to be my "Vanna White."

"Don't you mean Vanna Black?" Sharaud said sarcastically.

Melvin shot him a look, but Sharaud's sarcasm didn't deter Melvin from
putting on a grass skirt and a coconut bra.

I tried everything to get them up and out of their seats, from debates to
role-playing. Soon, they weren't just reading "boring" chapters or writing
"boring" essays—they were reading and writing about characters that felt
like their friends.

I stayed later and later after class, trying to figure out ways to make my
lessons more stimulating, more relevant. My goal was to find a common
ground every time a student asked me the question "What does *this* have to
do with my life?"

My silly persona was working. Slowly but surely, they began to swallow
To Kill a Mockingbird. Sharaud even validated my eccentric strategy when he
made a profound connection to a misconstrued character.

"I can relate to Boo Radley, Ms. G," he said introspectively. "People mis-
understand me all the time."

I was so proud of him at that moment that I wanted to hug him. But I
didn't. I sensed that Sharaud was masking some pretty deep wounds. I hoped
this could be the beginning of the healing process.

After we finished *To Kill a Mockingbird*, I decided to find another piece of literature that would make them think critically, question authority, and reexamine their own beliefs. I looked at the district's list of approved literature and was excited to see *The Catcher in the Rye*. I hoped that Holden Caulfield's sense of nonconformity would resonate with them.

When I went to the co-chair of the English Department to get the books from our storeroom, she told me that I couldn't use *The Catcher in the Rye* because the books were reserved for the Distinguished Scholars.

"But I think my students can really identify with Holden," I offered, picking up a copy of the book from the stack.

She took the book out of my hand and replaced it on the stack. Since I had all the "taggers," I was told that my students "would desecrate the books with graffiti." Another teacher in the bookroom chimed in, "What's the point? They won't get it anyway."

When I pushed the issue a little further, the co-chair simply said, "Your students are too stupid to appreciate it."

I felt sucker-punched.

Too stupid? I thought about the old saying that parents teach their kids, "Sticks and stones will break your bones, but words will never hurt you." And for the first time, I disagreed. What if a kid hears words like "dumb," "stupid," or "nothing" again and again and again? What if they hear it so often that they begin to believe it? Unfortunately, many of my students had heard such words and acted accordingly. A horrible, self-fulfilling prophecy resulted.

Maybe believing that her students were better than mine justified her control of the fiefdom. There was a movement in education that emphasized test scores over teaching. In fact, I'd been taught how to "teach to the test" rather than to the student. In this test culture, I was afraid teachers would lose their passion and creativity and become too rigid. I hated Scantrons and filling in the blanks with number two pencils. I believed that Salinger hadn't written *The Catcher in the Rye* so that a student could mark in "Holden wore a red cap" on the answer key. I was afraid that these kinds of multiple-choice tests were focusing on minutia. The tests were supposed to make everything equal—but I was beginning to realize that things were not equal. Not by a long shot.

The irony was that the co-chair's desire to preserve some archaic academic hierarchy would have put Holden Caulfield right over the edge. The fact that she was just going to let the books sit on the shelf collecting dust until her students were ready to read them made me want to challenge her. She didn't own the books—she simply had a key to the book closet.

Her blatant bias made me determined to get the books without having to grovel. If she wasn't going to share her secret stash with a student teacher and a bunch of "stupid" kids, then I'd have to find copies of the book from another source.

I'll show you "stupid," I thought.

Desperate times called for desperate measures, so I called my dad.

"Dad, can I have a cash advance on my Christmas present?" I asked. It was only October. "I really need to buy something."

"Sure, it'll save me a trip to the mall," he said.

He was on his way to the golf course when I called. Since he didn't want to be late for his foursome, he didn't push me for details. I think he assumed that I was going to buy another suit or some furniture for my husband and my minimalist apartment. He certainly didn't expect me to buy a bunch of books. When I got his check, with "Merry Christmas!" written in the memo, I immediately cashed it and headed to Barnes & Noble to buy every student a copy of *The Catcher in the Rye*.

When I passed the books out, many of my students were hesitant to open them. They were surprised to get books that hadn't been defaced by dozens of other kids. The books were brand new—there was no graffiti, the pages weren't bent, and the bindings were still intact. The pages were crisp, unlike the school's copies of *To Kill a Mockingbird*, which smelled like mildew with their yellowy aged pages. One student even smelled the pages.

I tried to downplay how I got the books, but my supervising teacher squealed on me.

"Ms. Gruwell bought these books for you with her Christmas money," he said.

"Why would you waste your money on us?" asked Sharaud.

"It's not a waste. I actually think it may be one of the best presents *I've* ever received," I said.

My financial sacrifice seemed to make my students respect me more. I'd gone out on a limb to prove that they weren't "too stupid," so in turn they wanted to reciprocate the favor by truly dissecting Holden's plight. They had no idea that people wrote books in which the protagonist was just like them. Since *The Catcher in the Rye* was "reserved for the Honor students," a guilty pleasure permeated the room each time there was an epiphany or personal connection. My students related to Holden's angst, for almost everyone had at one point or another been the outcast, the reject, the misfit.

I knew going in that my student teaching position was supposed to last only a semester, but as finals approached, I started getting anxious. There were still so many things I wanted to do, so many stories I wanted to read, and so many places I wanted to take them. But I was running out of time and would be leaving Wilson at the end of January.

My supervising teacher, who had been relatively incognito since the first day of class, must have sensed my anxiety. He would inherit my students the second semester. I don't know if he didn't want to deal with Sharaud's antics six months shy of retirement, or if he could see how engaged they were in my class, but he decided to give me a gift—another semester teaching my students. Unbeknownst to me, he went to the district office, worked out a golden handshake, and allowed me to teach until June.

He wanted it to be a surprise to the students, so on the last day of the semester, he announced that I would be staying until the end of the school year. I would even get paid a nominal salary. What had all the sentimental makings of a good-bye party quickly became a celebration.

"Now you're stuck with me!" I said with a smile.

CHAPTER 6

S hortly after the new semester began in January 1994, a controversial
story broke about students from Castlemont High School in Oakland,
California, who laughed while watching Steven Spielberg's new epic,
Schindler's List. An hour into the film, several students laughed during a
scene where a Nazi shoots a Jewish woman in the head. Some Holocaust survivors who were in the audience were incensed at the students' inappropriate behavior. Someone complained, and the theater's management stopped
the film. When all sixty-nine students, most of them African American and
Latino, were escorted out of the theater, the audience applauded.

Pundits on the nightly news asked, "How could these kids be so insensitive?" Newspaper columnists wondered, "How could anyone laugh at the
plight of the Jews?" A lot of misinformation and stereotypes circulated
around this story, adding fuel to the race debate prompted by the Rodney
King riots.

Having just studied the Holocaust with my students, I felt emotionally
connected to this story. I wondered how much these Bay Area students actually knew about the Holocaust before they saw the film. I brought a newspaper article about the story into class, hoping it would spark a lively discussion.

Since my students were in the midst of reading *The Catcher in the Rye,*
they were questioning everything as if they were the embodiment of Holden
Caulfield. Everyone was phony and everything was a damn conspiracy! So,
with Holden's sensibility, we tried to dissect what happened in that theater.

"The teacher must have failed to prepare them," Sharaud concluded.

It turned out there was some truth to his hypothesis. We later learned that the teacher had organized a field trip over Martin Luther King weekend but had not put the film in context. Her students were told they would "see a movie" and "go ice-skating" afterward. Some of the students did not know the film was in black-and-white, that it was three and a half hours, and that it was about the Holocaust. They also were not aware that many Holocaust survivors would be attending that particular showing.

"I really think the students were misjudged and placed in an awkward situation," Sharaud said, defending them. "When kids are desensitized to violence, they often use laughter as a coping mechanism."

His wisdom sparked the desire to take my students to see the film. On the drive home from school that day, I noticed that *Schindler's List* was playing at my local theater in Newport Beach. I wondered what it would be like to take my students to my neck of the woods. What would they think about my neighborhood? And more important, how would they react to the movie?

On Monday, I casually said, *"Schindler's List* is playing at my local movie theater. Would any of you be interested in going with me to see it this Sunday?"

Every hand shot into the air.

I had no idea how I was going to get all of them to Newport Beach or how we were going to pay for it, but I was impressed by their commitment. I had to think fast, because I had only a few days. I quickly got on the phone to request a few more shifts at the Marriott.

Our plan was to meet in front of the school on Sunday afternoon and caravan down Pacific Coast Highway. Instead of trying to commandeer a bus at the last minute, I tried to round up friends and family who could help me schlep the students to the Lido Theater by car. Surprisingly, my father was the first to volunteer. I suspected that he wanted to meet Sharaud and Melvin firsthand even more than he wanted to see the film.

"Is your husband planning to come?" my dad asked.

"No, he's going to Germany tomorrow on a business trip," I said. Every time my father asked me questions about my marriage, I felt defensive. *Why isn't he pursuing a career in architecture? When are you two going to buy furniture? Why couldn't you have waited to get married?* And so on.

"I just wish he was more supportive of you," he said.

"Dad, don't worry. He is supportive of me," I said. But the reality was that my husband was not particularly interested in my school projects or my profession, and I found myself turning more to my father for emotional support. I suppose that's why I chose to take the kids to the film on a weekend when my husband would be out of the country.

As Sunday got closer, I thought it would be wise to inquire if the theater would offer us some kind of discount. Not only were we a large group, but we were pretty poor by Newport's standards. Most of my students were on some kind of federal assistance and received free and reduced lunch. It was always a painful reality when their meal tickets arrived. I tried to be inconspicuous when I passed the booklets out. Since most of my students were absolutely mortified about receiving the booklets in front of their peers, they usually refused to take them. Their pride took precedence over their hunger pangs. I didn't want the students to feel bad if they couldn't pay for the movie, so I decided to put everything on my credit card and deal with it later.

When I visited the theater to scout out the logistics, the manager was really sympathetic. Even though we were going to the twilight viewing, she said she'd charge us matinee prices. She even recommended that we bring our own snacks. "I'll just look the other way," she said with a smile, acknowledging that the concession stand prices might be a little excessive for many of my students.

I decided we would also need a place to process what we'd seen onscreen. I drove down the street to the Spaghetti Factory, an inexpensive restaurant that had hosted several of my sorority functions in the past. The manager climbed on board and reserved a special section on the second floor of the restaurant just for us.

When Sunday arrived, a fleet of friends and family lined up outside the school. Sharaud was one of the first to arrive. Unlike his usual attire of a football jersey and baggy pants, he was dressed in his finest church clothes.

Sharaud immediately yelled, "I'm driving with Ms. G," and hopped into the front seat. This time, it was my turn to navigate our way through my neighborhood. As we made our way down the coast, their eyes widened. Newport Beach and Long Beach are only about thirty miles apart, but my students pointed out how they are worlds away in most other respects. They noticed how there were "no bars on the windows," "no cars parked on anyone's lawn," and there weren't "liquor stores on every corner." I had never seen my neighborhood in this light before.

"Do you ever ask your neighbors for sugar?" Sharaud asked facetiously.

"I guess I could, if I needed to," I said.

"If you go knocking on your neighbor's door in my hood, you might get shot," he said.

When we got to the theater, I dutifully passed out to each student an individual care package filled with popcorn and candy. A darling student named Nicole made chocolate-chip cookies for everyone, as well. The two of us went up and down the line passing out our care packages.

Melvin and a couple of the boys went to the gourmet market adjacent to the theater to buy sodas and candy bars. The manager took one look at them and assumed they were going to shoplift. He followed them all over the store. When they got to the register, the cashier asked, "Do you have anything in your pockets?"

The boys turned their pockets inside out. All eyes were on them.

When they told me about their public humiliation, I was mortified.

"I'm so sorry," I said.

"Don't worry about it, Ms. G. That kind of shit happens all the time when you're black," said Melvin.

There was relatively no diversity in Newport Beach, and my students began to feel a little out of place. People stared at the kids and muttered comments under their breath. LaKeisha said that a couple of the ladies in the bathroom were holding their purses uncomfortably.

Choosing a theater in my neighborhood wasn't a calculated decision to take on the establishment. I just wanted to introduce my students to my world. It wasn't supposed to be a big deal, so all of this scuttlebutt was pretty shocking.

When we got to our seats, I overheard some uptight women in the next row contemplating whether to get a refund.

"Dad," I whispered, "do you think my kids notice what's going on?" I asked, feeling guilty.

"How could they not? They're more sophisticated than you give them credit for," he said.

When the lights finally went down, I was relieved.

During the film, they were completely consumed. Unlike their counterparts in Oakland, nobody laughed, nor did they take the subject matter lightly. They hugged one another, they shared Kleenex, and they even gave the film a standing ovation.

After the movie, we headed to the restaurant. Although our section was reserved and unoccupied, we waited and waited and waited. Every time people left the restaurant and saw us waiting to be served, they looked uncomfortable or afraid. When my students finally walked into the restaurant, I overheard a server saying, "I'm not serving *those* people."

It felt eerie as we walked to our seats. It reminded me of a cartoon, when the music dramatically scratches across the vinyl—errrr! And everything stops. And errr—everything did stop. Everyone looked. And everything that I knew to be true changed. Everything!

As we followed the hostess to our tables, you could have heard a pin drop. The bustling noise had stopped. The students could sense that the other diners didn't want them there. People looked them up and down, disapproving, as if they were lepers.

I was given that same disapproving look while in college when I house-sat for my boss whose partner had just died of AIDS. Since I was slightly homesick and missed my dogs at my parents' home, I volunteered to take care of their dogs after the funeral. When I got home, my roommate's boyfriend said with a look of disgust, "Don't touch me, I don't want to get AIDS." He was serious. He didn't know any gay people, so he believed all the rumors about catching AIDS in the air were true. I wondered what the people at the restaurant thought they were going to catch.

I had witnessed some pretty ignorant things while I was in high school. In my honors English class my junior year, my study partners and I picked *Uncle Tom's Cabin* to present for our final. My popular partner volunteered to be Uncle Tom. On the day of our presentation, he wore an Afro wig and took on the persona of Eddie Murphy's Buckwheat. He said, "Otay!" and grinned like he was the star of a *Saturday Night Live* sketch. All the students laughed, and we got an A. I never realized that there were no black students in my class who would have been offended by the crude Eddie Murphy impression.

The same honors students went on to Advanced Placement English our senior year. Two Berkeley-bound boys, who were self-proclaimed "anarchists" rebelling against stifling, suburban values, began their Holocaust slide show by turning off the lights and playing Oingo Boingo's "It's a Dead Man's Party." When the first slide came on, the teacher yanked the cord from the wall and kicked them out of class. Without any Jewish kids in the class to admonish them, the two perceived it as an act of defiance, not anti-Semitism.

For the first time, I was a witness to the effect of racial bias. Sitting among my students, I heard the whispers, the voices of hate, and the derogatory comments being cast at them. I was overwhelmed with a sense of wanting to shield them from such ignorance.

While we were at dinner, my elderly landlady, Dolores, who had volunteered to be a chaperone, pulled me aside with tears in her eyes and said, "Erin, I want to pay for dinner."

"No, it'll cost you a fortune," I protested.

"I insist," she said sincerely. "I'm so ashamed at how these wonderful kids have been treated. I don't want them to go home and think that everyone that lives in Newport Beach is a racist."

She took a wineglass, tapped it with her knife, and told the kids that it would be "an honor for her if she could treat them to dinner."

With that, Sharaud ordered the most expensive thing on the menu— the steak.

CHAPTER 7

The following day, *Schindler's List* won the Academy Award. In the post-Oscar frenzy, a reporter at the Newport Beach *Daily Pilot* decided to do a story about our trip to the Lido Theater after the manager tipped him off.

When the reporter and a photographer came to our classroom, he asked a number of probing questions about our experience. "Did you notice that there aren't many black people in Newport Beach?"

They all nodded.

"How were you treated?" he asked.

I sensed the reporter's slant on the story and it made me nervous. His leading questions opened the floodgates. Suddenly, Sharaud and other students talked about how they were looked at with disdain, how some patrons at the movie theater asked for refunds, and how women clutched their purses. The photographer snapped away as the young reporter feverishly scribbled on his little spiral notepad.

Newport's local paper ran the article the following Saturday. A friend called me at 6:30 in the morning and said, "Holy shit, Erin, you're on the cover of the *Daily Pilot*."

I put on my slippers, ran outside, and picked up the paper. It was dewy from the ocean mist. I opened up the paper and there we were—smack dab on the cover! The headline read, "A Lesson in Tolerance—Ethnically Diverse Class from Long Beach Comes to Newport to Watch Award-Winning 'Schindler's List,' Test Racial Waters." Next to the headline there were two color photos: one of me hugging a student named Keiuana and another of our classroom.

My husband was still sleeping, so I called my dad.

"What are you doing up so early?" he asked when he picked up the phone.

"My students and I are in the paper. Can I read it to you?"

"I have a 7 A.M. tee time," he said. "I've got to be out the door in a few minutes."

I began to read the article. My dad listened intently. "Uh-oh," I said. "They're quoting me as saying, 'You could tell the people in Newport were very, very nervous.'" I took a deep breath and continued to read. "'I told the kids . . . that Newport Beach is very conservative and there's not a lot of diversity. But they wanted to go. Most of them had never been there.'"

"Oh boy," my dad said.

"This might shake up the neighborhood a bit," I said. "But wait, there's more," I continued.

"'The people were lookin' us up and down like we were criminals,' said Sharaud, an African American student. 'I was in the bathroom, and this one white guy comes up to me and says, "What up cuz?" like I was a gang-banger or something.' Sharaud said one woman clutched her necklace as she walked by the group. 'You could see the veins bulging out of her neck.'"

There was silence on the other end of the phone. I continued to read.

"Melvin, the captain of Wilson's football team, said he felt as though fifty pairs of eyes were on him when he went inside the Via Lido Plaza Pavilion to buy a candy bar. 'They looked at me, then they looked at my pockets,' he said."

"The reporter didn't leave any stone unturned," my father said.

I continued to read.

"[La]Keisha said an elderly woman in the bathroom at the theater immediately grabbed her purse when the African American walked inside. 'I just looked at her like, "What are you thinkin'? I'm not going to do anything to your purse."'"

"This is a controversial article, Erin. I wonder if there'll be any letters to the editor," my dad said.

"We won't have to wait for any letters, Dad, because there's a little box that states, 'If you would be interested in sponsoring the class, give Gruwell a call at Wilson High School,' followed by *my home telephone number!*" I said.

The calls started soon afterward. At 8 A.M., a man screeched into my phone, "If you love black people so much, why don't you just marry a monkey?"

"Who are you?" I asked. I was scared.

"You better watch your back," he threatened.

I hung up immediately. For the rest of the day, I continued to receive calls from irate people. I was in the middle of being berated by another racist member of the community when my call-waiting beeped. "Can you hold on for a minute?" I stupidly asked. The voice on the other end announced that his name was "Joey Bishop," as if we were long-lost friends.

"Joey Bishop?" I shrugged at my husband. "Sir, I'm on the other line. May I have your telephone number and I'll call you back?"

Although Mr. Bishop seemed a little put off, he gave me his phone number anyway.

When I got off the phone, my husband chimed in, "Joey Bishop? Isn't he kind of famous?"

"I don't know."

My husband had been watching the spectacle unfold all afternoon and was feeling fiercely protective of me.

"I'll give him a call," I said, and dialed his number. "Mr. Bishop, this is Erin Gruwell."

"Do you know who I am?" he demanded.

"Not really," I admitted.

"Have you ever heard of the Rat Pack?" he asked.

I looked at my husband and whispered, "Rat Pack?"

"Frank Sinatra," my husband whispered back.

"Oh, the Rat Pack," I said, trying to recover. "Yes, Frank Sinatra."

"Yes," he said. "And who else?"

"Sammy Davis Jr.?" I asked. My husband nodded and gave me a thumbs-up.

"Yes! Who else?" he baited.

"Dean Martin," I said confidently, feeling like I had completed the trio. Then I waited.

"You're forgetting somebody," he said indignantly.

"Who am I forgetting?" I asked. I looked at my husband for help, but he shrugged his shoulders. We were out of answers.

"Yours truly!" Joey said.

As it turns out, Mr. Bishop was my neighbor and lived a stone's throw from the Lido Theater. He had just read the paper and was absolutely appalled by our neighbors' reaction, but he was also not surprised. "Why don't you come over to my house, young lady, so we can have a chat?" he invited.

"But I'm in sweats," I said apologetically. I assumed that if he was famous, I should get all dressed up.

"That's okay, I'm in sweats too."

He gave me directions, and I hopped into my car to meet him. When I found his home, he greeted me at the door wearing a yarmulke and carrying a tub of licorice.

"Want some?" he offered.

Truthfully, I needed something stronger than licorice to support my shaking knees, but I thought *When in Rome* . . . As we munched on licorice, Joey took me upstairs to his office to show me pictures of Frank, Sammy, and the rest of the Pack. He told me that he used to host a variety show similar to Johnny Carson's, and his walls were filled with photos of famous people.

"This is a picture of me and JFK," he said. "Oh, this is my favorite letter from Jackie." He pointed out photo after photo. It was surreal.

When he was done showing off his memorabilia, he took me downstairs to the parlor.

"Erin, do you have any idea what you've done?" he asked.

"How could such a beautiful community be hiding such an ugly secret?" I asked.

"Don't be so naive," he said.

Joey Bishop saw my situation differently. He drew a parallel between our little pilgrimage down Pacific Coast Highway and Pandora's box. Once Pandora's box is opened, all societal ills come flooding out. In the parable, it takes Pandora some time to reach "hope"—nestled at the bottom of the box.

"Unfortunately, I only have a few more months to find hope," I said, "before the school year is over."

He seemed slightly annoyed that I didn't give more reverence to his parable, so he told me a more serious story, one that personally involved him.

"I used to be a member of a prestigious golf course in Newport Beach until a golfer began a joke by asking, 'Hey, Joey, why did Hitler stop gassing the Jews?'" Joey said he didn't respond. "The golfer continued the joke by saying, 'Because the gas bill got too high!'" There was an outburst of laughter from the other golfers. Joey said he turned around and canceled his membership on the spot. "Racism, anti-Semitism—it may be subversive in this zip code, but it's serious stuff. You need to be careful, sweetheart," he warned.

Now I understood why he'd called me. I had an ally. As he was walking me to the door, he told me that he and Frank Sinatra and a priest from Palm Springs had converted a bunch of badass Hell's Angels into "Bikers for Christ." "If anything goes wrong," he assured me, "I can have fifty Harleys on your lawn within an hour."

Fifty Harleys? I hoped I wouldn't have to take him up on his offer.

I arrived at class on Monday with a stack of *Daily Pilot* newspapers. One for each student. Manny was so excited that he read it aloud as if he were Tom Brokaw hosting *The Nightly News:* "'In tough areas of Long Beach, a Holocaust of sorts occurs daily, the students said. Intolerant teenagers killing one another because of racial, cultural, and ethnic differences aren't an unusual occurrence.'"

"Manny, have you ever read a newspaper before?" I asked.

"Nope, this is the first one," he said with a smile from ear to ear. His pride permeated the room. His excitement was contagious. When he got to the quotes from the students and the actual description of how they were treated, Sharaud blurted out, "Damn!" Enthusiastic nods followed.

"Look, they quote me too," Manny said. "'Manuel lost a best friend to a gangster's bullet,'" he read.

"What's it like to read about yourself in a newspaper?" I asked Manny.

"It's weird," Manny said. "But at least he kept it real." Then, without skipping a beat, Manny turned the tables and asked me, "What do you think, Ms. G?"

"Well, um . . ." I hesitated in sharing how "real" it actually was. I desperately wanted to minimize my part in all of this. This wasn't about me—it was about them. I wanted them to feel special about being on the front cover of a newspaper, seeing their names in print, and feeling validated for doing something positive. I wanted them to bask in the moment, not worry about me.

Unfortunately, I don't have a poker face. They could see right through me. "The phone number in that little box is not Wilson's, it's mine," I said.

"Did anybody call you?" Manny asked.

"Actually, a few of my neighbors did," I stammered.

The mere mention of my neighbors piqued their interest. They started drilling me for details.

"Really? What'd they say?" Sharaud asked. Suddenly, my boring suburban life wasn't so boring after all.

I wasn't ready to give them the graphic details about the death threats I had received over the weekend, so I gave them the watered-down version in hopes that we could move on. I didn't want to tell them that one caller referred to my students as "niggers"—a word that causes a visceral reaction in me every time I hear it.

I had never been good at confrontation. Ever since I was a child, I'd learned to suppress situations that made me feel uncomfortable, and I tried to avoid controversy at all costs. Over the years, I had perfected my role as the mediator in my family, and I was accustomed to smoothing things over. I wanted to smooth this over, too, but it wasn't as easy as getting my brother and sister to call a truce.

But the boys in my class were not used to having someone call a truce. They were much too perceptive, and they could tell that I was "holding out on them." The more evasive I was, the more they pursued. And simply paraphrasing the calls only whetted their appetites. They wanted to know what the callers said—verbatim.

Finally, I capitulated. I told them that one of the callers said, "If you love black people so much, why don't you marry a monkey?"

The street fighter in Melvin reared its ugly head. He didn't want someone "punking his homegirl" and wanted to protect me.

As much as I wanted to dismiss the calls as idle threats, two of my students told me stories that were so incomprehensible, I had to accept that skinheads and death threats should not be taken lightly.

Manny shared a horrific tale about how his best friend was kidnapped by a Caucasian gang from Poly High School called the Ace of Spades. They hog-tied him, stabbed him to death, and then threw him off a cliff in a neighboring city. Convinced that he was next, Manny stayed in his house for the next six months, refused to go to school, and failed all of his classes. But what did grades matter? He didn't expect to see his sixteenth birthday.

Everyone knew Manny's story already except for me. I looked at Manny, who always had a smile on his face, and my heart ached for his loss.

"Manny, that's so sad," I said. "I can't imagine what it's like to feel that hopeless."

"When you have nothing to live for, Ms. G, you look for reasons to die," Sharaud interjected. His comment struck me. I was surprised at how wise he could be at times.

Dan, a quiet blond kid who always sat in the corner, said solemnly, "Hey, Manny, I know the guys who killed your best friend. They were friends of my older brother."

Dan's brother was tired of being poor and picked on, so he joined a skinhead gang that promised him protection. His brother had been recently arrested for stockpiling weapons he intended to use to blow up a local synagogue. Before his brother's arrest, Dan said that his brother occasionally hung out with members of the Ace of Spades.

Manny was noticeably stirred.

Dan told the class that he couldn't believe his brother had joined a neo-Nazi group, especially after all that we had learned about the Holocaust.

"What is so weird," Dan said, "is that we're not even pure white. Our mother is Mexican."

"My mom is Mexican too," Manny said, sharing the moment.

Manny and Dan's connection seemed to calm down the mini-militia that Melvin had been mounting. When the bell rang, Sharaud came up to me and whispered, "We got your back, Ms. G."

I took comfort in my students' support. I hoped that people would toss out their weekend newspapers and all the drama would subside. On the drive home, I assured myself that all of this was bound to blow over.

But it didn't. It was just the tip of the iceberg.

CHAPTER 8

When I got home from school, my answering machine was full of vicious messages. After a message in which someone shouted, "We don't want their kind down here," there was a concerned message from the reporter at the *Daily Pilot*.

"I'm sorry for putting your home telephone number in the paper," he apologized. "Did you receive any phone calls?"

"I did. Some of them were pretty appalling," I said.

The reporter said that the newspaper received a few disturbing ones, as well.

"Where do you think these calls are coming from?" I asked.

"Who knows? Racists, skinheads, Holocaust deniers," he rattled off.

"People really deny the Holocaust?" I asked.

"You'd be surprised," he said. "There is a local group called the Institute of Historical Review that actually believes that Jews were not gassed at Auschwitz."

"You've got to be kidding me," I said. "This group is located in Orange County?" I asked.

"It's sad, but true. Their P.O. box is in Newport Beach."

I was stunned.

"In 1979, the Institute had the gall to offer any survivor of the Holocaust a fifty-thousand-dollar award if he or she could prove that Jews were gassed in gas chambers at Auschwitz," he continued.

"Oh my God, what happened?" I asked.

"A Holocaust survivor named Mel Mermelstein took the Institute up on their offer. The Institute wrote him a letter offering him fifty thousand dollars for proof 'that Jews were gassed in gas chambers at Auschwitz,' but when Mr. Mermelstein provided proof, the Institute refused to pay him."

"This is shocking," I said. "Then what happened?"

"Mr. Mermelstein sued the Institute for breach of contract. As a result, a U.S. Superior Court in California ruled that Mr. Mermelstein had provided proof and the landmark case declared that the Holocaust is an indisputable legal fact."

"What happened to the Institute?" I asked, as if he were reading me a cliffhanger.

"The Institute and some of their affiliates eventually had to pay Mr. Mermelstein ninety thousand dollars and offer an apology. Believe it or not, they're still around."

My stomach plummeted. The reporter speculated they might even be some of the people who were calling me. These weren't just a few isolated, angry Archie Bunker types.

It was hard to believe that in 1994, fifty years after the Holocaust, people still denied its existence. The reporter went on to tell me about some neo-Nazis in a neighboring city. These skinheads didn't just shave their heads and don swastikas; they defaced local synagogues, harassed people, and perpetrated hate crimes. I wondered whether these ignorant white supremacists would still be bigots if they heard Renee's or Mel's personal testimonies.

Since our article had caused an unexpected commotion, the *Daily Pilot* decided to run a follow-up article. Luckily, the second article triggered a wave of sympathetic callers.

Ron Wilson, the ombudsman from the University of California, Irvine, called and said, "Erin, I see you're still up to mischief!"

"Unexpectedly, yes," I said. Ron had been my confidant in college. I could always count on him, so I was thrilled that he was reaching out to me.

He wanted to know how people were reacting to the article in the paper. I knew I could cut to the chase with him.

"Ron, it's been crazy. All I wanted to do was take my students to see a movie about intolerance, and now I'm being threatened by absolute strangers," I said.

"That's why I called you, sweetheart," he said. "UCI is hosting a symposium on tolerance, and I think it would be a perfect follow-up for your students. The symposium is featuring the author of *Schindler's List,* Thomas Keneally, who is a visiting professor."

With *Schindler's List*'s recent Academy Award, Thomas Keneally's new addition to the UCI creative writing department was quite a coup. Ron offered to roll out the red carpet by hosting lunch in the dorms and arranging a private meeting with Keneally. The idea of taking my students to my alma mater to meet an acclaimed author was very exciting.

But then the reality hit me. How was I going to get permission to go on another field trip?

"Ron, I don't think they'll let me go on another field trip." I must have touched a nerve in Ron, because suddenly years of struggling against academic inequality came to the surface. He wanted to know why athletes get out of class early to take bus trips to score touchdowns, and why student council members get out early to plan assemblies, and cheerleaders get to primp for pep rallies. He continued his litany of exceptions, and I agreed with every single one of them, because I was the athlete who got out of fifth and sixth period for bus trips, as class president I got out of second period to plan assemblies, and as a cheerleader, I always went to third period late after our pep rallies.

I begged Ron to call my principal and discuss the field trip with him. If Ron could get my principal to agree to this worthy outing, then I could find the money for another bus somehow.

I'm not exactly sure what Ron told my principal, but somehow he agreed that we could attend the symposium. However, it left me in pursuit of financial help. It was a lot easier this time around, because when people like Polly Stanbridge called and asked if they could help me, I said, "Absolutely!" Polly lived a few miles from me, and her husband was an acclaimed scientist at UCI. She was heartsick about the racist reactions of our neighbors, so she offered to galvanize her friends and family to contribute to our cause.

Even though a couple of checks trickled in, we still didn't have enough money. I decided to speak to a gentleman I had befriended at the Marriott who was living on the twelfth story of our hotel while they remodeled his home. He'd created the bobblehead doll for Major League Baseball and had made a fortune. My dad had a Reds bobblehead on his desk, next to a baseball signed by Pete Rose and Johnny Bench. The rumor in the hotel was that he was a billionaire.

Over the course of a year, I had met his children and his grandchildren and received my share of wet kisses on the cheek. I had made his plane reservations and dinner reservations and I'd defended him to all the disgruntled bellmen.

After he read about my students' experience seeing *Schindler's List*, he told me about losing the majority of his family in the Holocaust. So one day I explained my dilemma about the field trip over a cup of coffee and the Sunday crossword puzzle. When I finished telling him my predicament, he pulled out his checkbook and wrote me a check.

"Wow! That's a lot of money!" I exclaimed, looking at the check in disbelief. "We don't need *that* much."

"Well, if I'm going to ride the bus with you," he offered, "we might as well go in style!"

So instead of taking the traditional yellow school bus, we were picked up by a charter bus, with our new patron sitting shotgun. As my students filed onto the bus, I was impressed with how they had dressed up for our excursion. Melvin even wore glasses, though his eyesight was 20/20. "They make me look smarter," he claimed.

While we were on the bus, I got on the PA system and asked, "How many of you have ever visited a college campus before?" Not many responded. Many of them didn't expect to graduate from high school, so why visit a college?

"Since you all look like college students today," I continued, "I think you should act like college students once we get off the bus!" I hoped that our college visit would make higher learning seem more attainable.

When we arrived at the university, Ron greeted me with a warm hug.

"Ron, this is Sharaud," I said as he got off the bus.

"I'm a history major," Sharaud said, sounding quite precocious.

I winked at Sharaud. Ron graciously played along.

At nearly seven feet tall and wearing a purple suit, Ron had a commanding presence. As we toured the campus, my students analyzed everything: what college students wore, the architecture, how college students interacted. They marveled that there were no bells and that no hall passes were needed. They couldn't believe students could walk around so freely without being followed by security guards.

We made our way to the dorms for lunch, and I noticed Sharaud had gravitated to Ron's side. Sharaud had seen his father only a handful of times in the last sixteen years; I could tell he craved Ron's attention.

As my students picked up their lunch trays, Ron instructed, "You can have anything you want. Burgers, pizza, salad bar. Heck, you can even have Lucky Charms!"

They were in awe of all their choices, heaping food on their trays and mixing concoctions like soft-serve ice cream with Froot Loops.

I asked Ron to tell them a little bit about himself.

"I am living proof," he said, "that if you're born in the ghetto, you don't have to stay in the ghetto." There was an instant connection.

"Where are you from?" asked LaKeisha.

"I was born and raised in Harlem. And like many of you, I've seen intolerance firsthand. In fact, one of my best friends was murdered when I was a kid. After he was killed, they suspended his body through a basketball hoop as a warning to the whole neighborhood."

We were all stunned.

"How'd you make it out?" Manny asked.

"It was hard work, my friend. Education was my salvation," he said.

Manny nodded sympathetically.

I was relieved that their acceptance of him came so naturally.

"Okay," he said, a glimmer in his eye, "it's time to meet Thomas Keneally."

Although Thomas Keneally was the keynote speaker for the conference, Ron had made special arrangements for my students to meet with him beforehand. He'd reserved the outdoor humanities arena for us to talk with Keneally for an hour. When he joined us—a jovial Australian in a floppy hat and a leprechaun beard—my students were spellbound. He had written the story that had transfixed us in that darkened theater. They acted like they were meeting a movie star.

Thomas Keneally told us the genesis of *Schindler's List*. He and his wife were on vacation and happened to stroll into a luggage shop in Beverly Hills.

When he told the shop owner, Poldek Pfefferberg, that he was a writer, the frail man began telling Keneally about the Warsaw ghetto, atrocities of the Holocaust, and how a righteous gentile named Oskar Schindler had saved his life. When he finished his moving story, the survivor begged Keneally to write about it.

My students had so many questions for him. How long did it take to write the book? Was the movie accurate? As the questions continued, we learned that telling the story had been an odyssey in and of itself. He talked about the process of turning his novel, *Schindler's Ark,* into a feature film. It took nearly a decade before his novel, published in 1982, became the basis of the Academy Award winner. He had no idea that once the story was told it would have such a profound impact on the world.

"Timing is everything," he told us.

Talking to a famous author made the writing process more relevant to my students. Whenever they were involved in the process, and not simply sitting at a desk, I noticed they asked fabulous questions and expressed themselves in meaningful metaphors.

Then Keneally began asking my students personal questions. His genuine interest validated them, and soon they were divulging emotional stories. Dan talked about how his brother defaced tombstones in a Jewish cemetery. Dara, a Cambodian refugee, talked about how some of her family members were killed by Pol Pot's political regime. The Khmer Rouge army forced her family to dig ditches, then climb into the holes they'd made. Once their bodies were covered with dirt, the young soldiers decapitated them. Keiuana spoke about witnessing urban genocide on the streets of L.A. She witnessed her first murder at the age of five, when one of her relatives told her to "duck" as he pulled the trigger on a sawed-off shotgun in a drive-by shooting.

As their vivid stories unfolded, I sensed Keneally was mesmerized. When I was in college, I never heard stories as tragic as my students'. Most of my peers came from suburban homes and talked about teenage angst or their parents' divorce. I imagined that Keneally had plenty of students like me who would rather write fictional tales than reflect on real life. I wondered if stories as gritty as my students' had ever crossed his desk.

Each story they shared seemed to relate to intolerance, whether they were the innocent bystander, the victim, or the actual perpetrator. And as they shared, I marveled at how respectful he was of them. He didn't placate them, try to exploit them, or even show them pity. He listened to them, really listened to them.

When they were finished sharing, he simply said, "You need to write your own stories."

On our way back to the bus, Keneally pulled me aside to tell me that our story was very touching and that I should share it with his friend, "Steven." I assumed "Steven" was another author or a professor, so I asked, "What does Steven teach?"

Keneally burst into laughter. Steven was neither a professor nor a writer. "He's a director," he said. My body went numb. Steven? As in *the* Steven? *ET* Steven? I had seen every one of Steven Spielberg's movies—from *Jaws* to *Schindler's List*—and referring to him by his first name seemed sacrilegious.

Keneally went on to say that Steven and I should meet. But as far as I was concerned, people like me didn't meet people like him. People like me read about people like him in magazines. I knew where Spielberg dined and what he'd named his children, but I never expected to carry on a conversation with him.

I went on to explain that I didn't feel comfortable contacting Spielberg— that just wasn't my style. I'd have been content to catch a glimpse of him on the red carpet, not meet face-to-face. I was sure I would say something stupid. Besides, what would a genius like him have to say to a clueless teacher like me? He was at the top of his game and I was fumbling my way across the bottom. He'd just accepted an Academy Award, while I wasn't even accepted in the teachers' lounge!

As a means to divert his request, I pointed out some of my flaws, like creating lesson plans on my way to work and scribbling essay prompts on a pizza napkin. Occasionally, I even taught on the fly.

Downplaying my capabilities didn't discourage Keneally. He was steadfast, and continued to press the issue.

To appease him, I wrote down my telephone number and handed it to him.

"If you want to share our story with your 'friend,' I would be honored," I said, "but in my opinion, the real honor was meeting you."

CHAPTER 9

Thomas Keneally said that you have a pretty compelling story," said
Marvin Levy, Steven Spielberg's spokesperson.

My stomach tightened into a little ball.

"We were wondering if you could write us a letter explaining what makes
your class so special," he said.

I was so nervous that I almost dropped the phone.

Mr. Levy asked if I could mail the letter to his office by Monday morning. Considering that it was nearly 5 P.M. on a Friday, I had only twenty-four
hours to write a compelling letter and then FedEx it to Marvin. My mission
seemed impossible. How was I going to write a letter that was interesting
enough to make its way through the stacks of fan mail Spielberg received
every day?

I turned to my husband in hopes of getting sympathy. He had studied
architecture in college, and he reminded me that Frank Lloyd Wright cranked
out the designs for his famous house, Fallingwater, in only four hours. I knew
he meant well, but this anecdote didn't console me much—I was no Frank
Lloyd Wright.

I didn't know where to start. I agonized at my computer for hours—starting over and over again. It was a daunting task. I felt absolutely inadequate
putting my feelings on paper. How could I encapsulate everything I'd experienced with my students?

I didn't want my letter to come across like a cheesy Hallmark card or
some dramatic after-school special. My students' "keep it real" motto would

be my compass. I wanted my letter to be so "real" that my students leapt off the page the way ET transcended the movie screen.

Suddenly, I could empathize with my students' reluctance to write! When trying to get them to pick up a pen, I used corny clichés to trick them into writing. The girls loved my miniskirt model: "Make your paper long enough to cover everything but short enough to pique someone's interest." The boys reveled in my toilet theory: "Make your paper interesting enough that you would want to take it into the bathroom with you." Since the days of living with four boys and my fiancé, I was convinced some males' best reading took place in the bathroom. I knew that if I made my writing analogies crude enough, I'd grab their attention. The girls all sang in unison, "Ew, Ms. G, that's gross!" but the boys gave each other high fives like I was privy to some secret code. Soon, the girls took great pride in showing off their miniskirt masterpiece, and the boys speculated as to whether or not someone would want to read their opening zinger on the throne.

While my clichés worked wonders curing my students' writer's block, it was the classic case of "do as I say, not as I do!"

At 4 A.M. on Saturday morning, it hit me. I needed to paint a picture for Spielberg in the same way that he had brought the Holocaust to life by spotlighting the little girl in the red coat. Spielberg was the master at saying so much by saying so little. I needed a metaphor that would bring my class to life in the same way.

"My class is as colorful as a box of Crayola crayons," I wrote. After hours of agonizing, and two pots of coffee later, I'd finally found my hook. Rather than identifying my students by a singular color—black, brown, yellow, or white—I described them as crayons. And even if they were rough around the edges, or were broken in the middle, they figured out a way to hold the pieces together, smooth out those rough edges, and even sharpen themselves.

I milked the crayon analogy until I felt like I'd painted an adequate portrait of my class. When I finished my manifesto, I was blurry eyed and grumpy. Craving a bit of reassurance and something to soak up all the coffee I'd consumed, I drove to my dad's house for some breakfast and a quick edit before I sent my letter off to Spielberg.

I sat across from my dad as he read my letter. Sometimes he nodded, which I took as a good sign, but then he began to shake his head. Not a good sign.

"You can't say 'bullshit' in a letter to Steven Spielberg!" he said sternly. "Do you want him to think that you talk like a sailor?"

"I guess I got a little carried away, huh?" I said over my scrambled eggs and toast. In the letter, I tried to describe how an English teacher had called my students "stupid" and wouldn't let them read the school's copies of *The Catcher in the Rye*. I struggled to come up with an eloquent description of how she made me feel, but in the wee hours of the morning, "bullshit" seemed to sum up the scenario.

"Erin, take the high road on this one. You're lucky to have a job. At the end of the day, you need to realize that those other teachers have tenure and you don't. If you don't lay low for the rest of the year, they're not going to hire you next year."

"But you taught me to question authority," I responded.

"At this stage in your career, you can't afford to be this much of a maverick."

I didn't want to admit that he was right. As usual. After some cajoling, my dad got me to admit that "bullshit" was a little "too colorful" and that it didn't quite fit into how I wanted to present myself and my students.

When I finally left his house, I doubted myself both as a writer and as a teacher.

Sealing the FedEx package, I felt like a kid putting a message in a bottle and sending it out to sea. Maybe my letter would be read, maybe not.

Marvin Levy called a couple days later and said, "Steven loved your letter!"

"Really?" I said in disbelief.

"He wants to meet you," he said assuredly.

A million questions ran through my head. What do I wear? What should I say? Should I bring examples of my lesson plans? Luckily, I didn't have too much time to obsess, because Marvin interjected, "How about tomorrow?"

"Um, sure. I can come right after school."

I did not tell my students about my meeting with Spielberg—I didn't want to get their hopes up. I think they could tell that something was going on, though, because I was a bit distracted and restless. Close to the end of the day, I made an announcement that I would not be available for any tutoring after school and left immediately.

I was a nervous wreck. And if visiting Spielberg wasn't daunting enough, I would have to make the ninety-minute drive to the studio without any air-conditioning. Someone had recently broken into my car, stolen my radio, and messed up the wiring to the air-conditioning.

Spielberg's office was located on the Universal Studios lot, the epicenter of where so many movies and television shows are filmed. I made my way past the billboards and back lots. Everything looked so different behind the scenes. I was used to the polished perspective on the screen, not the facades.

I drove past the guards and parked in the lot adjacent to his office. All the cars were so fancy, and mine wasn't. My convertible roof was starting to rust in spots, and it needed a new paint job.

As soon as I entered the lobby, I felt out of place. This was not a world I was familiar with, and I didn't know how to dress or how to act. I wondered if this was how my students felt each time I took them out of their comfort zones—to a restaurant in an affluent neighborhood, or to a college campus.

While I patiently waited in the lobby, I felt conspicuous in my clothes. I didn't have time to go shopping for something new, and I suddenly felt insecure. I was wearing a suit that was missing a button. Although I'd been accused of "overdressing" while in the teachers' lounge, now I felt fashion challenged. The stylish receptionist behind the desk made me painfully self-conscious. I noticed that my shoes were slightly scuffed, so I tried to hide them under the coffee table. Then I noticed I had traces of chalk on my butt. I began to rub off the chalk, when a pretty woman appeared. She was wearing a fancy headset that reminded me of a gadget I'd seen on *The Jetsons*.

"You must be Erin," she said enthusiastically. "Would you like something to drink?"

"No, I'm fine," I said, when in actuality I wasn't fine—I was about to implode.

"I'm Marvin's assistant, Becky," she said. "Marvin can't wait to meet you," she said with a reassuring smile.

As she led me to Marvin's office, I noticed all the movie paraphernalia decorating the office. I had to remind myself that I was there for a reason and I couldn't let all the fancy cars and designer labels throw me off. While I was waiting to be introduced to Marvin, I organized some of the photos I'd brought with me. I must have looked like Felix the Cat, pulling photos out of my bag of tricks. I was looking at a picture of Sharaud at the Spaghetti Factory when Marvin walked in and said, "Spielberg loved your letter, young lady!"

Suddenly, I was experiencing performance anxiety, knowing that my first impression could be my only impression. I had to make the best of it.

As Marvin talked, in his New York accent, I couldn't help but look around and see all the eclectic artwork in the office—an ET figure, some kind of dinosaur, an original Norman Rockwell painting, and a framed poster of *Schindler's List*. The environment looked more like a college dorm, with all the cool gadgets and fancy posters, than a business office.

When Spielberg casually walked in, I was taken aback. No fanfare, no bodyguards, no trumpets announcing his arrival or rose petals at his feet. Just a bearded man in jeans, a T-shirt, and a baseball cap.

"Hello, Erin," he said with a welcoming grin.

I was stunned. His mannerisms were more like those of an animated kid than a movie mogul. Reaching my hand out to meet his, I said, "It's such an honor to meet you, Mr. Spielberg." I wondered if he noticed the moisture in my hands.

"I loved how you described your class as being as 'colorful as a box of Crayola crayons,'" he said.

I was excited that he took note of my analogy. He seemed to be genuinely interested in the plight of my students.

"So what did you say to the teacher who told you that your students were 'too stupid' to read *The Catcher in the Rye*?" he asked.

"I should have told her to fuck off!" I said.

Oh my God, where did that come from? I completely froze. *Did I just say "fuck" in front of Steven Spielberg?* I wanted to run and hide behind ET.

The next few moments were like an out-of-body experience. The word "fuck" kept playing in my head like a broken record. It reminded me of *The Brady Bunch* episode where the vase shatters and all the audience hears is "Mom always said, 'don't play ball in the house!'" Instead of hearing naughty Brady boys admonish me, I heard my father. "Do you want Spielberg to think you talk like a sailor?"

My students must have been rubbing off on me. I was waiting for the bodyguards to throw me right off the lot. But, in a strange twist of fate, my internal monologue was interrupted by hysterical laughter from the big boy in the baseball cap.

In a desperate attempt to regain my composure, I asked him if I could show him some pictures of my students. Excitedly, he agreed. I pulled out photos of Melvin in a hula skirt, Sharaud with my father at the Spaghetti Factory, and Manny hugging Thomas Keneally. With each picture, I felt like a proud parent. It didn't matter what kind of clothes they wore, where they came from, or even what color their skin was—somehow Spielberg saw what I saw.

Then he asked me if he could meet my students. My knees got weak. But there was a catch—he didn't want any publicity. No press releases, no cameras, and absolutely no reporters. Just us. I understood his excitement to meet the students, tempered with his desire for privacy.

I began to worry about how I was going to arrange another field trip. I assumed there would be anarchy in our English empire. Without cussing this time, I reminded him that my department wasn't very supportive of our escapades outside the confines of the school. Their obstinacy didn't seem to faze him. He'd worked with difficult people along the way. His office would take care of everything—buses, tickets to Universal Studios, and a private meeting with him.

I made my way off the Universal lot and hit typical horrific L.A. traffic. Even though I'd just had an amazing meeting, I began to lose my confidence. I wondered how my colleagues were going to react to Spielberg's invitation. I doubted that the chair of the English Department would allow my students to take another trip, especially so close to the end of the year, when they traditionally inundated students with a series of standardized tests.

My intuition told me that the chair would say "No!" and that I was headed for a battle.

CHAPTER 10

I f my students were going to meet Spielberg, especially on his turf, then I
wanted them to feel as if they'd "earned" it. I'm a big believer in "earning
stuff," which probably stems from my parents making me do chores when I
was a kid. I spent a lot of time doing chores and picking up after our three
St. Bernards.

My business acumen kicked in at the age of thirteen, when my sister,
Gina, was told that if she wanted to have a car when she turned sixteen,
"she'd have to pay for it herself." With a sneak preview of what lay in store,
I became an entrepreneur. I mowed lawns, cleaned neighbors' homes, and did
a lot of babysitting. When my sixteenth birthday rolled around, I bought my
own car. Even though it was only a Mitsubishi without any air-conditioning,
it was mine. Three years of pooper-scoopers, grass clippings, and Comet
made me appreciate my car much more than some of my girlfriends who'd
been handed the keys to a brand-new BMW on their sixteenth birthday.

My two-door Mitsubishi Mirage lasted me through my senior year in college, and every time I crammed the cheerleading squad into it or loaded it up
with all my worldly possessions to move to a new apartment, it reminded
me how hard I had worked. I hoped that if I made my students work a little
harder for this field trip, maybe they'd appreciate it more. I wasn't going to
make them clean any houses or shovel dog poop, but maybe a poignant writing assignment that figuratively "cleaned house" would suffice.

To earn the field trip they would have to write about their journeys—their
own personal odysseys. In Homer's epic tale, Odysseus simply has to go

from point A to point B in hopes of making it home alive. Along the way, he faces adversity—a Cyclops here, Sirens there. But somehow, he makes it home in one piece. I wanted my students to understand that, like Odysseus or any other literary protagonist, they too were on a journey, and although they didn't face Cyclops or the Sirens, they had their own monsters to deal with.

Each protagonist we had studied since September underwent a similar journey and experienced a profound epiphany—Scout in *To Kill a Mockingbird,* Holden in *The Catcher in the Rye,* and even Oskar Schindler in *Schindler's List.*

Manny was the first student who dove into the autobiography project. It was as if he planned to get a Pulitzer Prize. Meeting Keneally made him see the power of writing, and this was his chance to tell his story to a sympathetic audience. He'd grown up thinking he was Mexican until kids on the playground started calling him racial names like "nigger." When he asked his mom what the word "nigger" meant, she told her five-year-old son some shocking news: The man he called "Daddy" was not his real father. His biological father was black, and he was in prison.

As he grew older, Manny's features became more like his father's, and kids in the predominantly white neighborhood stopped playing with him. Even his maternal grandfather disowned him. In response, Manny toughened his skin and began to react to people's stereotypes. When people made assumptions about him, he validated them. If people were going to call him names and treat him differently, he was going to act the part. If people called him stupid, he acted stupid. If people thought he might steal something, he would rob them just to prove a point. And if people looked afraid of him, he'd punch them to reinforce their fear.

By the age of fourteen, he still didn't know his father or his own identity. So when skinheads murdered his best friend, his anger consumed him. He wondered why they hadn't killed him instead. Manny convinced himself that he was either doomed to go to jail like his father or join his friend in the grave.

Manny had the strength to change his destiny, and his letter became a model for the class. Manny read his rough draft aloud with pride. When he finished, the class broke into applause. He got glances that said simply, "I've been there, done that." No look was more intense than the one he got from Khari.

Khari was the biggest kid in our class. He was pure muscle mass. I hadn't quite figured him out yet, which made me concerned because the year was almost over. He never said anything, rarely turned in his homework, but was always present, always engaged. Something in Manny's memoir had rocked Khari, so much so that he came up to me after class and asked if he could talk to me. He hesitated and then said sincerely, "I don't think I should go on this field trip. I haven't earned it."

I was shocked. "What do you mean you haven't earned it?"

"I can't write like Manny, and I'm ashamed of my story. I don't want to make the class look bad," he said sadly.

"What do you mean 'look bad'?"

"Ms. G, you don't understand. I've seen a lot of shit. I mean, I've been in drive-by shootings, I've pulled the trigger, and I've buried my share of friends. I came to Wilson to get away from trouble, but trouble seems to have a way of finding me."

Something inside me ached. I wanted to hug him and tell him everything would be okay. Instead of placating him, I decided to challenge him. "Khari, you are going to write your story and hand it in tomorrow, even if I have to go to your house tonight and help you write it," I yelled. "I don't care if you have to stay up until 5 A.M.—I expect you to write it. I won't accept any excuses."

We locked eyes and stared at each other for a moment. He was the first to look away.

"Okay, I'll do it," he said, noticeably shaken.

When he left, I was trembling.

In class the next day, I announced it was time to turn in their final drafts. Khari nodded his head. He didn't turn in his paper at the same time as the rest of them, though. He kept it at his desk, afraid to let it out of his possession. When the bell rang, he remained in his seat. I knew something was up; I asked everyone to leave so I could talk to him.

"Khari, what's going on?" He didn't look at me. Instead, he looked down at his paper. It was typed. No other paper was. None of my students had computers, so I didn't require them to type assignments unless we could all go to the computer lab together.

When he handed me his paper, he was shaking. He seemed so strong, yet he was so vulnerable. I sat down in a desk next to him and began to read.

"Dear Mr. Spielberg, My life is very different than yours . . ." As I continued to read, I couldn't contain my tears. I reached for his hand as I read about his first drive-by, the bullet that was still lodged in his knee, and his "38 special" handgun. He described a world that seemed like fiction, but it was his painful reality. At the end of his letter, he said, he would understand if Spielberg didn't want to meet him, because he was "bad."

By the time I finished the letter, Khari had put his head on the desk and covered his face with his enormous arms. He was trying to hide the fact that he, too, was crying. We sat there for a while without saying anything. I just squeezed his hand, as if I could send him some secret Morse code that said, "It'll be all right." But I didn't know if it really would.

When he finally lifted his head, I nodded. Then I put my hand on my heart. He nodded too.

"Khari, I'm going to put your letter on the top of the pile," I said. "I want Mr. Spielberg to read yours first."

Khari simply smiled and mouthed "thank you" as he walked away.

After Khari left, I felt desperate. Initially, my intention was to make my students believe that they'd "earned" the right to meet Spielberg. I didn't think there was any harm in tricking them to believe that Spielberg had requested their autobiographies, but now that they thought he was actually going to read them, I felt dishonest. After reading Khari's letter and envisioning him agonizing over a dilapidated typewriter, I felt like I had deceived them.

When I got home and saw all the different shades of ink my students had used on their lined paper—some crinkled or folded—I decided to sit down at my computer and type each one of their stories. I'm no whiz on the computer, and I have to look at the keyboard when I type, so typing their stories took all weekend.

On Monday, I handed each of their stories back to them, typed.

"Wow! Did you type all of our stories?" Manny asked.

"No. I got some help, from Khari." I looked at him and winked.

"That must have taken you forever," Sharaud said.

"Well, if Spielberg is going to read all these amazing letters, I wanted to make it a little easier on him," I lied.

"Do you think he'll actually read them?" Dan asked.

"Why wouldn't he?" I said, continuing the charade. "They're amazing. And after typing each of your stories, I feel like I know you all a little bit better. I'm proud of you," I said.

As my students filed out of class, chattering about what it was going to be like to meet Spielberg, I felt frantic. What if they asked him about their letters? Would they be devastated if he didn't read them?

I took the folder that Dara had used to turn in her paper, decorated with yellow sunflowers, and quickly put all the letters inside. Then I got in my car and drove straight to Universal Studios.

When I got to the guard at the Universal entrance, I asked him to call Marvin Levy. The guard looked annoyed. People were not supposed to visit Spielberg unannounced. What if Marvin turned me away? A man in a convertible Porsche and on a cell phone was behind me, and I could see in my rearview mirror that he was getting agitated while the guard thumbed through the directory to find Marvin's number. Once he made the call, we had to wait a few more minutes for his assistant, Becky, to track him down. More cars started to pile up behind me. The man in the Porsche honked his horn and waved his hands in the air. Maybe this was a bad idea. Then the gate went up and the guard told me that Marvin had given permission for me to come onto the lot.

I made my way to the office feeling awkward. Marvin met me in the foyer, looking surprised that I had shown up without an appointment.

"Erin, we weren't expecting you. Is everything all right?" he asked.

"I brought something for Mr. Spielberg," I stuttered.

"What is it?" he asked, sounding protective of his boss.

"Stories. My students' stories," I said, clutching the folder.

"Was he expecting them?"

"No. But I wanted my students to feel like they earned this field trip, so I tricked them into writing them. Now I feel really bad, because my students poured their hearts out to him and I feel like such a liar."

"Let me take you to Spielberg's assistant, Bonnie. Maybe she can help you."

On the way to Bonnie's office, Marvin explained that Spielberg was leaving for Washington, D.C., the next afternoon, shortly after the meeting with my students. He planned to testify about the validity of teaching the Holocaust in public schools.

When we got to Bonnie's office, she looked surprised to see me as well.

She was clearly overwhelmed with work. Her phone was ringing off the hook with calls from politicos and members of Congress.

"I know this is unsolicited," I said, "but I had my students write Mr. Spielberg a letter that gives a glimpse into who they are and how he's touched them. I want them to feel like they've earned this trip." I handed her the meager folder with the silly sunflowers on it.

"Oh honey," she said with a tinge of a southern accent, "he gets handed scripts every day. See this pile?" The pile seemed to be a foot high. "This is what he's taking home with him tonight."

I wanted to disappear. I felt foolish and impulsive. Shouldn't meeting Spielberg for a few minutes be enough? I shouldn't have imposed on him like this. I should have just gone through the motions and let my students think Spielberg had read their stories.

Sensing my discomfort, she said with a smile, "I can't promise he'll read them, but I'll put your package on the top of the pile."

Then Bonnie's phone rang. I took that as my cue. As I was about to leave, she stopped me and said, "Ya know, he really likes you."

"Really?" I asked, slightly stunned. "Why?"

"Anyone that can say 'fuck' in front of him without batting an eye is pretty gutsy in his book!"

I never thought of myself as gutsy before. I must have fooled him.

The next morning, chartered buses arrived at the school to pick us up, courtesy of Mr. Spielberg. We were all anxious. To help ease the tension, Melvin talked the bus driver into playing a Snoop Dogg CD for us, and we sang all the way to Universal.

Marvin met us at the gate and said that Spielberg would meet up with us in the afternoon. In the meantime, he'd arranged a VIP tour of Universal Studios for us.

After we had gone on every ride and seen every attraction, we got escorted to the front of the food line at a burger stand. Most of my students just stood there. A few of them ordered a soda.

"Sharaud, don't you want something to eat?" I asked, trying to nudge the others along.

"Nah, I ate earlier," he said, looking down.

Then I realized why my students were too timid to order. Most of them were on free and reduced lunch, and clearly this hamburger joint wasn't going to accept their cafeteria meal tickets. I whispered to Becky that my students didn't have any money, and she instantly lit up.

"Tell them they can have anything they want! This is on Mr. Spielberg."

"Well, in that case, I'll have a cheeseburger combo with extra fries and a large Coke in the souvenir cup!" Sharaud said. The rest seemed to follow Sharaud's lead.

When lunch was over, Becky said, "I think it's time." We followed her to Spielberg's private screening room. It resembled a miniature movie theater—except that the floors weren't sticky from spilled soda and the seats were plush recliners.

I knew that meeting Spielberg would be an incredible opportunity for my students, and to remind them of how far they had come in a year, I planned a little surprise. When I was typing all their letters, one story really struck a chord. Will, one of the only Caucasians in my class, was legally blind. He used a voice recorder to tape all of his classes and had a personal tutor transcribe all of his work. I remember when he came into my class the first day how timid he was in finding a seat, and how he would hold his tape recorder in the air to follow my pacing.

On "Back-to-School Night," his mother admitted that she was really nervous about Will being in such a tough class because he had been home-schooled for the last four years. Although he was fragile, he wanted to be mainstreamed into a traditional school program, rather than attend a school for the sight impaired. His mother told me that "something horrible had happened to Will in middle school," and that she hoped he would be okay in my class. I envisioned that he'd been tripped or bullied because of his size and walking cane. I became fiercely protective of Will and didn't want Melvin or Sharaud to pick on him.

In his letter to Spielberg, Will revealed that "horrible" incident. When he was in middle school, some schoolyard bullies stole his tape recorder and left him messages like "You're a freak!" and "You don't belong here, retard!" When he sat down to transcribe his homework with his tutor, the messages incapacitated him. He was so traumatized that he didn't want to leave the safety of his home.

My class was his first attempt at coming back to school. When we had done a poetry assignment earlier in the semester, I encouraged everyone to bring in the lyrics of their favorite song and dissect its poetic devices. After two days of Snoop Dogg blaring on my boom box, Will brought in a guitar that was half his size and proceeded to belt out George Thorogood's "Bad to the Bone."

With Will strumming the guitar and singing "ba-ba-ba-bad," something beautiful erupted: Melvin stood up and started cheering. Sharaud began to sing along with the chorus. Next thing I knew, everyone was on his or her feet, clapping, cheering, and singing "ba-ba-ba-bad" in their best George Thorogood impersonation. Some of the students even lit their lighters—the same lighters that were considered contraband at Wilson—as if they were at a concert. In his letter to Spielberg, Will wrote that it was "the single greatest moment of my life."

After typing Will's letter, I called him and asked him to bring his guitar with us on our field trip to Universal. "I want you to warm up the crowd," I said. He was thrilled. So was his mother. She met me at the school early that morning and we snuck his guitar onto the bus. Becky had someone sneak his guitar into the theater while we were on the tour.

As the students anxiously awaited Spielberg's arrival in the miniature theater, Becky escorted Will to the edge of the stage. He confidently began to strum his guitar. As if on cue, Melvin and Sharaud started a wave.

Amid the music and the camaraderie, I saw Spielberg slip into the back of the theater. He was absolutely unassuming. He began to tap his feet.

Once Will finished his song, Spielberg said, "You must be Will," as he made his way to the stage.

The students gasped. There he was—no paparazzi, no bodyguards.

"Where's Khari?" he said, looking around the audience. "And Sharaud?" My heart felt like it was going to burst.

"You'll have to excuse me," he said, "but I'm a little tired. I stayed up all night getting to know you."

Chapter 11

Standing before an audience of my adoring students, Spielberg shared with them how powerful and real he found their stories.

"Your letters exposed me to a world I've only seen in movies," he said.

Khari turned to me and whispered, "Did he read *my* letter?"

I wanted to scream "Yes!" at the top of my lungs so every cynic who ever doubted Khari could hear me, but I simply nodded.

Khari stared at me intently for a moment and then shook his head in disbelief. "Thanks," he mouthed.

While trying to play it cool, I winked at Khari as if I knew Spielberg was planning to read his letter all along. For the first time, I understood why my father always cried at award ceremonies. At that moment, I felt like a proud parent whose son was about to receive a medal of honor.

Over the course of an hour, Spielberg and my students exchanged stories of survival, moviemaking, and the struggle to get *Schindler's List* made. Although they lived in different worlds, everyone managed to find common ground. At one point, Spielberg remarked, "Pain is pain." His validation made my students sit a little taller, raise their hands a little higher, and listen more intently.

After Spielberg explained that he was heading to Washington, D.C., to meet with our nation's leaders to discuss the importance of Holocaust education, Keiuana raised her hand and asked if we could take a group photo with her disposable camera. I cringed. I remembered being warned against bringing cameras with us. Marvin wanted our meeting to "fly under the radar," and he didn't want any stories about our visit leaking to the press. I assumed that Marvin would politely say no, but Spielberg said, "Sure." Within a nanosecond, my students leapt from their seats and surrounded Spielberg. On cue, Spielberg put his arms around the giddy students as if they were old friends.

Ironically, it turned out to be Marvin holding Keiuana's camera to take the picture. He promptly handed the camera to Becky. I stood next to her, directing the students to stand a little closer. Right before she said, "Cheeeese," Khari came over to me, grabbed my hand, and pulled me into the photo.

"The picture wouldn't be complete without you, Ms. G," he said.

After the photo, Spielberg asked mischievously, "So, Ms. G, what are you going to do for an encore?"

In the movie world, when someone like Spielberg has a smash hit, be it *Raiders of the Lost Ark* or *Jurassic Park*, there's usually a sequel. So when Spielberg enthusiastically said, "Imagine all the things you could do if you had one more year together," it planted the seed for a sequel of our own.

Before we arrived at Universal Studios, Marvin must have shared the news with Spielberg that my principal had just offered me a teaching position at Wilson in the fall. This was information that I had not yet shared with my students. I was ecstatic that I would be an "official" English teacher, but teaching the same students had never really crossed my mind. Spielberg's suggestion that we stay together another year made my students giddy about their senior year. After all, they had come so far in nine months that the prospect of building on this momentum was exhilarating.

I left his theater feeling like my students and I could do just about anything, especially if we were together. Unfortunately, that feeling was as realistic as the facades on the Universal back lot. As a rookie teacher, I didn't carry Spielberg's clout.

Once we were back at Wilson, I realized that my desire to stay with my students would put me in a precarious position. I had heard rumors that all new English teachers started at the bottom rung of the teaching ladder, and I expected that to be my fate as well. Since my principal had supported my field trips, I hoped that I could make a compelling case to him about continuing with my current students, in addition to teaching incoming freshmen.

"Since I already know my students' strengths and weaknesses, I figured we could hit the ground running come September," I told him.

"You'll have to ask the head of the English Department," my principal said. "We have site-based instruction, so she is in charge of the master schedule."

My stomach dropped, knowing that I would have to ask the chair of the English Department for permission. She had a reputation for being inflexible, so appealing to her directly made me nervous, perhaps even a little afraid. I had not gotten over the fact that she'd called my students names, so I'd made a point to avoid her at all costs. I heard she was upset about my buying copies of *The Catcher in the Rye* for my students and taking them on field trips. And although I had intentions of keeping a low profile until the end of the year, I supposed that taking my students to meet Spielberg put her over the edge.

When I finally mustered up the courage to go into the teachers' lounge, I could feel resentment in the air. My intuition told me that I was asking a favor from someone who was not predisposed to grant it. I stood next to the coffee machine for a moment while she muttered something under her breath. As I approached her, she rolled her eyes.

"May I speak to you about the master schedule?" I asked.

Without looking at me, she said, "Yes."

I stammered a bit before I was able to blurt out, "Can . . . can I stay with my students for an additional year?"

"Absolutely not!" she said without even considering my request. "We do things based on seniority here." She reminded me that teaching juniors and seniors at Wilson was a coveted position. "You are a brand-new teacher, and therefore you will teach freshman English and freshman English only!"

She insinuated that it was audacious of me to think I could waltz in after student teaching and take on senior English. She had seniority, and she was going to teach seniors—period.

But what if the process wasn't working? If it had been, Melvin wouldn't have spent the beginning of his high school career thinking that his only option was scoring touchdowns, Manny wouldn't have dropped out, and Sharaud would never have brought a gun to school.

Couldn't she differentiate between where the students were at the beginning of the year and where they were now? Students who once made paper airplanes out of my syllabi were now turning in their homework, writing profound essays, and getting A's on their assignments. An amazing transformation had taken place in the span of one academic year. Hardened kids who had been told that they were "stupid" by the educational system began to feel smart, and now they had the grades to prove it. Why should the system want to impede their progress?

"I'm willing to sacrifice my conference period or teach them before school," I said. My groveling didn't move her.

I felt helpless, like a child begging for something from an unreasonable parent who says "No!" simply because they can. I was stubborn, and "No!" without an explanation never satisfied my inquisitive nature. I always wanted to know why—I wanted everything explained to me. But clearly, she did not feel the need to explain why new teachers always taught the classes that nobody else wanted.

Her icy glare focused on my pearls, and she said, "You're making the other teachers look bad!" I stood there dumbfounded. How? I wanted to ask her to explain, but I didn't say anything. I just stood there, silent.

As I turned to leave the lounge, she said, "Let's see what you can do with those kids, hotshot."

It seemed to me that I had spent most of the past year fighting battles with my students. Now here I was in a battle with my supervisor, and I was at a clear disadvantage. My skin was not that thick, and I found myself fighting back tears. I just wanted to escape. If I tried to fight her, I'd not only lose the battle, I'd probably lose my job as well.

My future at Wilson seemed bleak. I called my dad for a little consolation.

"I don't understand why she won't let us stay together," I said.

"Erin, what did you expect? You're lucky to have a job," he said. "You've gotta play by her rules."

"But you know how long it takes for a team to gel. Once you have a winning team, why break it up?" I said, trying to appeal to my father's sense of baseball.

"Sharaud is no Johnny Bench," he said. "And besides, there will be plenty of other players."

I had called him hoping that he'd make me feel better, but I got off the phone feeling worse. Suddenly, I was wondering whether I should transfer to another school or if I should just quit altogether. Rather than give up, maybe I could look to my students for advice.

I had only a week left of the school year, but giving my students a final exam and taking down the photos from my bulletin boards seemed like admitting defeat. My students had become much more than test-takers; we had evolved into a family. Saying good-bye would be devastating.

Although I was taught that a "teacher should not get too close to his or her students," I decided to throw a farewell banquet in the library. My parents, my landlady, and even my neighbor, Polly, volunteered to bring food to our potluck.

At the end of dinner, there was a startling show of emotion. Keiuana stood up to say good-bye and burst into tears. "You are the only real family I've ever had," she said. Her teary testimonial created a domino effect. One by one, students began sharing their feelings too.

For the first time in their lives, my students had empathy for their peers, and the outpouring of love made our impending separation that much harder.

"When I first saw you with your polka dots and pearls, I wondered if you were for real," Khari said. "I couldn't understand why you were so damn happy. I wanted to make you as miserable as I was. But now I can say that for the first time in my life, I'm not miserable."

Khari gave me a hug and the entire room erupted in applause. Then the custodian came in and told us that it was time to leave. I stood by the door and hugged each of them on their way out. Part of me felt like I was saying good-bye to sailors about to ship off to sea.

Sharaud lingered behind as everyone left. He couldn't understand why we couldn't stay together next year, but this wasn't the time for politics. It was a time for good-byes. As he headed out the door, he said, "I'll call you some-time . . ."

With the students gone, I felt a familiar void. My parents divorced when I was seven, and ever since then, I was used to awkward good-byes. Saying good-bye to my students reminded me of saying good-bye to my dad after each weekend visitation. I suppose that if I could learn to accept those visitations every other weekend with my dad, then maybe I could learn to accept stolen moments with my students as well.

I guess my class had become my family, and without them I was feeling like a martyr, projecting my past onto my present. As a child, I did everything to fill the void by cramming a lifetime into those weekends with my dad, but it never was quite the same. I feared that the situation with my students might mirror those childhood experiences.

In the past, when I felt such a void, I could turn to my siblings for support. Unfortunately, in my new marriage, my husband didn't understand my feelings of emptiness or my attachment to my students. When I was teaching, my life seemed to make sense. I felt fulfilled. In the classroom I felt useful, but at home I felt inadequate.

I appreciated how honest my students were, sometimes painfully so, but I noticed that my home life wasn't as straightforward. That night, when I got home, I noticed that I had my students' essays on the kitchen table instead of a four-course meal.

"I brought you some leftovers from our potluck," I offered my husband.

"It's okay, I already ate," he said, pointing to a pizza box.

I wanted to tell him about our farewell dinner, but since he didn't have an emotional connection to his job, he couldn't understand why I brought my job home with me, why I wanted to take my students on field trips, and why I was sad to say good-bye.

Since my phone number had been previously printed in the *Daily Pilot* newspaper article, it didn't take Sharaud long to keep his promise. Summer had started and he wanted to know if he could come to Newport Beach to visit me. Without asking my husband or thinking about the logistics, I invited him to come over for a barbecue.

Sharaud didn't have a car or a driver's license, so he asked if he could hitch a ride with someone from class who did. Without hesitation, I said, "Sure. Why not?"

Much to my surprise, about ten former students crammed into two cars and made the pilgrimage to my apartment. I lived about a mile from the art deco theater where I had taken my students to see *Schindler's List*. I was a little nervous over how my students would feel about returning to the same neighborhood where they had been met with suspicious glances and such hostility.

Sharaud must have read my mind, because as he entered my apartment he said, shaking his head and smiling, "I did not see one black person on the drive down."

"You don't have to worry about me grabbing my pearls," I said to Sharaud, returning his smile, as he and the boys walked in.

He looked surprised and perhaps even a little disappointed when he saw that I lived in a small, two-bedroom apartment without much furniture. I think he assumed I lived in a big house.

It was a little awkward when my students met my husband for the first time. Since he had been MIA with everything that we had experienced outside of the classroom, they were in denial that I was actually married. I caught Sharaud sizing him up and giving him a once-over.

"Hey, Mr. G!" Sharaud said, extending his hand.

"Actually, it's Mr. Sherman. Erin, I mean Ms. Gruwell, didn't change her name when we got married," he said.

"Oh, so Ms. G is as hardheaded at home as she is at work," Sharaud said.

"Absolutely," my husband agreed.

As we ate dinner on our picnic table in the backyard, we reminisced about the highlights from the last year. Our laughter and storytelling became louder and more animated, and I could sense that my husband was feeling left out. To include him, I tried to change the subject, but it inevitably went back to our classroom.

"So what's the plan for next year?" Sharaud asked.

I was at a loss. Although I had spent the entire summer planning my curriculum, I was feeling anxious about my new students. "I'm still working on it," I said.

"What is there to work on?" Khari asked. "Why don't you just do what you did with us?"

"What if it's not that easy?" I asked.

"You'll find a way, you always do," Khari said.

"What if I just got lucky with you guys?"

"I'm sure you have a lot of luck left over," Sharaud reassured me, reaching for his fourth burger.

"She sure doesn't have a lot of food left over!" my husband said, chuckling.

"What if I get a class full of Sharauds?" I asked.

"Don't worry, Ms. G," Manny assured me. "We'll help you keep those freshmen in check."

"Yeah, we'll help you regulate," added Sharaud, flexing his biceps.

CHAPTER 12

Thexe students aren't ADD, Ms. G; they're B-A-D!" Sharaud said on the first day of school after taking inventory of my morning class. He resembled George C. Scott in *Patton*, standing before the flag, addressing the troops.

Since Sharaud had a history of being "bad," I considered him an expert. Now a senior, it appeared to me that he had grown several inches taller over the summer. He rolled up the sleeves of his football jersey and said, "Check out these guns," showing off his muscles while eyeing the immature lot before him.

I was overcome by an eerie feeling of déjà vu. The classroom was a mirror image of my first day last year. The students had once again separated themselves into racial comfort zones and were throwing up their respective gang signs.

As if on cue, Sharaud began to identify each clique in a drill sergeant's cadence. "You've got your Latino gangstas in this corner and your wannabe rappers in that corner. You see, there," he said pointing to the front left corner, "that's your Asian crew, and right there," pointing to the front row, "is *one* scared white boy." He described the troop to a tee, at least superficially. Who needed rap sheets or disciplinary folders? Sharaud had single-handedly profiled each kid and each potential problem within a matter of minutes. As he swaggered out the door toward his first class of the day, Sharaud muttered, "Freshman . . . fresh meat," shaking his head dramatically.

"Damn!" a student said, taking a seat. "Why am I in the stupid class?"

"You must have fucked up last year!" said a student from the back, followed by laughter and high fives.

Breaking down barriers and creating a family atmosphere was going to be much more difficult than I had anticipated, because I had kids who solved their problems with violence. Before I headed off to school that morning, my dad had made a sarcastic remark about Sisyphus: "How long are you going to roll that rock uphill?"

"Maybe this year will be different," I said, trying to sound optimistic.

Actually, it was different—it was worse. Much worse!

My roll sheets were filled with all the "undesirable" students that no one else wanted: kids who just got out of rehab, had run away from home, or had been previously incarcerated.

I was taken aback when Maria, a feisty Latina, sauntered into my class escorted by her probation officer. The officer told me that she was on house arrest and was wearing an ankle bracelet to monitor her whereabouts.

"You'll have to fill out this form every day to ensure that she's in school," the officer told me. "If she misses school, gets into another fight, or isn't home by 4 P.M., she'll violate her probation and go back to juvie."

She glared at him for sharing this information with me. Underneath her thick black eyeliner, I could see the remnant of a black eye. She must have used an entire can of Aqua Net hair spray, because her bangs rose nearly three inches above her forehead. Her hardened exterior was accentuated by her dark lipstick.

"She just got out of Juvenile Hall. She's a repeat offender, so she'll be on probation for a while. If she gives you any trouble, don't hesitate to call me," he said, handing me his card.

Trying to gain my composure, I said, "Okay. Maria, why don't you find a seat?" As she headed toward a seat near the other Latinos, I got a glimpse of boy's boxers beneath her big, baggy pants. She was wearing a tank top, covered by a Dickies jacket. Although she was diminutive, probably less than five feet tall, she had a presence about her—a swagger that clearly demonstrated that she owned the place.

For the remainder of the period, she glared at me from the back of the room.

By lunch, I was exasperated.

After my encounter with the chair of the English Department at the end of last school year, I had decided it would be easier to eat lunch in my room. Her comment, "Let's see what you can do with those kids, hotshot," played over and over in my head. I imagined her smug satisfaction with my roll sheets. The deck had clearly been stacked against me.

Halfway through my sandwich, Sharaud popped back in. "Freshmen suck!" he said matter-of-factly, as if he were a wise sage. Short of wearing a smoking jacket and puffing away on a pipe, he seemed professorial and authoritative. "Just accept the fact that they hate you," he said.

Sharaud was probably right, because the classes after lunch weren't any better. There was total apathy. No one raised a hand to answer a question, no one laughed at any of my corny jokes, and no one wanted to be there. Some students asked for a hallway pass to the restroom and never came back. And between each period, the floor of the classroom was strewn with copies of my syllabus, marked up with graffiti.

I asked my students to journal about their first day, and even though I told them to be honest, I was still a bit stung by their assessments. One student wrote, "My freshman English teacher is way out there. I wonder how she got this job. The administrators should have known better than to give her this class, but I guess she didn't know any better than to take it. How is she going to handle four classes full of this school's rejects?" Others made comments about how "English sucks!" or had journal pages that were laced with drawings.

While I was reading their journals after school, I discovered that some of them were disciplinary transfers, some of them had learning disabilities, and some just wanted to get the hell out. One student wrote, "This school is asking for trouble when they put all these kids in the same class. It's a disaster waiting to happen."

After football practice, Manny and Sharaud stopped by my classroom to see how I'd survived the first day of boot camp. They were the perfect yin and yang. Sharaud was like the devil on my shoulder, spewing stereotypes about my students, while Manny was the angel, offering his condolences.

"No matter what kind of PC label you teachers try to give a class like this, everyone that walks through your door knows that they're in the bad class," Sharaud said. "You should just expect them to be a pain in the ass."

"Come on, Sharaud, they're just putting up a front. Don't give up on them yet, Ms. G," Manny said, ever the voice of reason. "If you met me when I was fourteen, I probably would have robbed you or jacked your car."

At seventeen, Manny sounded like a preacher, so his assessment had merit. "Don't you remember Sharaud on his first day?" he reminded me.

Manny and Sharaud made it their mission to check up on me daily. They were my "moles." They informed me that there had been several drive-by shootings over the summer and now the ongoing racial feud was felt on campus. Several Latino students were jumped by Asian and African American gang members at the bus stop after school. In retaliation, several Latino gang members from the community jumped the fence at Wilson High to initiate a fight. Although the problems initially started between gang members, it quickly escalated to innocent bystanders. Within moments, a race riot erupted on the quad.

Several of my students were involved, including Maria. She was suspended for a week, and although she was all bruised up, she narrowly escaped being sent back to juvenile hall because they couldn't prove her degree of involvement.

The riots on campus encouraged me to compare the civil strife on the streets of Verona in *Romeo and Juliet* to the gang warfare on the streets of Long Beach. It became apparent to me that I could use such parallels to link my curriculum to the lives of my students, reinforcing the concept that we could learn lessons from history and literature.

Sharaud convinced me that if I wanted to make any headway teaching Shakespeare, I needed to know a little "somethin' somethin'" about Snoop Doggy Dogg.

"Ms. G, everyone from Long Beach claims that they know Snoop," Sharaud said. "Sometimes it's true, but most of the time it's not."

Snoop had put Long Beach on the map. His music videos, filmed on the streets of the LBC, were in constant rotation on MTV. Snoop gave kids in suburbia a taste of "gangsta rap," and for those living in his former "hood," it gave them validation. My students idolized Snoop and aspired to follow in his footsteps. If invoking Snoop would give me a little "street cred," then I was willing to give it a try. But since it was obvious that I wasn't "kickin' it" with Snoop, I had to walk a fine line.

"Don't go overboard," Sharaud warned.

I learned to run down each academic concept with Sharaud first, then he would figure out a way for me to feed it to my students. Racial gangs like the Crips and the East Side Longos were akin to the Montagues and Capulets. But rather than sporting colorful tights and biting their thumbs, my students were differentiated by skin color and their weapons were more lethal than swords.

I knew the language in *Romeo and Juliet* would seem foreign to my students, so I decided to do an exercise that analyzed how we use words in different contexts before we dove into the literature. I started with a passage in the play that begins with "Ho!" I knew controversy was inevitable, but I thought it might be interesting to have a play on words.

"Ho!" they each read, followed by giggles. A Shakespearean "ho" and a street "ho" were two very different "ho"s. The "ho"s they knew stood on Pacific Coast Highway, one of the main arteries of their city, turning tricks and soliciting all those who passed by, even kids on their way home from school.

Where I grew up, there was a guard at the entrance gate to my neighborhood who would give the grand inquisition to anyone who didn't live there—even pool cleaners and gardeners. Since "working girls" never made their way through our gates, the only prostitute I'd ever seen was Julia Roberts in *Pretty Woman*.

"Ho" was just enough to hook them, and now I had to reel them in carefully. Dissecting language was the first step, but it would take me only so far. Since my students seemed to have a strong affinity for slang and four-letter words, I decided that I'd have to teach them better ways to communicate the same sentiments. I knew that language was part of the power struggle for them and using irreverent words was an attempt to upset their teachers. It was part of the rebellion. Knowing that their goal was to get a rise out of me, I decided not to react to their profanity by punishing them, but instead by making a lesson out of it. We would begin by deconstructing simple words first.

"What does it mean if someone is 'bad'?" I asked.

"That they fucked up," someone muttered from the back.

"Oh, that's jacked up," someone else blurted out.

"What else?" I said, trying to ignore the chaos in the back.

"That you're wrong."

"What does 'bad' mean in this case?" I asked while turning on my CD player to blast Michael Jackson's "Bad." The class went nuts. They all sang in unison, and some of the boys even got up to imitate Michael's signature dance moves—moonwalking, grabbing their crotches, and kicking their legs in the air—forgetting for a moment that we were in an English class.

"Okay," I interrupted, turning off the music and trying to calm them down a bit, "what does 'bad' mean for Michael Jackson?"

"He's da bomb."

"The bomb," I repeated while writing it on the board.

"*Da*, not *the*," another student rushed to my rescue.

"Oh? Duh," I said, trying to look cool, knowing all the while that I wasn't.

I was thrilled they were teaching me something. This was the perfect segue into my lesson on how language changes. We discussed words like "good" and "bad," and I gave them the homework assignment of interviewing someone in their twenties, thirties, forties, and fifties to see how words changed through the years.

The next day was hilarious. Between "peachy keen," "groovy," and "dope," I knew that I was onto something. We practiced different ways they would address their friends, their grandmothers, and even their principal.

"If words like 'good' and 'bad' can change so much over forty years, imagine how much they could change in four hundred?" I said, trying to casually lead them to Shakespeare. "And if you talk one way to your friends and another to the principal, could you imagine if you had to address a queen? Could you imagine Shakespeare going up to Queen Elizabeth and saying, 'Baby, you're *da bomb*'?" I said playfully, trying to incorporate their slang.

"Ba da bum, ching," Henry mimicked, throwing his index fingers in the air and rolling his eyes at my joke. Although Henry had a tough exterior, he was always engaged and ready to make the class laugh. He would be the perfect character for the following lesson.

"Now, Henry, could you imagine if you hooked up with Maria and took her home with you?" I asked. I knew this imaginary tryst would light a fuse, since Maria was Latina and Henry was African American. "What would happen?" I prodded.

"Oh, no she didn't!" an African American student blurted out. Apparently, I had tapped into a social taboo.

"Ms. G, you're trippin'," said Henry. "Everyone knows she'd get mad-dogged if she went to our hood."

"Maria, what would happen if Henry came to your house?" I asked.

"He'd get his ass kicked by my homies," Maria said.

"What would happen if you two went on a date together?"

"Please, don't get me started," Maria said. "Black girls would definitely trip on me."

"Interesting. Things haven't changed that much over the years," I said. "Now, we're going to read one of Shakespeare's plays about two teenagers that fall in love and—"

"Get their freak on?" a kid from the back blurted out, followed by laughter.

"Actually, they did get their freak on," I said. "But their parents and friends tried to keep them apart."

"Why?" Henry asked.

Good, he took the bait. "Because people began to trip," I said.

"So Shakespeare is an OG?" Henry asked with an impish grin.

This scenario spawned a lesson in rewriting certain Shakespearean scenes in contemporary street slang. Later, they role-played. Suddenly, Romeo said to Juliet, while standing at the balcony, "Yo, yo, baby, you look so hot! Ya know what I'm sayin'?"

Their play on words didn't desecrate Shakespeare but actually brought them closer to his work. It wasn't long before they became curious about and even began to appreciate the original language.

Shakespeare allowed me to make lessons out of language, out of love, and out of the concept of civil strife. Why did words change? Why did people fall in love? Why did people fight? It all seemed so elementary.

As a way to capture my students' attention, I offered to show *West Side Story* at lunch for anyone who was interested. It was a disaster. The musical version didn't resonate with them in the same way it had with me while I was in high school. When the Jets and the Sharks began throwing salad fixings, I lost all credibility. "I don't know what happens in your hood, Ms. G, but 'round here, gangstas don't dance or throw cabbage."

I needed to find a version of *Romeo and Juliet* that was more relevant. A colleague gave me a documentary called *Romeo and Juliet in Sarajevo*, in which two "star-crossed lovers" try to escape ethnic cleansing in Bosnia. The girl is Muslim and her young boyfriend is Serbian. When they try to escape the bloodshed, they are shot in "Sniper Alley," the main corridor dividing Sarajevo. They die in each other's arms in the middle of the street and remain there for a week before they are dragged away by soldiers.

The documentary was so gritty and so horrifying that it riveted my students. When I turned on the lights after the video, some of them were embarrassed because they were crying. They had no idea that the war was currently raging on the other side of the globe. When they watched TV, they usually whizzed past CNN and Christiane Amanpour reporting from the trenches in Bosnia to get to MTV. I hoped that *Romeo and Juliet in Sarajevo* could be our rallying cry.

"Why were the lovers left there for so long?" I asked.

"Because no one puts their life on the line for anyone," one of my students said. Stories started pouring out of the students about horrific things they'd seen where no one did anything. "People get murdered all the time around here, and people don't do shit!" Maria said.

"Shit goes down every day and people just look the other way," Henry said.

I was shocked by how callous and blasé they sounded. In my neighborhood, we were nosy. We'd stick our heads out the window or walk outside every time we heard a siren. In my students' neighborhoods, hearing sirens or even helicopters overhead was an everyday occurrence. They stopped looking out the window or even gathering on the street. They were numb to it.

"We see violence all the time. You just get used to it," Henry said.

"Used to it?" I asked.

"Yeah, it's normal," he said matter-of-factly.

"Normal?"

"Maybe it's not normal where *you* come from, but where *we* come from, it is."

"But that doesn't make it normal," I tried to plead.

"Shit, lady, wake up and realize what kind of world we live in," he said.

Henry was right. Our worlds were different. Very different.

That evening I told my brother, Chris, about my troubling conversation with my students. Chris had just returned from four years of active duty in the army, and had moved in with me and my husband for a couple of months to help him make the transition from the military to a community college.

When the Gulf War started, my brother was a senior in high school and had no plans to go to college. Since my parents had gone to college, it was just expected that we would go to college too. It was quite a shock when my brother decided to enlist in the army shortly before his graduation. He was inspired to be like my grandfather, who had fought in World War II. My father, who had been vehemently opposed to the Vietnam War, was not supportive of my brother's decision to join the service, let alone the Special Forces.

Other than my brother, I didn't know anyone who joined the military. During his four-year stint, he was sent to Somalia and Sarajevo. We never talked about what happened in Bosnia before. I guess part of me didn't want to know. After showing the documentary about Bosnia to my students, I had more empathy for his experience and I suddenly wanted him to tell me everything.

"Hey, do you want to come to class with me tomorrow and tell my students about your tour in Bosnia?" I asked. I hoped that his talking about his experience with my students would be mutually beneficial.

"I don't know, your kids sound kind of tough. They probably wouldn't listen to me," he said with a shrug.

"No, I think they would. They were fascinated by the documentary about Sarajevo," I said. "They had a ton of questions that I couldn't answer."

He was silent for a moment.

"If you come, I'll help you with your English paper," I bribed.

"Okay," he succumbed. "I'll do it."

Chris came to class the next day wearing khaki pants and a button-down oxford, rather than his battle fatigues. It took my students a moment to warm up to him, since he looked more like a preppy than a soldier. He began by telling my students a brief history of Yugoslavia and why the war started in terms they could understand. He seemed to make a real connection. Then he described what his role was and some of the horrors of ethnic cleansing.

"I saw this couple lying in each other's arms in the middle of 'Sniper Alley,'" he said, "and I felt absolutely helpless." Everyone sat up. "No one did a damn thing for a week. Everyone wanted to do something, but rival soldiers were lined up on either side, and we feared for our lives," he said tearfully.

I had no idea that Chris had actually seen the couple from the documentary. My heart sank. We talked about Bosnia in broad strokes at home, but now he was giving my students graphic details that reinforced the film. Hands went up in the air and questions flew. He had them in the palm of his hand. Chris had never commanded that kind of respect before, nor had my students ever been so engaged. They wanted to know how he felt, if he had nightmares, if he would recommend the military to them.

The more questions my students asked, the more I began to understand my brother. No one ever asked him questions like this at home. No one gave him the respect that he so desperately longed for. Suddenly, I realized that Chris, like my students, just wanted to belong. Chris didn't join the army to kill people or to dodge sniper fire, but he, like my students who had joined gangs, craved an identity and the feeling of acceptance. There was comfort in conformity. By wearing those medals, or that beret, he had an identity. Once the violence started, the identity was in question, but how can you get out of it without being called a coward? It all made sense to me: my sorority, Chris's platoon, Maria's gang—we all wanted to belong to something.

CHAPTER 13

Our discussion about Bosnia encouraged me to select stories about "real" issues my students would understand: tagging, living in housing projects, being incarcerated, even murder. The grittier the stories were, the better.

Reading realistic stories started to have an impact on my students' journal entries. They began making comparisons between themselves and the complex characters they were analyzing. The short story "The Tagger" prompted my graffiti artist to fess up to his creative additions to my classroom, "The Last Spin" prompted a discussion on Russian roulette, and *Durango Street* reminded some of them of their stints in juvenile hall.

It probably looked like I was on the pulse of pop culture, when in actuality I was getting tipped off by Manny in the hall. He was my version of Watergate's "Deep Throat." Manny had a hand in selecting several of my literary selections, so when he asked me for help with his college applications, I jumped at the chance. Helping him would give me the opportunity to share some of the tips I'd learned from a recent workshop I attended called "Writing the Perfect College Essay." I invited him to my house for dinner so we could discuss his choices and fill out the applications together.

Manny was the first person in his family to apply to college, and the process was daunting to him. The counseling department at Wilson gave Manny fee waivers to apply to two colleges of his choice. At some of the private colleges he had researched, the tuition for a semester was probably more than his mother made all year. Since I was a product of public universities, I suggested that he apply to Berkeley.

He looked at me blankly and asked, "Where is it?"

"It's near San Francisco."

At first he was hesitant, but the more I told Manny about Berkeley's legendary reputation, the more excited he became. My uncle used to tell me tales about Berkeley, his prized alma mater, and I thought it would be ideal for Manny. He had overcome so much and would be an asset to any campus, especially Berkeley. Besides, if any college could see how Manny strived to turn his F's into straight A's, Berkeley would.

"I think it would be perfect for you!" I said.

"Okay, I'll apply."

I didn't want him to lose an opportunity to apply to a college he'd already researched or use up his free waiver, so I offered, "If you apply, I'll pay for the application fee."

"No, Ms. G, you can't do that," he said.

I knew Manny was proud, and I didn't want him to think I was giving him a handout. "Come on, Manny, after all that you've done for me this year, it's the least I can do!"

"Okay, Ms. G, but I'm still going to help you with your students."

"I'm counting on it," I said. "Now let's work on your application essay."

"My mom wrote it for me," he said, pulling out an essay from his backpack. She had glued his football picture in the right-hand corner. Unfortunately, it was two pages of fluff. It read like a narrative résumé that only skimmed the surface, hardly revealing his life experiences or showing Manny's true potential.

His mom's version did not present his "whole story," nor was it the story that would get him into Berkeley. If Manny was to stand a chance of getting through the door of any college, he had to be painfully honest about his past.

"Manny, you need to explain to the admissions officers why you once had a 0.6 GPA. You'll be competing against people who have had a 4.0 since birth," I said.

The fact was that he was competing against people like me, children of privilege who would be traumatized if they ever got a B+ on a report card.

I told Manny that we should rewrite his essay from scratch and try to divulge all that he'd overcome—racism, homelessness, and the murder of his friend.

I wanted Manny to tell his story using his own voice, so I needed to gently coax the real story out of him while I took notes. The more we began to peel back the layers of his story, the more I was in awe of him. If admissions officers actually read about his tumultuous adolescence, they'd realize he was an amazing candidate for their college.

When we finished writing his essay, I gave him a high five. Manny seemed exhilarated, and so was I.

After I dropped him off, it hit me how different our experiences were. I'd gone on college tours, had tutors help me with my essay, and even enrolled in special SAT prep courses. I talked about college with my parents at the dinner table and even lounged around the house in college sweatshirts.

Compared to Manny's, my college essay had no grit or adversity. I didn't have to overcome anything. I'd simply written up a laundry list of my trivial triumphs: lettering in field hockey, being crowned the Winter Formal Princess, and planning prom as class president. If I'd been an admissions officer, I would have puked at how superficial my college essay sounded.

As soon as I got home from dropping Manny off, his mother called me. "Why doesn't Manny just come and live with you?" she yelled. "Obviously, you think you're a better mother."

Her anger caught me completely off guard. "I'm not trying to replace you," I stammered, completely dumbfounded.

She had read his new essay and was furious. Apparently, I had trespassed on sacred maternal territory by helping Manny rewrite his essay. My help was an insult to her. I'd overstepped my boundaries.

She had never gone to college and didn't want to admit to her son that she didn't have the answers, but I didn't want her to think that I had all the answers either.

The more I apologized and explained that I wasn't trying to replace her, the more she screamed. "You think you're better than me just because you went to college."

"No, Bonnie, I don't," I said. "I'm just an English teacher trying to help my student write an excellent essay," I tried to rationalize. "When I was applying to college, I went to my English teacher's house for help too."

My actions must have touched a nerve, because even though we had a common interest in Manny's success, my explanation fell on deaf ears.

"We don't need your pity," she said. Then she hung up.

I felt nauseated. I had never intended to alienate a parent or pass myself off as the "Great White Hope." I had no intentions of stepping on their pride. All I wanted to do was be an advocate for my student, but in this case, it seemed to have backfired.

Talking to Manny's mom was a real wake-up call. I didn't want to reinforce her negative stereotypes—about class, about race, and about education. I wanted this woman to know that I didn't pity her or her son. I didn't think I was better than her, and I certainly wasn't passing judgment.

The following day, Manny came by my classroom and said, "Don't worry about it, Ms. G." I could tell he was caught in the middle and must have felt like his loyalty was being tested.

"I feel horrible, Manny," I said. "I couldn't sleep last night."

"My mom will get over it."

"What can I do?"

"Nothing. She just hasn't come to terms with my past. Seeing it on paper was too much for her to take," he said calmly. "It'll blow over soon."

Even though Manny seemed blasé, I couldn't be. I agonized about my role as a teacher and where I should draw the line.

My outlook on parents changed and I was nervous about mutiny at the impending Back-to-School Night. What if more parents were angry at me? Would there be more screaming, more name-calling? That night, I waited in my classroom expecting the worst.

"Excuse me, could you direct me to Ms. Gruwell?" a vivacious mom wearing lots of colorful jewelry asked me.

"I'm Ms. Gruwell."

"But you're so young!" she said.

"I know," I said self-consciously, and shrugged my shoulders.

"Ah, now I know why my son loves your class!" she said, smiling.

"He loves my class?" Now I was the one in disbelief. "Who's your son?"

"Dane."

"Oh, I love Dane. He sits right here in the front row."

"Dane sits in the front row?" she asked. "He's never sat in the front row before."

I didn't want to tell her that he was one of the few Caucasians in my class and that his chair had been the only seat left on the first day of school. When I started to mix up the room a bit, he asked if he could remain in the front.

When I found out that he was on the Long Beach Little League team that won the World Series two years in a row, he became the perfect person to test my sports analogies on. Since he was a star baseball player, I could swap stories with him relayed to me by my dad. Baseball helped create a special bond between the two of us.

"My name is Debbie," she said, reaching out her hand to shake mine. "I've heard a lot about you. Dane keeps talking about Ms. G this and Ms. G that. So I'm really excited to finally meet you!"

I was a little shocked, since I was still stinging from my encounter with Manny's mother. I had to fight the urge to solicit more compliments, because I didn't want to come across as too desperate.

At that point, she was the only parent with me in the room. Just then, Debbie recognized a friend of hers across the hall who was heading into the Distinguished Scholars classroom.

"What's Dane doing in this class?" her friend asked.

I immediately recognized her friend's tone, and I knew that the rest of her sentence should have been "with *those* kids?"

"I don't know how Dane got into this class, but I'm thrilled that he did," Debbie said. As her friend walked away, Debbie turned to me and said, "If you haven't noticed already, there are two different Long Beaches."

"What do you mean?"

"There are the *haves* and the *have-nots*," she said, pointing across the hall. The majority of the parents across the hall appeared to be upper-middle-class Caucasians.

"A lot of those parents stick together," she continued, "and sometimes they can be cruel. Dane never fit into those classes. He's not a good test-taker," she said.

It was ironic that she was trying to justify Dane's academic ability to me, because I was about to tell her that he was one of my best students. He never missed a day, always did his homework, and he was getting a solid A.

"A lot of Dane's friends tease him for being in your class, but I think that must come from their parents," she said.

I never imagined that he might be ridiculed for being in my class.

"A lot of those parents think that their kids are better than everyone else's."

"Debbie, your son is fantastic," I said. "I mean it. He's doing great."

As she was about to leave, I asked her if I could call her sometime. "I may need your help."

She instantly lit up. "Absolutely!" she said, followed by a big hug.

Debbie's enthusiasm reminded me of my parents. They never missed a Back-to-School Night and were involved in all of my extracurricular projects: carpooling me back and forth to field hockey practice, buying candy bars for the student council fund-raiser, and cheering in the stands at all the home games.

I hoped that Debbie could give me insight into the community that I drove in and out of each day. Her son was a celebrated Long Beach Little Leaguer, so she really had a good sense about Long Beach and its divisions—racial, economic, and geographic.

I left Back-to-School Night wondering what the other parents were like. Were they divorced? Were they working? Did they have too much on their plate? Did they speak English? Or did my students simply forget to tell their parents that it was Back-to-School Night?

I decided that if I wanted to learn more about my students' parents, I'd have to be subtle. The following day, I enlisted Sharaud's help to play a nonthreatening icebreaker called the Line Game. Sharaud came in early to help me move all the desks against the walls. In the middle of the room, I put a huge piece of duct tape, creating a straight line from wall to wall.

When the students filed in and didn't have a place to sit, I knew I had instantly grabbed their attention. "We're going to play a game," I explained. Several students smiled. I suppose they thought they were going to get away with mischief. I numbered them off into "ones" and "twos." The ones were to stand on the right of the line, and the twos on the left.

"Each time I ask a question that pertains to you, you have to walk to the center and stand on the line," I said, pretending this was a simple game. In reality, it was much more than that. I went on to explain that there was to be no talking or discussions during the course of the game. Knowing that some kids didn't like to draw attention to themselves, I warned them, "This is not the Hokey Pokey, where you stick your leg out. You've got to shake your 'groove thang' and walk all the way to the middle of the room and stand on the line." Acting corny was an attempt to lighten the mood and throw them off my scent. In order for this game to work, my students had to trust me and let go of their inhibitions.

While they were standing in the two lines facing one another, someone said, "It looks like a *Soul Train* line."

To add a little levity, I asked, "Henry, why don't you dance down the center and 'bust a move'?"

Some students laughed, others rolled their eyes. Henry obliged my request, though, and began to dance down the center of the lines. Someone started clapping and singing, "Go, Henry, it's your birthday!" Henry moved his body like a contortionist down the center, while the class swayed and cheered.

"Okay, are you ready to play?" I asked, excited to see that my experiment was working. "Here's the first question: Who owns a copy of Snoop's CD?"

Nearly everyone went to the center, and some of them started singing, "Ain't nothin' but a G thang, baby . . ."

"Okay," I said enthusiastically. "You've got it. But there's no singing needed. Or high fives, for that matter. Let your body do all the talking. Next question: Who's a Laker fan?"

Once again, nearly the entire class went to the middle. Perfect. I continued for a while with a series of easy, pop-culture questions that Sharaud had helped me devise that morning that would get my students in the routine of stepping out of their comfort zone. I asked questions about food, video games, Hollywood stars, fashion trends, and their siblings. Once I was convinced that they knew the routine, I switched gears to more serious questions.

"How many of you have parents who are divorced?" I asked.

A vast majority of the students walked to the center.

"How 'bout those of us whose parents never got married in the first place?" someone shouted from the line.

"Good question. How many of your parents never got married?" I asked.

Many students stayed on the line and others walked to the center.

As the questions intensified, so did the students' moods. They wanted to see who stepped on the line with them. There was comfort in knowing that they were not alone. To make it seem less intrusive, I rephrased the questions so they began, "Step on the line if you know someone who . . ." Asking if they knew "someone who" was in a gang or had been homeless made the process less threatening.

Their willingness to step on the line was uncanny. The more serious a question was, like "Step on the line if you've known somebody who's an alcoholic" or ". . . somebody who's taken drugs," the more serious their demeanor was. After each question, they looked at one another and nodded their heads. They recognized their vulnerabilities, and there was a reckoning, an acknowledgment, and a bond. Maria was one of the few students who stood on the line after almost every question. I was impressed by her honesty.

"Does anyone want to ask a question?" I said, trying to get further participation from my students.

Henry was the first to take the bait. "How many of you have been shot at?" Half the class walked to the line.

One after another, the questions seemed to mirror the individual who was asking them. "Who knows someone doing time?" asked another.

"Who's ever buried a friend?" asked another. Nearly every student stood on the line. They looked at one another and shared a moment of silence.

When the bell rang, no one was anxious to leave. "Hey, Ms. G, that was tight," Henry said. "Can I stay next period and do it again?"

"No," I laughed, "you've got to go to your next class, but I'm glad you liked it."

As students were leaving and others were coming in, I overheard some students say that the game was "dope."

The Line Game gave me a glimmer of hope. The students' willingness to be exposed encouraged me to be less guarded. Maybe, if I wanted to truly connect with my students, I would need to step up to the line as well.

CHAPTER 14

S hortly before school started, Manny came parading down the hallway with his chest puffed out, shouting, "Look, Ms. G, I have something to show you!" He was waving a thick white envelope like it was a winning lottery ticket. He was giddy as he handed it to me, still shaking. I opened it and read, "Congratulations! You have been accepted to the University of California, Berkeley!" Our eyes locked, and we both started jumping up and down.

"I knew you could do it!" I said.

"I wasn't as confident as you were," he said. "I just thought applying to Berkeley was another one of your crazy ideas."

"They would have been crazy not to accept you!"

"Thanks, Ms. G, I couldn't have done it without your help," he said, giving me a hug.

"Hey, it was a team effort," I said. "You did all the hard stuff!"

The class bell rang, and as Manny headed off to class, I shouted, "We'll have to celebrate later!"

He stopped, turned around, and said, "My mom wants me to thank you."

I never expected an apology or a thank-you, so her sentiments struck a chord. Fighting the tears, I said, "Manny, she deserves all the thanks!"

As I walked into my class, I felt such sadness. Manny's acceptance was bittersweet. Last year, my students and I would have celebrated Manny's success together. But looking around at my current class, I felt so disconnected. We did not share the same kind of emotional bond. Although I had an occasional breakthrough with a student, I had not managed to make my entire class into a cohesive unit.

I had invested so much in my students last year, but I felt burned by the educational bureaucracy. To avoid ridicule or scorn from my colleagues, I didn't buy them new books or take them on field trips. As a result, I was overly cautious and guarded with my new students.

I suppose that holding back caused me to lose some of my passion. In doing so, I hadn't really connected with my students. I may have scratched the surface a few times by bringing my brother in to talk about Bosnia or by playing the Line Game, but I knew I hadn't fully engaged them.

With the end of the year fast approaching, I decided to extend myself more and follow some of the success we experienced last year—where the lessons ignited a desire to go beyond the walls of our classroom.

Manny's acceptance letter planted a seed. I would hold him up as a role model and have my students write an essay about an individual like Manny, who had overcome adversity. Following their essays, I would assemble a panel of inspiring adults, whose triumphant circumstances could reach my students in a way that I couldn't.

I called Renee Firestone to see if she could help me create a panel consisting of inspiring speakers who persevered through tragedy in their teen years. She was thrilled to help and suggested inviting a Japanese gentleman by the name of Mas Okui. As a teenager during World War II, Mas was placed in Manzanar internment camp. With Renee and Mas anchoring the panel, I decided that we would need a room large enough to seat all my students.

Renee suggested, "Why don't you use the theater at the Museum of Tolerance?"

"That would be perfect," I said.

Then she asked, "How are your darling students from last year?"

"They're wonderful, but I miss them. I only have chance encounters with them in the hall. Melvin is the rally chairman, Manny just got into Berkeley, and Sharaud has helped me motivate my new students. I don't know what I would do without him."

"Spielberg spoke very highly of them," she said. Since the success of *Schindler's List,* Renee had been working with Spielberg's Shoah Foundation, interviewing fellow Holocaust survivors all over the world. She spent a great deal of time with Spielberg, and I was flattered that he would mention my students to her. "Why don't you invite them to the panel?" she suggested.

"That's a great idea. A field trip would be a special reunion for them. Maybe they can help me manage my unruly freshmen," I said.

With Renee on board, I began to fine-tune the assignment. Since I was still wary of the chair of the English Department and her reaction to any extracurricular activities, I planned to have an after-school field trip, and scheduled the panel for five o'clock in the evening. I figured that if we left after the school day ended, she wouldn't complain about my students missing classes.

When I told my husband that I was thinking about working a few extra shifts at Nordstrom to pay for the bus, he suggested that I ask his boss, John Tu, for help.

"John Tu offered to help you at the holiday party, remember?" he said.

"I know, but it was a party, and sometimes people say things they don't really mean just to be polite."

John Tu was the CEO of Kingston Technology, a successful computer company in Southern California. We had talked briefly about my students, and he seemed genuinely interested, but several months had passed and I was nervous that he may have forgotten me.

"John is really sincere. I don't think he would have offered if he didn't mean it. Besides, it beats selling bras," he said.

With my husband's encouragement, I set up an appointment with John Tu. When Mr. Tu finally came down to the lobby, he had a big smile on his face. He was impeccably dressed. I expected him to take me to a fancy office, but he showed me his desk, which was nothing more than a cubicle in the middle of hundreds of employees. As we walked to a conference room, he told me that he didn't like hierarchies or stuffy titles. His philosophy was to be approachable, so he put himself in the middle of the action, rather than removed in a corner office.

His approach to power structures seemed like the perfect opening to tell him about my students. "Mr. Tu—" I said.

"Call me John," he interrupted.

"John," I said, taking a deep breath. I realized that I was incredibly nervous, but I pushed forward. I was not used to asking for help. "I've struggled to teach English at a high school in Long Beach, which is only about twenty-five miles from here. Most of my students are bused in from dangerous neighborhoods and their parents don't seem too involved in their education."

"What are their parents like?"

"I don't know. Only a handful of them have returned my phone calls or come to Back-to-School Night. Many of them don't live with their fathers. Some are in jail, some are on the streets, and tragically, a few of them don't even know their fathers at all."

"I'm a father, and I couldn't imagine not being there for my kids."

"I can't imagine going through life without my father. He's my rock, and I know I'd be lost without him. I think my students crave positive male role models. I brought my brother into class one day and that really resonated with them. Especially the boys."

Luckily, John Tu had compassion for my students' plight. Although his father was a successful businessman, John told me of how he had seen poverty firsthand as a boy growing up in Taiwan. Now it was his mission to give back to people in need. "Is there anything I can do to help?" he asked.

"I want to take my students on a field trip where they can learn from individuals who have come from great hardship to become successful adults. Last year, I raised the money to take my students to see *Schindler's List*, to visit my alma mater, and I took them to a museum. I had two extra jobs to help pay for all the trips. I still pick up an occasional shift at the Marriott, but I don't have enough time to raise the money for a field trip before the school year is out. Is there a way you could help?"

"I'll help fund your trip, if your students work for it," he offered.

"I don't believe in handouts, Mr. Tu," I said. "They will have to earn it."

As I was about to leave, I asked, "Would you join us on the field trip? I'd really like my students to meet you."

"I would be honored," he said.

I was so excited that I tripped on the stairs on my way to the lobby. Fortunately, John had already returned to his cubicle and didn't see me stumble. I tried to play it cool, but I was slightly mortified nonetheless.

I knew that the conventional ways to get my students to write a heartfelt essay would not be as successful, so I needed to sell the idea to them in a different way. They had to work hard and earn this trip. As with the Line Game, I tricked my students into thinking that the way to write with heart was through their stomach.

I brought in a gourmet ham sandwich from a local French bakery in Newport Beach. The sandwich was bulging with honey-glazed ham, provolone cheese, heirloom tomatoes, butter lettuce, and Dijon mustard, between halves of a freshly baked baguette. I also had a regular sandwich on plain white bread with one measly slice of ham.

I set up a desk in the front of the room and made it look like a table at a fancy restaurant—with a tablecloth, some china from my wedding that we had yet to use, a candle, and a vase with a flower. I wore an apron and a chef's hat that said, "Chef Boyard G." I chose Henry and Maria, my Romeo and Juliet, to sit at the table and taste each sandwich.

Once they unanimously agreed that the sandwich on the fancy bread with all the fixings was better, I explained to them that "a good essay is like a sandwich." I dissected each element of the sandwich in terms of literary devices. The bread was what held an essay together, the meat was the important stuff, and the lettuce, tomatoes, and cheese were all the details that made a sandwich taste better.

"The 'meat of your sandwich' must be about a courageous character who has overcome adversity," I instructed.

"I don't know anyone who's overcome adversity," Maria said definitely. "Everyone's still caught up in it."

"Well, then, you can write about a character in one of the stories we've read, like the little girl who went to the Japanese internment camp," I suggested.

"Can I write about myself instead?" she asked. "My life is more dramatic than any of the stories you've made us read."

Sensing that her essay could lead to a real breakthrough, I agreed.

After she turned it in, I read how her father gave her a pair of shining red boxing gloves on her fifth birthday. He told her, "Maria, life is tough, and when it knocks you down, I want you to get up swinging." So she learned to swing first, swing fast, and to keep a stiff upper lip.

After reading the first paragraph, my stomach sank. I tried to picture her as a five-year-old, going to kindergarten with a box of crayons, the kind with a sharpener in the back, and turning a piece of paper into a masterpiece. But in Maria's case, I quickly learned that not all five-year-olds start off with a blank canvas.

Her education didn't come in the classroom; it came on the streets, when Maria watched her eighteen-year-old cousin get shot five times in the back by the Los Angeles Police Department. As I continued to read, I wondered how a little girl could go off to school and concentrate on her ABCs and 1, 2, 3s when she didn't even know what post-traumatic stress disorder was.

Her dad, with his sixth-grade education, taught his daughter to be proud of her roots. And since the men who shot her cousin didn't look like her, didn't talk like her, and didn't come from where she came from, she quickly learned that "they" were the enemy. Suddenly, "they" weren't just two men wearing blue suits with shiny badges; "they" were anyone who looked like them—anyone who was white.

When the LAPD stormed into her home and handcuffed her dad on suspicion of murder, it was just another reminder to Maria to keep her dukes up. Although there was only circumstantial evidence, her father refused to testify against one of his homeboys and was sentenced to serve time in a maximum-security prison for a murder he didn't commit.

If Maria wanted to see her dad at the notorious maximum-security prison, she had to climb in the backseat of a lowered Chevrolet Impala and drive close to eight hours. Her father, dressed in a jumpsuit, with shackles around his ankles, would pick up a telephone, put his hand on the Plexiglas, and groom his daughter "to be a strong, woman warrior, his Aztec princess." And that's exactly what Maria did.

She bounced from school to school and soon realized that she could learn sophisticated math skills on the streets, rather than in a classroom. When Maria turned eleven, she was jumped into a gang. In her essay, she wrote that ten people, twice her size, surrounded her and beat her up. She emerged from the circle with a shattered nose, cuts, bruises, and broken bones. Even though she had to lie on a hospital bed for over two weeks, she felt empowered. She was just like her daddy. Soon, she was following in his footsteps and was behind bars herself.

Reading Maria's essay made me understand why she was so angry. I went to John Tu's office armed with Maria's essay, so he could truly comprehend the kids he was helping. As I read him Maria's essay, he kept shaking his head in disbelief.

"I had no idea," he said, noticeably moved. "I would love to talk to her at dinner."

"Um, Mr. Tu," I hesitated, "I wasn't planning on taking them to dinner. A lot of my students are on government assistance, and the only meal they may have is the free breakfast and lunch that our school cafeteria serves."

"I would like to buy them dinner, then," he offered.

"There's a Marriott close to the museum," I said. "Maybe I can get an employee discount."

"That's a great idea, Erin. Why don't you ask the panelists to join us for dinner too?"

As I described the details of our upcoming field trip to my students, everyone seemed excited about it. We discussed what was appropriate to wear, how they should act on the bus and at the theater, and audience etiquette.

I had a meeting after school with my former students, and I asked if they could act as unofficial chaperones and keep a watchful eye on the freshmen. Sharaud volunteered to sit next to Henry since they were both on the track team, and Manny said he'd watch over Maria because her feistiness reminded him of his mother.

I was going through the parent permission slips the evening before the trip. I noticed that Maria was the only one who hadn't turned in her slip. Perhaps she forgot. I called her home to remind her to bring the slip with her to school or she couldn't get on the bus.

"I'm not going," she said curtly.

"But your essay was so good."

"It was just a stupid essay."

"Can I talk with your mother?" I asked in the hopes of her convincing Maria to come.

"She's working. And besides, my mom could care less. My fu—" She caught herself midword and said, "My stupid p.o. won't let me go."

"Maria, I'm so sorry. Can I call him on your behalf?"

"For what?"

"To tell him this an important school event."

"He doesn't give a shit. A rule's a rule. To him, I'm just another case number."

"You're not just a number to me. Let me at least try?" As I pressed the issue, she got annoyed.

"You don't get it, Ms. G. I already asked him and he said no. So don't waste your time."

When we hung up, I felt helpless. Students like Maria needed to go on meaningful field trips, needed to hear inspiring panelists, and needed to meet people like John Tu who cared enough about students to pay for the field trip.

As we boarded the buses the next afternoon, Manny asked, "Where's Maria?"

"She can't make it," I said disappointingly. On the bus ride up, I felt sad. Although the students were all on their best behavior, something was missing.

Although John Tu was disappointed that he couldn't meet the "little girl who wrote the essay," he was excited to meet the rest of my students. He sat next to them during the panel and asked them a lot of questions during dinner.

When I read their journals the following day, one of my students wrote, "The biggest treat of all was when John Tu sat at my table. Here was this man who had so much to say but wanted us to do all the talking. . . . How could someone who doesn't even know me be so interested in me? Here's this gazillionaire treating me as if I'm the belle of the ball, when my own dad is treating me like I don't exist. John Tu gave me more attention in seven minutes than my dad has given in seven years."

Their journals pulled at my heartstrings. As I continued to read, the head counselor, Dave Beard, popped his head into my room.

"Uh-oh, what'd I do now?" I asked. Usually, when Mr. Beard visited my class, it was because someone in the English Department had registered a complaint.

"You didn't do anything wrong," he said, chuckling. "I wanted to see if you would be interested in teaching sophomores next year."

"Really?" I said, sounding surprised. "I assumed that I'd be teaching freshmen forever."

Mr. Beard explained that the school district had decided to offer any teacher close to retirement a "golden handshake." Teachers could retire a few years early and still keep all of their retirement benefits. Several teachers from Wilson decided to take it, leaving an opening in the English rotation.

"I'd love to," I said, jumping at the chance.

"If any of your students want your class again," he offered, "you can just send around a sign-up sheet and I'll plug them into the master schedule."

Although the idea of staying with my students an additional year was intriguing, I didn't want to get my hopes up, especially after being denied the opportunity to stay with my students the previous year. I tried to manage my expectations in case they didn't want to endure another year with me and only a few signed up.

The next morning, I asked my students to sign up if they wanted to be in my class again next year.

When the clipboard made its way back to me, I was surprised to see that they had all signed up, even Maria.

CHAPTER 15

"Sometimes I feel like I live in an undeclared war zone," Darrius said during a lively class discussion at the beginning of the school year about the rites of passage.

Over the summer, I had looked forward to seeing how my students from the previous year had matured. I was a little nervous because Sharaud and his posse had graduated and left me to figure out the subtleties of teaching sophomores on my own. Darrius's comment was most certainly not the way I had envisioned the school year to begin.

The principal told me before school started that Darrius had spent much of the summer in juvenile hall and to be "extra careful." The principal, however, wouldn't tell me much more than that. I figured the true story would arise eventually.

Darrius's comment struck me. When I thought of a war zone, I thought of tanks and battle fatigues. Long Beach is thirty minutes from Disneyland— the happiest place on earth—and forty-five minutes from Rodeo Drive and those palm trees. There are no tanks going down the streets. No one is wearing battle fatigues. But rather than interject, I listened.

Sadly, Darrius truly believed that he lived in a war. So much so that every time a lowered Chevy drove down his street, he perceived it as a tank, a possible drive-by shooting. And every time Darrius put on his battle fatigues, a blue jersey, symbolizing his affiliation with the Crips, someone else would put on red, the color of the Bloods.

Darrius stood up. "I've buried two dozen friends to senseless gang violence," he continued. Although Darrius looked menacing, he was actually quite amiable. He hadn't quite grown into his body yet, and his size made him a little clumsy.

When Darrius was thirteen years old, he was given $25 by his mother, with strict instructions to go to Target and buy school supplies. Darrius called his best friend to join him, but his friend did not want to be called a "schoolboy" or a "sellout." So rather than buying school supplies, he convinced Darrius to buy a used .38 Special handgun.

Later on that same day, they went to Martin Luther King Jr. Park, a park in Long Beach that is usually filled with people doing drugs, working girls turning tricks, and homeless people sleeping in cardboard boxes. On this particular day, there were two teens admiring their new prized possession.

Darrius told the class that they had power that day, and that they were invincible. Since their entire frame of reference was pop culture, what they saw in movie theaters or watched on TV, his best friend suggested, "Hey Darrius, I want to show you a game I saw in a movie. It's called Russian Roulette."

His friend volunteered to go first. Darrius reenacted how his friend put one bullet in the chamber, gave the cylinder a spin, and put the gun to his temple. And with one pull of the trigger—*boom!* He blew his brains out—all over Darrius.

Several of the girls in class gasped in shock. Seeing that his peers were noticeably stirred, Darrius continued by saying that he was covered in blood and that he, in a state of shock, cradled his friend until the police showed up.

"Since there was a gun, a dead body, and a nigga," he explained that the cops cuffed him and took him off to juvenile hall.

I realized that for young men like Darrius who desperately try to escape their reality in darkened movie theaters or with rented movies, this was one movie that he couldn't pause, stop, or eject. In all actuality, it was playing over and over again in his mind.

"Even if I stand in the shower and I scrub myself raw with a Brillo pad and Comet," he said, "I still feel my friend."

While my students were looking down or diverting their eyes, Maria stood up, locked eyes with Darrius, and said, "Darrius, I feel you. I've seen more dead bodies than a mortician."

They looked at each other intently. Then he nodded at her and took his seat. Although he had no knowledge that Maria was on probation, I knew they shared uncanny similarities—among them, a deep sense of hopelessness and loss, and the belief that life was unfair to people who looked like them.

The exchange between Darrius and Maria had a profound effect on me. I didn't want them to perpetuate the cycle of violence by reaching for those shiny red boxing gloves or using a .38 Special. I wanted them to reach for a pen and find another way to fight back.

Maybe having my students read stories about teens who had overcome similar circumstances, or even worse, war, would resonate with them. Stories written by, for, and about teens who lived in real wars. Teens like Anne Frank, who in her tiny little attic looked out her window and watched her friends being led off to concentration camps like sheep to slaughter. Or Elie Wiesel, who as a teen was crammed into a cattle car, transported to Auschwitz-Birkenau, and then watched his parents perish in the gas chambers. But instead of reaching for a gun, these courageous teens reached for a pen.

Even though I was confident that these texts would appeal to my students, I went to the chair of the English Department with some reservation to check out the books. As expected, my request for books was rejected. More determined than ever, I searched for a bookstore that would give me a discount. Luckily, the bookstore manager at Barnes & Noble felt sympathetic to my plight and offered me a discount I couldn't refuse. I ordered 150 copies of Anne Frank's *The Diary of a Young Girl*, Elie Wiesel's *Night,* and two additional books, *Zlata's Diary: A Child's Life in Sarajevo,* about a Bosnian teen named Zlata Filipović whom critics hailed as the modern-day Anne Frank, and *The Wave* by Todd Strasser, about a teacher whose class experiment goes awry when his high school students begin emulating Nazis.

As the manager was ringing up all the books, I was afraid that I might max out my credit cards. I worried that I may have gone overboard by buying four books and wondered if my students would actually read them. The manager must have sensed that I was anxious, so he threw in 150 book plates, bookmarks, and individual plastic bags.

I wanted my students to find themselves within the pages of each book and not resort to Cliffs Notes or renting the movie from Blockbuster.

Hopefully, reading the actual book, and not a watered-down version represented in a magazine, would mark a rite of passage.

By setting the bar high for my students, I wanted to challenge them to break away from their pattern of low expectations. No matter what mistakes they may have made in the past, I wanted them to see reading a book from cover to cover as an opportunity to change. Suddenly, the presentation of these books seemed very important.

I started to think about doing something ceremonial. In my life, every time I had experienced some sort of symbolic change, my family celebrated with a toast. My graduation, my wedding, even my first job—we would raise a glass and celebrate with a toast. Unfortunately, my students didn't make many toasts because they didn't have much to celebrate. I wanted to share the experience of making a toast with them, so I decided we would have a "Toast for Change."

With a "Toast for Change," maybe students like Darrius and Maria could wipe the slate clean. It didn't matter to me that Darrius had a D average or that Maria had been kicked out of nearly every school she ever attended. Maybe they could start anew.

I went out and bought plastic champagne glasses and sparkling apple cider. The next day, I arrived at school earlier than usual to rearrange my classroom. I pushed all the desks and chairs against the wall. I blew up some balloons to make it look a little festive, and I lined up the champagne glasses and the books. When the students came in, they were a little taken aback.

Maria took one look at me, rolled her eyes, and said, "Ms. G, you really need to stop going to Starbucks. You've had way too many lattes."

I guess it was transparent how eager I was to kick off my experiment. I envisioned that the toast would encourage my students to actually read the books from cover to cover, engage in class discussions, write the perfect five-paragraph essay, and get better grades. I asked them to stand in a circle, hold up their champagne glasses, and make a personal toast.

Maria shocked us all. She picked up her glass and with a very serious tone said, "I don't want to be pregnant by the time I'm fifteen like my mother. I don't want to spend the rest of my life behind bars like my father. And I don't want to be six feet under by the time I turn eighteen like my cousin. I want to change!"

For a moment, I was dumbfounded. My idea of change seemed more simplistic, more academic. Maria's allusion to a life change started a chain reaction, though. Her honesty encouraged others to open up. There were more testimonials, more confessions. Students were tired of being picked on, tired of being poor, and tired of following in the footsteps of their parents. One student said she was tired of being like her mom, "standing on the corner of Pacific Coast Highway with a cardboard box that said 'Will Work for Food.'" Another was "tired of bailing out his deadbeat dad," while another was not "going to ignore his mom being beaten by her new boyfriend anymore."

As the toast went on, I realized that this moment meant a lot more than a promise to read books. Suddenly, panic set in. How was I going to help them change on such a dramatic level? I wasn't a counselor or a therapist. I didn't even have tenure.

"These books will help you change," I said, handing Maria Anne Frank's diary. Maria didn't see it that way. She was excited about the concept of change; she just didn't want to read a three-hundred-page book to do it.

She flipped through the pages and said, "Why do I have to read a book about a little girl who doesn't look like me?"

"Maybe you'll find yourself within the pages of the book," I offered.

"Yeah, right! She's not even Latina," Maria said defiantly. "She knows nothing about surviving in my hood!"

"Why don't you try opening the book first, Maria? Then you can decide."

I must have been talking in some kind of teacher code, because Maria was disgusted by my feeble attempt to bring any kind of relevance to the book.

I asked the rest of the students, who looked more excited than Maria, to pick up the new books and all the other accoutrements. Although most had backpacks, suddenly carrying a plastic Barnes & Noble bag was like toting a Louis Vuitton purse. I think they wanted to show off to the other kids at school that they were given brand-new books. The first book they were assigned was Anne Frank's *The Diary of a Young Girl*. Since they had met the Holocaust survivor Renee Firestone the previous year, I thought this would be a perfect place to start. From Maria's body language, I could tell she was not happy about having to read. I overheard her mutter something in Spanish and watched her storm off.

Later on, Maria told me that when she got home that afternoon, the electricity had been turned off in her apartment. Because she was still on house arrest and couldn't go outside due to her ankle monitor, she was stuck inside her tiny apartment. With the lights out, she lit a candle, crawled into her bed, and began to read. Her sole purpose was to come back to class and tell me *she was not going to find herself within the pages of a book.*

Some of the language in the book was difficult for Maria because her reading level may have been as low as a fourth-grader's. Although Maria struggled with the diary entries, she continued to read. When Maria read a passage about Anne Frank feeling like a bird in a cage, something clicked within her. It was as if a tiny little bulb went on, like the kind she had seen in cartoons. Maria realized that she was in a cage too. She felt like Anne, in her tiny little attic, had written that sentiment fifty years ago just for her to read.

The diary seemed to have an immediate impact on Maria. She seemed less defiant. She doodled less. She stopped making up excuses to go to the bathroom. And she started dropping by after school to ask me questions like "When is Anne going to smoke Hitler?"

Now, I know I'm not cool, and just when I think I've mastered their slang, my students go and change it on me. "Smoke Hitler? What does that mean?"

Annoyed by my ignorance, she said, "Ya know, take him out."

Suddenly, it made sense to me. Maria was projecting her gangster mentality on the book and expected Anne to take out Hitler.

"Keep reading, Maria. . . ."

When Peter entered the attic, she wanted to know if Anne and Peter were going to "hook up and do a little somethin' somethin'."

"It's not that kind of book, Maria. Keep reading."

Maria clearly admired the relationship that Anne shared with her father, Otto. Although Maria's father was in a maximum-security prison, she said she could relate to their father/daughter bond. Maria, like Anne, shared a secret language with her father, who tried to shield his little girl from danger.

Then one day Maria came into class and threw the book across the room. Outraged, she started calling me names in Spanish, so I reached for my cheat sheet to find out exactly what she was saying.

She had tears in her eyes and said, "Why didn't you tell me that she dies?" she said.

I thought that everyone knew that Anne dies at the end. I felt horrible. In the movies, the good guy always makes it, but that was not the case in real life. Maria believed that if Anne, who was such a good person, didn't make it, neither would she.

"If Anne doesn't make it, what are you saying about my chances?"

Before I had a chance to answer, Darrius intervened. "Maria, Anne Frank is gonna go on living even after her death, just like it said in the book."

"Shut up, Darrius, I'm not talking to you."

"Come on, Maria, how many of our homies have died and we've never even read an obituary? They're not on the cover of *Newsweek* and their parents aren't on TV sitting next to Larry King."

Maria stood there silently. I think Darrius got under her skin, talking about Anne's legacy and the power of writing. "She did make it. She wrote about it!"

The next day, Darrius came to class with several books from the local library: books about World War II, the Holocaust, and Anne's attic. He was like a kindergartener ready for show-and-tell. He was so excited that he reminded me of a Coke can ready to explode. I envisioned him missing this kind of excitement as a five-year-old, so it appeared that he was making up for lost time.

"Wow, Darrius, did you get all those books at the library?" I asked.

"Yep!" he said, proudly shaking his head.

"Did you check all those books out?"

"Um . . . no," he said, kind of elusively.

Darrius had never been to the library before, so he treated these books like contraband. Apparently, he and his "associates" had shoved these books down their size-60 jeans or inside their Raiders jackets.

He had done a little research and found out that the woman who hid Anne Frank, Miep Gies, was still alive. She was eighty-seven years old and living in Amsterdam. "We should invite her to our class!" he said, as if all we had to do was pick up the phone and invite her. This was not as simple as his bootlegged copy of *Field of Dreams*, where "if you build it, they will come."

But I had to admit, this could be an interesting English assignment. Instead of writing a book report, we could write letters to Miep Gies.

The next day, Darrius came into class with a jug from a water cooler. Knowing that Darrius didn't actually own a water cooler, I decided it was best not to ask. "This jug is what we're going to use to raise the money to get Miep Gies here!" He reached his hand into his pocket and pulled out some fuzz and a couple of coins. Into the jug went seven cents. He looked up at the class and held out the jug, as if to say "Ante up!"

But I knew they would have a hard time anteing up. They were not going to be able to convince their parents to pull out their Visas or their checkbooks. Or even go to the ATM and get a crisp twenty-dollar bill. Most of them were on free and reduced lunch and had meal tickets in lieu of dollar bills. I overheard one student say, "American Airlines probably won't take our lunch tickets, huh?"

"How many of you have ever been on a plane?" I asked.

Most hadn't. They had no concept of how much a ticket cost or all the other expenses related to travel. Working as a hotel concierge gave me a more realistic insight into travel expenses, and I knew that we were never going to raise enough money. But Darrius's idea presented the perfect writing assignment. If they perceived that Miep may actually read their letters, it may raise the quality of their writing.

A couple of days later, Darrius put me on the spot. "Ms. G, what happens if we raise all this money and she doesn't come?"

There were all of eighteen dollars in the jug.

"Um," I said, trying to stall. How could I placate him and the rest of the students long enough to get really good letters from them? "If she doesn't come and we've raised all of this money, then we can buy more books or even go on a field trip, so it really is a win-win situation."

I stopped and looked deeply at Darrius. He wanted this so badly.

"But if she does come," I said, "your lives will never be the same."

CHAPTER 16

T he first day back from the winter holiday, I ran into Tommy in the hall.
"Hey, Ms. G, do you have any more books?" he casually asked.

"What?" I was about to lose it! I figured he'd lost all the books and was ready to read him the riot act. "Did you lose them?"

"No, I, um, actually read all of them and was wondering if you had any more."

"Really?" I was surprised. Most of the students were still reading Anne Frank's diary, the first book of the collection.

"Yeah, well, I was grounded over the holidays and the only thing I could do was read."

"You read all four books?"

"Yeah, can you believe it? I really liked the one about the little girl from Sarajevo. I could relate."

I was stunned. I wanted to hug him but decided to make an important phone call instead. Tommy had transferred into my class midsemester because his previous English teacher was afraid of him. Ms. Broadway, the tenth-grade vice principal, poked her head in my class one day to see if I would take Tommy. She caught me on a bad day, and I said, "Why do I have to take the kids that nobody else wants?" Then I realized that Tommy's only option was my class or another school. So I took him.

At first, I didn't know what to think of Tommy. He was ominous, and he sort of scared me. He never volunteered to read, never asked a question, and was silent during the Toast for Change. But since he had read all four books, I suddenly had a new outlook on him.

I practically ran to the office to seek Tommy's emergency contact card. "Mr. Jefferson, this is Tommy's English teacher . . ." and before I could finish my sentence, he said, "Uh-oh, what did Tommy do this time?"

"No, it's not that kind of call, sir. I just wanted to tell you that I am really proud of Tommy. He read all of the books I assigned." As I kept bragging, there was a silence over the phone. "Mr. Jefferson, are you still there?"

He cleared his throat, not to give away that he was pretty choked up. "It's just I've never got this kind of call before."

"Could you do me a favor and give him a hug for me tonight?"

"Um, sure," he said hesitantly.

The next day, I heard Tommy's booming voice coming down the hallway. "Ms. G, did you call my dad?"

"Yeah, I did. What happened?"

"He gave me a hug."

"He did?" I could hardly contain my smile. "How'd it feel?"

"It felt good, I guess." As he was about to storm away, he turned and said, "Um, my dad hasn't done that since I was a little kid. It meant a lot. Thanks."

A few days after that, Tommy disappeared.

After two weeks, I was really worried about Tommy. I wondered why he was missing. Was he ditching? Was he hurt? Was he in jail? The more I thought about it, the more I panicked. I tried calling his home, but there was no answer. I wondered if he had moved.

Calling my students was a source of frustration for me because it was always hit-or-miss. I had moved only once during my childhood, so our phone number had been the same since I was seven. That wasn't the case for many of my students, because many of them were transient and moved often. They got evicted, or they had problems with neighbors, or something else. Their emergency cards were almost always inaccurate. I tried Tommy's home phone—disconnected. Then his pager—inactive.

When I couldn't reach him by phone, I started bugging his friends for information on his whereabouts. They hadn't heard from him either, so I started imagining the worst.

When Tommy finally showed up at school, I was furious. No note. No explanation. No apology. "Tommy, you've missed a lot of assignments, so would you stay after school today to find out what you've missed?" I said with an edge.

He didn't say anything. He just nodded his head "yes" and sat down. That only made me angrier. I wanted him to tell me where he'd been and explain to me why he was missing, but he gave me the silent treatment. His whole demeanor was different. It looked like he had lost a little weight, and he looked sullen.

To make matters worse, I was sick. I had gotten sick a few days before Christmas and hadn't been able to shake it. At the beginning of the holiday season, I was obsessed with trying to locate Miep, and I think this obsession was genuinely affecting me. "Stop taking your job home with you," my dad warned. But I couldn't turn off my class, even during a holiday. "You're too stressed, Erin," my dad said. "You need to lighten up or you're going to get really sick."

When I couldn't make it past nine o'clock on New Year's Eve, I knew something was wrong. Turns out I had walking pneumonia. My defenses were still down, I still hadn't been able to locate Miep, and I was grumpy. Tommy's demeanor really triggered me.

When Tommy came into my room after school to talk about his hiatus, he was completely devoid of emotion.

"Tommy," I asked, "where have you been?"

He stood there in silence.

"Tommy, have you been ditching?"

He shook his head.

"Then what's your excuse?" I was short with him.

He stood in silence and looked down and whispered, "My cousin was murdered."

"Oh, Tommy, I'm so sorry." Suddenly, my anger turned to empathy. I wanted to hug him, console him, but he just stood there as if he was anesthetized.

"How did it happen?"

"He was shot five times in the head by a rival gang."

I wanted to ask a million questions, but I could sense that he didn't want to talk.

"A lot of shit is going down right now and there are too many fucking funerals. All these *cholos* are killing my homies."

I lived far away from Long Beach, so I was often oblivious to the battle-field my students were subjected to. Since he was sharing, I didn't want to interrogate him for fear that he'd shut down.

"It's just too much for me to take right now, Ms. G. I'm still trying to get over my friend who got murdered before Christmas, and now this. . . ."

"Your friend got murdered too?"

I wondered why he didn't tell me about his friend in December. It certainly wasn't in the newspaper. In my city, the death of a teenager would have been a headline. When my friend died during our senior year in high school, it seemed like the entire town shut down. Sam's death was all we talked about. Every paper covered it. It was even on the nightly news. Support groups sprouted up. Everyone went to the funeral. And his death seemed to affect everyone in its wake.

I stood there dumbfounded. Then I remembered Tommy coming back after the holiday and telling me he "was in trouble" and all he did was read. I wondered if he had been with his friend or why he was in trouble. Clearly, he wasn't going to tell me the details, but I wanted him to tell somebody.

"Honey, I'm so sorry. Do you have anyone to talk to?"

"No, I don't really feel like talking," he said, looking down at his feet.

"Do you feel like writing about it?"

"I don't know. You really wouldn't understand. Your life's too perfect."

Even though my life was far from perfect, this was no time for a debate. This wasn't about me. "What about Zlata Filipović? She'd understand. Maybe you could write her a letter."

"Do you think she'd read it?"

"I don't know, sweetie, but it's worth a shot." I immediately caught myself and thought, *You idiot, why did you have to say "shot"?* "Zlata would definitely understand."

Zlata's Diary was the next book in our series, and it was Tommy's favorite. Since she and Tommy were both fifteen, I assumed it would help him get out his feelings if he wrote to someone whose life was not so "perfect" in his eyes. After all, Zlata lived in the middle of a war in Sarajevo and had witnessed her friend Nina being shot by snipers.

"You can use my computer if you want."

He sat down at my desk and started typing:

"Dear Zlata. They say America is the 'Land of the Free and Home of the Brave,' but what's so free about a land where people get *killed*?"

It was a powerful introduction. He went on to compare how they both had lost friends and family to senseless violence. He ended his first paragraph with a chilling sentence: "The strange thing is . . . my country is not at war, or is it?"

As he wrote to her, tears began to roll down his face, as if he was reliving their deaths. He ended his letter with "Until this undeclared war has ended, I am not free."

His letter was a passionate plea to Zlata, this teenage girl from war-torn Sarajevo, to learn about Tommy's America. Tommy didn't need to take a test or write a book report to prove to me that he understood the book. When he finished, he'd written more than the normal five-paragraph essay. It was a masterpiece. It was also a catalyst for something bigger.

As he was about to leave, he asked, "Hey, do you think we can invite Zlata to come here too? I have to meet her."

"I don't know, Tommy, let's see what happens with Miep first."

CHAPTER 17

My students' latest projects usually followed me to my weekend job at the Marriott. My concierge shift started at 6 A.M. on Sunday mornings, and it was generally pretty quiet until around 9 A.M. This downtime gave me the opportunity to read the newspaper and catch up on world events that would be applicable to my lesson plans. While I was reading the film reviews in the *New York Times*, an article about the documentary *Anne Frank Remembered* caught my attention. The documentary featured interviews with many of Anne's friends, including Miep Gies. The documentary was playing only in select theaters, but it had recently been nominated for an Academy Award. I was so excited, I could hardly contain myself. I called my husband, but he wasn't home.

I looked around the concierge lounge for a friendly face. Then I spotted one of my regulars, Bill. He was a CEO who had been staying at our hotel for years. Guests of the lounge were generally surprised that I could put together words that were not monosyllabic. Some of them were really patronizing, because they assumed that there was a correlation between my polyester uniform and my IQ. I got tired of men talking down to me when they came in for their morning coffee or a request to upgrade their airline tickets. Their condescension was particularly frustrating since I spent my week trying to dispel stereotypes and, on the weekends, I was the one who was being judged.

Bill was not like that. His daughter was studying to be a teacher, and in many ways he reminded me of my dad. Since I had exhausted my father with my Miep obsession, I needed a new confidant. Maybe Bill would be a sympathetic listener and give me some good advice.

I told Bill that my father thought I was being "completely irrational" and that "buying books should have been enough." But it wasn't enough. My dad told me to "let it go," but I couldn't.

"Why don't you find out who made the documentary and see if Miep's coming to Los Angeles for the Oscars," Bill suggested. "If she is, maybe you could coordinate something with her people."

The concept of "her people" cracked me up, because I constantly had to deal with our guests' "people." Their nannies, chauffeurs, secretaries, and even their mistresses. I wondered what kind of "people" Miep had. Would her "people" even return my call?

When I told my husband about Miep later that evening, he said he didn't feel like talking about my job. It was clear that he'd had enough. I think the stress was taking a toll on me, because suddenly a wave of failure rushed over me. I wondered if I was a bad wife and a bad teacher.

My husband's indifference really affected me. So much so that I couldn't sleep. If I was going to pursue Miep, I would have to do it without confiding in him. It was after midnight, so rather than toss and turn, I got out of bed and called the Anne Frank Museum in Amsterdam. I expected them to speak Dutch and hang up on me, but the receptionist's English was perfect.

I asked her if she knew if Miep Gies would be coming to America to promote the documentary. The receptionist got very animated and said, "Yes, Miep is visiting to a city in California called Newport Beach." Newport Beach? I was astonished. Luck must have been on my side, because I never envisioned a midnight search leading me to my own backyard.

That was the first of several serendipitous moments.

The receptionist told me to call the Orange County Museum of Art located in Newport Beach for more information. In the morning when I called the museum, which was only a block away from the hotel where I worked, they told me to call the director of the program, Vincent Guilliano.

As it turned out, Bruce and I were neighbors. I suggested that we meet at my favorite coffee spot. A few minutes into our lattes, Bruce began to tell me about Miep's upcoming visit. A few years earlier, the Newport Beach Art Museum had hosted the traveling "Anne Frank in the World" exhibit. Sal

Deliema, a Holocaust survivor living in Orange County, had befriended Otto Frank at Auschwitz and remained friends with him until Mr. Frank passed away. Otto Frank had asked Sal to call him "Papa" while they were at the concentration camp, and as a tribute to his beloved friend, Mr. Deliema was instrumental in inviting Miep to be the featured speaker at the Anne Frank tribute. Due to the recent interest in the documentary, the Museum organizers were planning to bring Miep back a second time.

"My students really related to Anne's diary, and they have this crazy idea that they can write letters to Miep and entice her to come to Long Beach. They have been trying to raise money to get her here."

"How much have they raised?"

"Only about twenty dollars so far," I said, embarrassed.

"What were you planning to do with their letters?" he asked.

"I don't know. Grade them. Give them back. Move on to the next book. But I feel like I tricked them."

I went on to explain how I felt guilty because their letters were so passionate. They desperately wanted to meet her.

"Most of my students are on free or reduced lunch, so it'll be hard for us to raise enough money for plane fare." I went on to tell him how panic had begun to set in. True, unadulterated panic.

"Aren't inner-city teachers always panicked?" Bruce asked me with a laugh.

"Well, I can't speak for the masses, but it certainly keeps me on my toes."

"Did you always want to be an English teacher?"

"No. I planned to be a lawyer, but, much to my father's chagrin, I realized my calling was in a classroom, not a courtroom. Since I was an English major at UC Irvine, it seemed like a natural fit."

There was an awkward silence. "My son was an English major at UCI. He would have been about your age."

I could sense something awful had happened, so I looked down at my latte. I didn't want to prod. After an awkward moment of silence, Bruce told me that his son had tragically drowned in the San Francisco Bay shortly after graduation. His death was the impetus for Bruce to immerse himself in the "Anne Frank in the World" exhibit. It was a legacy to his son.

His dedication to his son's memory seemed to mirror Otto Frank's. Both fathers wanted to pay homage to their children. Since his son was a poet, he asked if he could read me a poem his son had written called "Moment." Bruce choked up while reading the last stanza of the poem:

> *To live forever*
> *And never feel a thing*
> *To wait a million lifetimes*
> *Only to erode and become sand*
> *Wish not for the stone*
> *But for the fire*
> *Last only moments*
> *But Change everything.*

"May I use this poem with my students?" I asked.

"I would be honored."

Bruce understood why my students wanted to meet Miep and agreed to help make it happen. When I left the coffee shop, I was giddy. Besides my making a new friend, Miep was going to visit my students!

Bruce and I agreed that it would be better if I didn't tell my students that Miep was already planning a trip to California. We believed it would mean more to them if they thought they were responsible for her visit. She was due to arrive in less than a month, so I had my students revise their original letters in the computer lab. Once revised, we bound them into a book at Kinko's. The book of letters looked really impressive.

"After she reads these letters, she's gonna come for sure, Ms. G," Darrius said.

I bit my tongue. I planned to keep the charade going a little longer. Although I wanted to tell them she was coming, I wanted them to think it was because their letters were so good.

To help build suspense, I had them study the poem Bruce had given me. It was really touching, and once again they could see the importance of writing their thoughts and stories on paper.

I waited a week before I finally announced that she was coming. Everyone went crazy. They were cheering so loudly that the teacher across the hall popped his head in to complain.

"Sorry," I said, shrugging my shoulders. Then I shut the door and let the students continue to celebrate.

They decided to host the event at the Bruin Den, a community center across the street. Darrius didn't want Miep to have to "deal with metal detectors at our school," so he suggested the center, since it would fit all 150 of us perfectly.

With their newfound purpose, my students stayed after school even later and later. Self-appointed committees began to pop up. My tagging crew decided that they would be in charge of decorating the Bruin Den. I had the majority of the graffiti artists in my class, so I gave them butcher paper, paint, and markers to transform the dilapidated center into their version of the Museum of Modern Art. White butcher paper became their canvas, and Guillermo and Geraldo became Diego Rivera and Pablo Picasso.

As they were decorating the Bruin Den, Darrius said, "I heard airplane food sucks. We should probably feed her."

This seemed like a perfect excuse to get hesitant parents involved too. Darrius convinced us his grandma could make a mean sweet potato pie. Not to be outdone, Maria said, "My mom can make tamales." It would be an eclectic mix of food, showcasing who my students were and where they came from.

When my students came to school the next day, it was as if they were headed for church. Girls who generally wore big baggy pants were wearing dresses. They didn't look as hardened without their caked-on eye shadow and dark lip liner. There was softness about them. Even Darrius was wearing a creased shirt and a belt. I didn't even know Darrius owned a belt.

"Boy, you guys clean up well," I said in amazement.

Darrius had volunteered to be one of the official "greeters" and escort her to the podium. After all, it was his idea in the first place. I think he envisioned that the ceremony should resemble the MTV music awards. "It's too bad we don't have a red carpet," he said, shaking his head in disappointment.

"Its okay, Darrius," I said. "I don't think she's expecting that."

Then Maria walked up. She had lost her cocky swagger and looked surprisingly innocent. Her bangs weren't as high and her lipstick wasn't as dark. She looked so soft and feminine, like it was her Quinceanera.

In her hand was her most valuable possession. A $4.99 book. The same book that she had thrown against a wall a few weeks earlier.

She averted her eyes and asked, "Ms. G, is there any way that you can buy this book in Spanish?"

"Sure, honey, how come?"

"Because my mama wants to read about the little girl that changed my life."

CHAPTER 18

As Maria anxiously awaited Miep's arrival, I noticed that she was wearing a skirt. Since she generally dressed in oversized boy's clothing, I commented, "You look really pretty today, Maria."

"I finally got that damn thing off," she said, pointing to where her ankle monitor used to be. "I wanted to look nice when I ask Miep to sign my book. I never turned in my letter to Miep," she said, handing me a handwritten letter on a slightly crumpled piece of notebook paper. "Do you have time to read it before she gets here?" she asked.

I looked around the Bruin Den, and although it was sheer chaos—students were still setting up the chairs and hanging posters, and Darrius was pacing—I said, "I would be honored to read it."

Maria's letter to Miep described the complexities of her two worlds. Shortly before she began reading Anne's diary, she was jumped by members of a rival gang. They beat her pretty badly. Her homeboy decided to take vengeance by finding the people who beat her up. In an act of revenge, he shot one of the boys in cold blood.

Although she was able to escape the scene of the crime, she was subpoenaed and would have to testify in the murder case. Since the police hadn't recovered the weapon, she would have to be her friend's alibi.

In her world, there was an unwritten code of silence. She was prepared to lie in court and send an innocent person to prison. But when she read Anne's words that "in spite of everything, I still believe that people are truly good at heart," Maria decided to break her allegiance to the code and speak the truth.

I was just about to tell Maria how amazed I was by her courage, when Darrius shouted, "She's here, she's here!" pointing to a black Town Car.

Miep Gies gingerly stepped out of the car. She appeared to be five feet tall. She looked like a cherub, with alabaster skin and white hair. Darrius took a deep breath and walked over to greet her. Miep had no way of knowing that Darrius's father had died of AIDS, that his brother was in and out of jail, and that his best friend had shot himself in the absurd game. She didn't know and it didn't matter.

Although she was several feet shorter than Darrius and several shades lighter, he acted as if he were escorting Michael Jordan himself into the Bruin Den. When Miep stepped up to the podium, it was as if she were a movie star, a professional athlete, and a pop icon all rolled into one.

She reached for the microphone and welcomed us in a soft voice. My students and I were transfixed, clinging to each word. She began by telling us that "Anne Frank was a Jewish girl, but that doesn't mean her history is only of importance for Jewish children."

Miep was in her early twenties when she became Otto Frank's secretary. Once the Nazis occupied Amsterdam, Otto Frank asked Miep if she would "front for the Franks" while they were in hiding in the secret annex above their office in the pectin shop. Without hesitation, Miep gladly accepted. For two years, she hid the Franks even though she knew that the consequence for helping a Jew was to be sent to a concentration camp.

During the two years, Miep told us about all the things she tried to sneak into that attic—books, paper, pens, and food. She told us tales of riding her bicycle in the snow to dig up turnips when there were no rations. As she described her sacrifice, it reminded me of all the things teachers do behind the scenes for their students—driving across town to Target to save fifteen cents on markers, or staying up all night to grade papers. Just as Anne had no idea how much Miep sacrificed, my students had no idea how much their teachers sacrificed for them.

Miep warned us against living a life "filled with regret for refusing to help people." Then she tearfully told us that someone in Amsterdam had discovered that she and the other pectin employees were hiding Jews in the secret annex. The bounty at that time for a Jew in hiding was about $2 a head. Someone with hate in their heart, or desperate for money, alerted the Gestapo that there were eight individuals hiding in the attic.

Miep choked up as she described the events of August 4, 1944, the day that Anne Frank was captured. The Gestapo stormed into Miep's office and threw her against the wall.

"I saw a gun pointed at me by a man who said, 'Not one sound. Not one word,'" she explained.

As she was describing the scene, I pictured the contrast between this diminutive little woman and a strapping soldier. I envisioned Ralph Fiennes from *Schindler's List* threatening to take her life.

"Then they headed straight to the attic," she said.

As the soldiers stormed up the staircase into the attic, she described how helpless she felt. She heard objects being thrown against the wall and Anne scream. She stood at gunpoint as the eight people were taken as prisoners.

Miep described how she desperately ran home to her tiny apartment to find anything of value that she could use to bribe the Gestapo. She found an earring, a frame from her recent wedding, and a couple of knickknacks. She delicately wrapped them up in a kerchief and proceeded to the Nazi headquarters. Her plan was to bribe the soldiers to let go of Anne.

"She's just a baby," she said, holding out her hand containing her meager belongings toward the soldiers.

Rather than feeling sympathy for this humble secretary willing to sacrifice her worldly possessions, a soldier pulled out a gun, put his finger on the trigger, and pointed it at her head.

A nearby soldier who had overheard the conversation recognized Miep's accent and asked her if she was Austrian. She was. When Miep was young, she had been adopted by a Dutch family but never quite lost her accent. As fate would have it, the soldier was a fellow Austrian. He told the other soldier to let her go. He walked her outside and told her she was "lucky that he didn't kill her on the spot."

Miep went back to the attic, tried to straighten up the mess, and found Anne's beloved checkered diary scattered across the floor. She picked it up, hoping to return it to Anne someday. After all, the BBC had just announced the D-Day landings; the war would be over soon. Miep put the diary in her drawer and never read a word until she and Otto discovered that Anne had died of typhus at the concentration camp Bergen-Belsen.

Miep promised Otto Frank, her courageous boss and sole survivor from the attic, that she would keep Anne's spirit alive. She was faithful to her promise for nearly sixty years.

"There is not a day that goes by that I don't remember August fourth and think about Anne," she said.

She commanded us to follow in Anne's footsteps and do something noble. "You must act when injustice happens. We should not wait for leaders to make the world a better place. We should make this change now, in our homes and our schools. Make sure that Anne's death was not in vain."

I sensed that something had changed in all of us. At that moment, Darrius stood up. He looked so vulnerable, like he was fighting back tears. Miep's description of Anne's capture had clearly shaken him.

"I've never had a hero before, but you are my hero," he declared.

"No!" she said adamantly. "I am not a hero," she said while pounding her little fist on the podium. "I simply did what I had to do because it was the right thing to do!"

CHAPTER 19

After Miep's visit, Darrius, Tommy, and Maria began to bond. They had all experienced incredible loss and had a mutual understanding of the significance of Miep's words. They felt like Miep had passed the baton to them to stand up to injustice, so when they began reading *Zlata's Diary*, they felt like Zlata's story was echoing their own lives.

"Zlata would understand what we're going through," Tommy said one afternoon. "She's seen a lot of crazy shit."

"Maybe we could meet her too," Darrius suggested.

"Yeah, Ms. G," Maria chimed in. "Why don't we get her to come too?"

Although I was excited that my students were bonding, I had no idea how to find a Bosnian refugee, and even less of an idea of how to pay for it. I had kicked in a lot of my own money for Miep's event and I didn't think my husband would be supportive of another extracurricular project.

I told Renee Firestone my dilemma over dinner one evening. She was quickly becoming a surrogate mother, and I found myself calling her for advice quite often. She invited me over for dinner. She lived within walking distance of the Museum of Tolerance, which made it convenient for all the volunteering she did there. She had recently been interviewed for a documentary about the Holocaust called *Survivors of the Shoah* and was hopeful that my students could see it.

I told her some of the ways my students had changed after meeting Miep. They were more inquisitive, they stayed after school doing their homework, and the racial tension seemed to dissipate. They were so involved and empowered.

"They question everything!" I said with a laugh.

"Good for them," Renee said. "It's better than regurgitating facts and figures, isn't it?"

"I know. But now that we're reading *Zlata's Diary*, they want Zlata to come visit us too."

"That's a great idea," she said.

"It would be a great idea if I knew where she was, and if we had the money to pay for a visit."

"Well, I can't give you advice about financial matters, but I can help you find her," Renee said with great confidence.

"How?"

"She just sent me a holiday card."

"She did?" I asked, rather puzzled. "You know her?"

"Yes," Renee said with an impish grin. "I met her at the Museum of Tolerance while she was on her book tour. The museum hosted an exhibition comparing the similarities between the Holocaust and the ethnic cleansing in Bosnia. Zlata and I were on the panel together."

I sat there dumbfounded. Renee never ceased to amaze me.

"Let me go find the holiday card," she offered.

The return address on the card was from Ireland.

"I thought she lived in France," I said. "The back of her book jacket said that she was living in Paris after she escaped Sarajevo." After reading her book, I just assumed that Zlata was shopping at the Champs Élysées and hanging out with a hip literary crowd in coffee shops.

"She moved recently. It's a bit difficult to live in France, especially if you're a refugee."

Renee picked up the phone and requested to speak to an international operator. She read off the address and handed me the phone. For a moment, I was stunned. It couldn't be that easy, could it? The phone went directly to an answering machine, and so I quickly hung up.

"What happened?" Renee asked.

"An answering machine came on," I said.

"Why didn't you leave her a message?"

"I don't know. I got scared. I need to come up with a plan first," I said.

I left Renee's house armed with Zlata's address and telephone number. Now all I had to do was figure out what the hell I was going to do with them.

I started by having my students write Zlata letters. The letter that Tommy had written after his cousin was murdered was used as our model letter. Ironically, his letter was the perfect sandwich. After the students wrote, peer-edited, and perfected their letters, we went to the computer lab to type them. Along with the bound letters, I included photographs of my students with Miep and Renee. I also included a card from Renee, hoping it would give us some credibility. Once the package was complete, I mailed it to her home in Ireland.

In my personal note to Zlata, I asked her to call me collect if she was interested in coming to Long Beach. When she actually called, I was taken aback.

"Hello, Erin, I received your students' letters and I would love to come," she said in flawless English.

"This is so exciting!" I was giddy.

She sweetly asked if she could bring her mother, her father, and her best friend Mirna with her on the trip because she did not like to travel alone.

"Absolutely," I said, trying to hide my embarrassment that we hadn't invited her family in the first place.

All of a sudden, I realized that our efforts were going to have to be quadrupled. We would need help. Lots of help. To pull it off, I would have to ask everyone I knew to pitch in. The first on my list was my dad.

"Dad, I have amazing news," I said over the phone. "Zlata just called me and she accepted our invitation."

"Wow, bringing authors to your class seems to be turning into a cottage industry," he said with a chuckle.

"I know. But I'm going to need some serious help. She wants to bring her parents and her best friend with her."

"Why?"

"She's only fifteen."

"She's the same age as your students?"

"I know—isn't a coincidence? I think that's what makes her book so powerful," I said. "Can you help me get some autographed baseball stuff?" Since we needed enough money for airline tickets, hotel rooms, and food for four people, I would organize a raffle.

"Sure," he offered. "I'll muster up some stuff that you can raffle off."

My dad worked for the California Angels baseball team, and he was able to score some signed baseball paraphernalia: a ball, a jacket, a bat, and even some game tickets. Once I had the Angels gear secured, I encouraged the students to donate other items for the raffle. They were ingenious. They donated free oil changes, car washes, housekeeping services, homemade tamales, ice cream scoops, and even tickets to the movies. I suspected that my students didn't actually have their boss's approval for some of the raffle prizes because the free ice cream and movie passes included the caveat that they could only be redeemed on the days my students were working.

We called the raffle a "Read-a-thon for Tolerance," and each student agreed to comb the community with raffle tickets. John Tu generously agreed to help with any extra costs that our raffle couldn't cover.

I talked with the manager at the Marriott to see if she could help us. She donated two of their luxury suites for Zlata and her family to stay in for the duration of the trip. I was shocked. Her donation would save us hundreds of dollars.

Once the momentum was under way, I decided that this would be a perfect opportunity to get their parents involved. I called Debbie to help me galvanize the parents. "I want everyone to bring their families. How can I do it?"

"Maybe you can do something that will make the parents proud of their kids. If you make it into a party, parents may come," she suggested.

I loved throwing parties. When I was in college, my apartment was synonymous with theme parties. I had nonstop parties leading up to my wedding, and after we were married, my husband and I continued to entertain. But since I lived in an apartment, I couldn't invite four hundred people to my backyard for a barbecue.

"Can you help me?"

"I'll put a call out to some of my girlfriends and see what I can do."

A couple nights later, she managed to get me on the agenda for the upcoming Booster meeting. Debbie and I walked into the library, and I didn't recognize any of the mothers. They were wearing designer suits and their kids were in the Honors program. Debbie seemed to know all of the women.

Debbie did most of the talking. She passed around a picture of my students that we had taken with Miep. One of the less-than-interested mothers said, "I don't recognize any of these kids. My son doesn't hang out with any of them."

"Debbie, your son is in that class?" another asked.

Debbie became agitated. "Look, these students are amazing. And Erin is willing to show these kids a side of life that they've never seen before. For the first time in his life, Dane is talking about what he learned in school."

Debbie made a passionate plea, but only three mothers agreed to help. But it was a start. Now all I had to do was find a place to have a party.

While I was discussing the prospect of Zlata coming during my lunch break at the Marriott a few days later, Chai, the head chef, suggested, "Why don't you have it here?"

"Because it would be ridiculously expensive," I said. I had gotten married at this hotel, so I knew that a dinner for all of my students and their parents would cost more than a down payment on a house.

"Why don't you find a sponsor, and I'll nudge the manager to cut the costs," he suggested.

Luckily, it wasn't wedding season and the ballroom was available. Chai said he might be able to finagle a huge discount.

I decided to call John Tu for help. Since he had really enjoyed the dinner with my students last year following the panel, I asked him if he'd be willing to help me do something similar this year that included their parents. He thought it was a great idea and generously agreed. With his blessing and the behind-the-scenes encouragement of my friends at the hotel, I began to plan an elaborate affair. It was like planning a wedding, without the tacky brides-maid dresses or drama.

I was a member of the concierge association, so I went to our annual meeting to describe how my students and I were planning to host Zlata and her family. All the other concierges from local hotels agreed to help. By the end of the evening, the association had donated a free limousine to pick Zlata up from the airport, certificates for restaurants for each of Zlata's meals, and several items for our raffle, like tickets to Disneyland.

With all particulars finally aligned, I announced to my students that we would be having a celebration dinner at the Newport Beach Marriott on a Sunday afternoon. I passed out brochures so they would share the information with their families.

"Wow, Ms. G, this is really fancy!" said Darrius.

"I know. It's so pretty. Now you can see where I work on weekends and where I got married!" I said.

"Are we going to meet your husband?" Darrius asked.

"Yes. You're also going to meet my parents and some of my best friends," I said. "And since Zlata and I are sharing this experience with our loved ones, I want all of you to do the same. I've arranged for charter buses to pick all of you up at Wilson High at 2 P.M. on Sunday. Everyone has to bring someone special with them—whether it's your parents, your grandma, your favorite aunt, or someone who looks after you. It's mandatory!"

"Mandatory?" Henry asked.

"Yes, there are no exceptions," I said, trying to sound stern. "But there's a catch. Before you and your loved one step on the bus, you have to teach them everything you know about the books we've been reading."

"We can't make our parents do homework!"

"Yes you can. I'm going to make my dad do his homework, and my dad is a lot older than yours. I am going to sit him down at his kitchen table and I'm going to teach him everything I know about the Holocaust and Bosnia," I said.

"Are you serious?" Tommy asked. "You really want us to teach our parents?"

"Okay, think of it more as sharing," I said. "And to make it easier for you, I assembled a package of articles that will guide you through the process. Darrius, can you pass these out?"

Darrius gave each student a thick package containing articles relative to what we were studying: "Bosnia's Ground Zero," a *Vanity Fair* article by Peter Maass that described the horrors of Bosnia firsthand, an article about Renee Firestone's experience at Auschwitz, an article about Miep Gies that had recently run in *People* magazine, and an article about Zlata Filipović from *Newsweek*.

"What if they don't wanna learn?"

"Now you know how I feel," I said with a smile. "So be creative and figure out a way to bring these subjects to life!"

Over the next few weeks, the students taught their families about the war in Bosnia and the Holocaust. They shared anecdotes about renting movies, like *Schindler's List*, together, or sitting at the kitchen table reading the various articles I gave them. The more they taught someone else about our lessons, the more it reinforced what they were learning in class.

Since the students were both emotionally and intellectually invested in Zlata's visit, I decided to do a few extra things to make the occasion more special. I had invitations printed for the parents, and I even found a professional photographer willing to donate his time to take photos of the students with their families. The Marriott chefs were preparing to pull out all the stops—which meant there would be several courses and lots of silverware.

The Friday before Zlata arrived, I prepared an "Etiquette 101" crash course. I coerced Guillermo, a former graffiti artist, to replicate a dining diagram that I found in my Marriott handbook on the chalkboard. I made a copy of the page for each of my students and brought in all the accoutrements to make the class see what the setup for a five-course meal looks like. With student volunteers, I walked them through the entire evening—from pulling out the chair for their mothers to which forks are used first. After describing how to go from the outside in with their silverware, I noticed some of the students scribbling notes.

"Bread plates go on your left and drink glasses go on your right," I demonstrated. "I'll show you a little trick I learned as a banquet server." With my thumbs and my index fingers, I formed a *b* with my left hand and a *d* with my right hand. "*B*s go on the left and *d*s go on the right."

I was amused watching them practice making *b*s and *d*s. If anyone were to waltz into my room unannounced, they'd think that I was teaching my students how to throw up gang signs.

"What if we forget any of this?" Darrius asked, looking very concerned.

"Then bring Guillermo's diagram with you as a cheat sheet," I said, smiling.

The next day, I headed to Los Angeles International Airport in the donated stretch limo to pick up Zlata and her family. As I saw Zlata wheel out her luggage on a chart, I recognized her immediately. Her hair was a little longer than it was on the cover of the book. She looked like a typical American teenager wearing Levi's, a hooded sweatshirt, and Vans tennis shoes. For a moment, I was a bit starstruck. Somehow, in all the hoopla, I had made Zlata out to be larger than life, when in reality she was just an unassuming teenager. When she hugged me, I felt an immediate kinship.

Zlata introduced me to her father, Malik, her mother, Alicia, and her best friend, Mirna. Malik looked like the war had taken a toll on him. He appeared to have lost a lot of weight, and his glasses were now slightly too large for his face. Alicia was a beautiful woman. She wore a Burberry scarf. Mirna had a pixie haircut and also looked like any American teenager, with her Doc Martens boots, jeans, and T-shirt.

Although they were a little tired from the long flight, we spent the entire ride back to the hotel asking questions of each other. When we arrived at the Marriott, I felt like I was escorting royalty. Everyone I worked with went above and beyond the call of duty to make everything perfect. I felt so proud of my colleagues for going the extra mile.

We had the opportunity to merge our two families at dinner. We sat in a bustling section of the Hard Rock Café—one of the restaurants that donated a free dinner to us. While Zlata and Mirna walked around, oohing and aahing over the guitars and outfits from iconic performers they'd seen on MTV, I couldn't help but think about all the horrors that they once had to endure. Loss of electricity, hunger, sniper fire . . . and yet they seemed so resilient.

Mirna was of Serbian descent, and she was lucky to escape Sarajevo with the Filipovićs once Zlata's book was published. Although she deeply missed her family, who stayed in Bosnia, her parents wanted her to be in a safer place.

Talk quickly turned to the savage war thousands of miles away. My father was fascinated by Malik and Alicia's story. Malik had been a lawyer in Sarajevo, and he told my father that he was devastated by the war. Many of the intellectuals tried to escape to save their families, and he felt particularly torn about leaving his friends behind. Although he was of Muslim descent, he had never practiced any particular religion. He was, however, traumatized that so many Muslim men were stripped of everything and sentenced to ethnic cleansing camps.

Alicia was a former chemist and her family's lineage went back to Croatia. She said it was common in Sarajevo for couples to marry for love and not along ethnic lines. Sarajevo was a poly-ethnic community that truly celebrated diversity before the war broke out. Although their country was at war, Malik and Alicia were still proud to be Sarajevan and were optimistic that when the war was over, they could rebuild their lives together.

The following day, when my father and I walked into the hotel ballroom, a wave of nostalgia washed over me. Just a few years earlier, my father and I had danced in the same ballroom to Louis Armstrong's "It's a Wonderful World" in front of three hundred people. Nearly four hundred people would be assembling in here soon, but this time, there would be no bouquet toss or "chicken dance."

"Erin, you realize you could have had a down payment on your house for what we spent on that wedding," he said.

"So I've heard," I said playfully, rolling my eyes. "But you have to admit, it was one hell of a party."

"Yes, you do know how to throw a party, my dear!" he said. "How'd you manage to pull this one off?"

"Everyone I know pitched in."

The ballroom looked like a five-star affair. My friend, the maître d', generously threw in extra amenities, such as a carved ice statue and a punch waterfall to add ambiance.

"Too bad they couldn't have pitched in for your wedding," he said, smiling.

When the buses pulled up, I couldn't believe my eyes. My students were dressed as if they were headed to a prom, in ball gowns and suits. The girls had gotten their hair and nails done, and the boys were wearing ties and polished shoes.

Maria's father had just been released from prison, and she couldn't wait to introduce him to me. Since his English was limited, Maria translated that he was very proud of his daughter. Tommy's father came up to me and gave me a huge bear hug, and Darrius's mom grabbed my hand and whispered, "Thank you."

As the servers escorted everyone into the ballroom, I watched my students pull out chairs for their mothers and put the linen napkins on their laps. I could overhear many of my server friends speaking to the parents in Spanish, telling them how proud their "maestra" was of her students.

Several of the boys pulled out their cheat sheets. "This is how you know which bread plate and glass is yours," they said, showing them *b* and *d* hand signals. They also explained that "as you eat, you use the silverware on the outside first."

When it was time for the presentation, I had asked several students to read the poem "Moment" at the podium and present gifts to Zlata. I chose Sonia to be one of the presenters, not realizing how terrifying it must have been to read poetry in front of four hundred people. Just years earlier, she had been in an English as a Second Language class. She came to America when she was eight, not knowing a word of English. In third grade, students and her teacher laughed at her lack of English, leaving behind deep scars.

As she got up to the podium, I could see her hands shaking. I wondered if she saw a room full of caring people or a classroom of naughty third-graders. As she read, she transformed before our eyes. She was poised, eloquent, and one couldn't detect an accent. I realized she must have read that poem aloud to herself a hundred times.

When Zlata rose to the podium, there were gasps and applause from the parents. I looked around and I could see mothers reach for their sons' and daughters' hands. They, too, felt like they knew her and had gone on this journey with us. She, like Miep before her, was so humble and gracious. She and her family were honored that they were the impetus for bringing all of these different people together to "celebrate humanity." She told us how excited she was to be in America to shed light on her country.

After her presentation and a standing ovation, I watched several parents congratulate Zlata and her parents. Some even asked for an autograph. Even my father asked her to sign his copy of *Zlata's Diary*. He looked like a starstruck kid asking for an autograph from Hank Aaron.

When the last bus had departed and the Filipovićs had retired to their rooms, my father pulled me aside and said, "You hit this one out of the park, kiddo. I've never been more proud."

CHAPTER 20

W hen Zlata and her family returned home to Ireland, I felt like we should do more with the lessons we learned about Bosnia.

"Since so many people helped us with Zlata's visit, why don't we do something to help Sarajevo?"

The class broke out in discussion of all the things that we could do. We voted on having a tournament titled "Basketball for Bosnia" in Zlata's honor. It would be a way for my students to feel like they were contributing to a cause that was bigger than themselves.

The president of the local university donated the basketball arena. We had several teams, three of which were named "The Bosnian Beauties," "Miep Mania," and "Anne's Angels." We even had jerseys donated with their team name embroidered on the back. Each team would consist of students, family, and community members. John Tu even volunteered to play.

The students researched what was most needed in the war-torn region and went door to door collecting Band-Aids, aspirin, tampons, toothpaste, and other necessary items. The Croatian club in a neighboring city volunteered to send over all the items we collected.

The day before the tournament, we received a letter from Zlata.

All the memories you gave me will be with me forever, as they are something one should not forget. And I just want to thank you for all that, for your friendship, your understanding—that is something mankind needs desperately. And you cer-

tainly have it together with your strong ambition to make the world a better place by starting with yourselves and your surrounding. You are real heroes.

But I also want to thank you for doing what you are doing today for my country, for children and young people who truly need people like yourselves, who will unselfishly and in a 100% humane way do something for them. Thank you for not forgetting them, for shadowing the feeling of being abandoned the rest of the world gives them.

Zlata's letter inspired a heightened sense of philanthropy at the Basketball for Bosnia tournament. Charlie walked up to the sign-in table with two of Wilson's star basketball players. Because Charlie talked to them about the war in Bosnia during practice, both seniors donated brand-new tennis shoes to our cause. "Somebody could probably use a pair of shoes," Big Roy said as he handed over a pair of Air Jordans. Since Charlie was a sophomore on the varsity team, he spent most of the time on the bench. But for this game, he walked around our tournament full of pride, because not only was he going to be a starter, but he also taught his teammates a valuable lesson.

The tournament was incredible. We had nearly a dozen teams and even a cheerleading squad. Several of the parents who had met at the Zlata event even reconnected and exchanged phone numbers.

The next day, Charlie Booker came sauntering into class wearing his "Basketball for Bosnia" jersey and announced that we should go for a "three-peat."

"What's that, Charlie?" I asked.

"The Chicago Bulls are trying to win their third championship in a row. Everyone's calling it 'three-peat!' If we stay together one more year, we can have our own three-peat."

"Charlie, I'm really flattered that you would want me three years in a row, but I haven't been here long enough to have seniority."

"What do you mean? You're not going to be our English teacher next year?" Darrius asked.

"No, I haven't been here long enough to teach juniors or seniors."

"That's jacked up," a student said.

"Unfortunately, that's just the way it is," I said.

"But we're a family."

"We can still be a family if we're not in Room 203," I said, trying to sound sympathetic to his apparent angst. I'd seen that disappointed look before with Sharaud and his classmates, and I didn't have the heart to set up unrealistic expectations.

I knew the chair of the English Department's resentment for me had grown over the year. Since Zlata and Miep had visited, her attitude toward me had gotten worse. I had overheard her complaining to other teachers about the picture of my students hugging Miep Gies in *People* magazine and some of the other stories that were written about Zlata's visit. I assumed that she would never agree to my teaching juniors.

As she had done with my previous requests, she immediately told me, "You don't have seniority and I will not displace other teachers."

When I told my students, many of them took it very hard. Several of them began to mope around. It was as if they were experiencing the first steps of separation anxiety.

In an act of desperation, I made an appointment with the superintendent, Dr. Carl Cohn. I had met him only once and was incredibly intimidated by him. He had a deep voice that sounded like James Earl Jones and had a commanding presence. I had invited him to Zlata's event, but he could not attend.

I looked around his office and saw all kinds of awards and photos of him with mayors, governors, even President Clinton.

"How can I help you?" he asked.

"Well, I know that there are almost a hundred thousand kids in this district, and probably thousands of teachers, but I wanted to ask you for a favor."

"I generally don't get involved in school politics," he said.

"I realize that, Dr. Cohn, but I think this is a unique circumstance. I have a hundred and fifty students who desperately want to stay together an additional year. They have it in their mind that we can create our own 'three-peat.'"

"Three-peat?" he said, chuckling. "Are you a basketball fan?"

"I'm a fan of anything that will help me connect with my students. Initially, one of the ways I made Bosnia come to life for my students was through basketball. Vlade Divac from the Los Angeles Lakers and Toni Kukoc from the Chicago Bulls used to be roommates on the champion Yugoslavian team.

Since Toni is a Croat and Vlade is a Serb, their friendship has been torn apart by the war in the Balkans. Once my students could see how even famous athletes were affected by this war, it put things into more perspective for them.

"Well, I have to admit, Ms. Gruwell, I am impressed by your guile. You've found a way to connect with students who are often written off. I'll help you grease the wheels a bit by talking to your principal. But if I get involved, be prepared for backlash."

A week before summer vacation, the principal called me into his office to tell me that he was going to give me permission to continue teaching my students for another year. As predicted, several teachers in the department were very upset.

"You will not be able to teach them their senior year, though," my principal forewarned me. "So don't set yourself up for a fall."

CHAPTER 21

I was elated to teach my students again, but I sensed that my passion for them might be alienating my husband and pushing a wedge into our marriage. I was beginning to see the strains my schedule had on our relationship. I got home late during the week, often graded papers until the wee hours of the morning, and worked on the weekends.

During the summer, I decided that my students should take a cue from Anne Frank and Zlata's diaries and write a class diary during their junior year. To prepare for the assignment, I made arrangements to visit Miep and Zlata in Europe at the end of the summer to get their blessing. I hoped that my husband would join me so we could spend some quality time together.

When my husband decided that he would rather go on a rock-climbing trip alone than go to Europe with me, I was devastated. After a heated argument, I took my wedding ring off. Even though it was a juvenile act, our relationship had slipped into a series of passive-aggressive stunts that would make any therapist wince. I thought he would come around, but he never did. So while he headed off to the great outdoors, I headed off to Anne's attic.

On the day of my departure, my father volunteered to take me to the airport. When he arrived at my apartment, half of my laundry was still in the dryer. I decided I would just leave my clothes in the dryer and buy socks and underwear when I got to the Netherlands, rather than listen to my father lecture me about "always being late." But I got a lecture anyway, and it wasn't about wet socks.

"Why are you two taking separate vacations?"

Since I didn't have the heart to tell my dad that my husband just didn't want to go with me, I said, "He's working really hard, Dad, and can't take that much time off."

My dad didn't buy it. Neither did I. Maybe if I had poured my passion into being the perfect wife instead of the perfect teacher, we'd be admiring the Dutch canals together. I tried to rationalize that the distance would be good for us, but it wasn't.

The trip to Europe was bittersweet. Although I had an amazing time with Miep in Amsterdam and Zlata in Dublin, I wished I could have shared it with my husband. He and I only spoke once during the two weeks I was gone. Unfortunately, the silence continued once I returned. Even though I spent my day emulating good communication skills with my students, my communication with my husband at home was deteriorating. It was the proverbial "do as I say, not as I do." We ate our meals in silence, and I started sleeping in the spare bedroom.

When I confronted him about the state of our marriage, he told me that he wanted different things and he felt like we had been growing apart for a while. When divorce was bandied about, I felt frantic. Since my parents got divorced when I was seven years old, I had made up my mind that divorce was not an option. But that decision was not mine to make. He had already made up his mind that he was leaving.

I tried to convince him to stay, but my "tough love" approach, the same I had used on my incorrigible students, wasn't working. I couldn't convince him to stay in the same way I could Maria when she threatened to storm out of my classroom. I couldn't dangle a grade over his head, and setting up a parent conference would not have the same desired effect.

When my husband left our apartment with a duffel bag in hand, my first reaction had been to call my dad, but I was afraid of the usual "I told you so" and "You were too young and immature to get married."

It was only six days into the new school year when he walked out, so my strategy was to pretend that nothing was wrong. I tried to convince myself that once he got tired of crashing on our friend's couch, he'd be back by the weekend.

When he didn't come back, though, I threw myself into work. That way the apartment wouldn't feel so empty and I wouldn't feel like such a failure. None of my friends were divorced, and I was too embarrassed to tell a soul. I was afraid they would judge me or not want to spend time with me anymore. So much of my social network was spent with happily married couples who talked about mortgages and day care. I was too mortified to show up single and talk about separation. To make matters worse, within a couple of months, I was going to be a bridesmaid and my husband a groomsman in the wedding of one of our best friends.

In an act of desperation, I called Debbie for support. She and I had spent a lot of time together planning Zlata's visit, and she often commented on the lack of support my husband gave me. I always made excuses for him and tried to rationalize how busy he was, but in reality, he was just not interested.

Debbie met me at a café after work, and once I saw her, I broke down: "My husband left a few days ago, and I haven't heard from him since."

"I hate to say that I saw it coming," she said, wrapping her arms around me. She reminded me how my husband refused to help me at the end-of-the-year party at the Bruin Den. The night before the party, I purchased 150 sunflowers, one for each student because they represent "deep loyalty and consistency," a theme that would carry over into our next school year.

The florist gave me several tubs to keep the flowers fresh. Rather than have the flowers wilt in my car or put them in my class, I asked my husband to bring them with him when he joined us for the celebration that evening. Since he worked much closer to home than I did, I asked him if he could swing by the apartment and pick them up on the way to the party.

An hour before the party began, in the midst of blowing up balloons, putting tablecloths on tables, and delegating tasks to my students, I called my husband to ask what time he was going to arrive with the flowers.

"I'm not coming," he said flatly.

"What do you mean, you're not coming?"

"It's been a long day, and I don't feel like driving."

I was stunned. "When were you planning to tell me this?" There was silence on the end of the phone. "But what about the flowers?"

"They're just flowers," he said snidely.

But no matter how much I pleaded, he would not budge.

I told Debbie that when I got home that night and saw the tubs of sunflowers on the kitchen floor, I felt hopeless. Since I wouldn't see my students until the fall, and I realized the flowers would soon wilt, I felt emotionally abandoned. I ended up sleeping in our spare bedroom that night.

When he refused to address the issue, the tension in our marriage grew. Feeling alone, I found myself sleeping in that room off and on for the remainder of the summer.

Debbie shook her head, then asked, "Is there someone else?"

"No," I retorted, having never given that a thought. "At least I don't think so."

"We could follow him one day after work and see where he goes."

"That's not necessary, Debbie."

A few days later, John Tu's secretary called. When I told John Tu about my plans to go to Amsterdam and Ireland, he encouraged his executive assistant to help me plan the itinerary for my trip. She asked if I would meet her for a drink after work. I assumed since I'd been home a couple of weeks that she wanted to see the photographs from my trip, but when she whispered, "It's serious," I got nervous. Maybe John had heard the news that my husband had left and thought it would be inappropriate to continue helping me. Maybe she was sent to do the awkward "breakup."

Moments after we ordered margaritas, she blurted out, "Your husband has a girlfriend."

A girlfriend? I was stunned. How could he have a girlfriend when his shoes were still in our closet, his toothbrush was still next to mine, and our heart-shaped waffle iron was still in the box? How could he already be dating when I hadn't even administered my first pop quiz?

I wanted to cry, scream, and ask her questions. What does she look like? Is their relationship serious? When did this all begin? Yet I couldn't ask any of those questions aloud. I sat there, numb.

"She works with him," she said. "You've actually met her."

Suddenly my world felt like it was coming apart at the seams. Reality crashed in on me. I hadn't touched a thing since my husband left, shamelessly hoping that he would come back. Now I knew he wasn't coming back. I couldn't run away from it anymore. I knew my marriage was over.

As I walked into my empty apartment, all the logistics of a divorce overwhelmed me. It was now time to call my father. Instead of a litany of "I told you so"s, he said, "Oh, honey, I'm so sorry." His compassion was unexpected but comforting.

I went on to tell my dad about a heartbreaking phone call that should have sent up a flare about the status of my marriage the day that Zlata departed. My husband's grandparents called to catch up with him, and when I overheard them ask what I was up to, he said, "She's just teaching." The words "just teaching" and his tone were devastating. I felt like he minimized who I was and what I did.

I wish I would have had the confidence to confront him. I had suppressed my emotions for so long that I suddenly found myself lamenting my fears to my father for hours. Rather than giving me answers, my father just listened. Could I afford the rent on our apartment, should I move, should I get a roommate, should I get another part-time job? How were we going to divide our furniture? How should I tell our friends? Will they take sides?

Since my husband worked for John Tu, I presumed John's loyalty would be with his employee, not a soon-to-be ex-wife. Bowing out gracefully would make it less awkward for everyone. I made an appointment with John under the pretense that I wanted to give him the present I bought him while I was in Ireland with Zlata, when in actuality I planned to part ways.

As I sat in the lobby waiting for John Tu, I felt so transparent with my ring conspicuously absent. I put my hand in my pocket, wondering if anyone knew that we were separated. I suddenly felt so embarrassed. What if I ran into someone who didn't know and I would have to try to explain the unexplainable? Or worse yet, what if I ran into my husband and his new girlfriend?

When John finally emerged, he took me into a small conference room and shut the door. I had gotten in the habit of chatting with him in his cubicle in the middle of the sprawling office. No partitions needed. Today, however, a wall or two was necessary.

As I sat across from him and his perfectly creased shirt and polished shoes, I felt like a naughty sixteen-year-old who had taken the keys to his hot rod and returned it with a door ding.

"I'm getting a divorce," I blurted out.

"I know," he said solemnly. "Unfortunately, there are not enough walls around here to contain that kind of gossip."

Apparently, sitting in the middle of that office, John Tu had heard all the rumors swirling about the demise of my marriage. Sitting across from him made me feel like a disappointment. A failure. I assumed that he would think that I had spent too much time on my work and not enough on my marriage. As a preemptive strike, I said, "I would understand if you don't want to help my students and me anymore."

"Of course I want to continue helping you, Erin." He got up to give me a hug, then said, "If you need anything, I will be here for you."

The next day, I noticed that some of my students were in cahoots about something. They were acting weird, whispering in the halls, conspicuously passing notes and looking at me strangely. I had made it a policy to always get to the bottom of my students' shenanigans—so much so that one of my students said, "Ms. G, you're like Jason from *Friday the 13th*! Wherever we go, you're always right there!" I wasn't sure if that was a compliment, but I decided that their conspiratorial behavior demanded a little intervention. I confronted Charlie first, hoping that he would sing like a canary.

"Charlie, what is going on?"

"Um," he paused. "Nothing, Ms. G," he said, exchanging glances with Ramiro.

Charlie and Ramiro were inseparable. They began interning at John Tu's company shortly after Zlata's visit. Since getting the job, they dressed more professionally, always offered to help me carry things in from my car, and treated me like I was the catalyst for their newfound paychecks.

"Ramiro, I know something is going on, so you might as well tell me."

"Um . . ." And with his pregnant pause that seemed to last an entire sixty seconds, he looked at Charlie for some kind of guidance. Charlie just shook his head. He did not want to be the bearer of bad news.

"Ramiro, what's wrong?" I demanded.

His eyes got watery and his voice cracked. "Charlie and I saw your husband kissing somebody at work. But don't worry; we're planning to go jack his car after school."

My heart sank. I imagined that Charlie and Ramiro thought they had caught my husband in the midst of cheating on me. Their first reaction was to protect me—an eye for an eye.

This situation, like so many others, would have to become a teachable moment. I had to be honest with them. I had to tell them that my husband and I were separated, and that I already knew about his girlfriend. At this point, telling them the truth would be more effective than shielding them from reality.

"What do you want us to do to him?" Charlie asked, invoking chivalry.

"Do you want us to kick his ass?" Ramiro chimed in.

"No, you can't go around jacking people's cars or beating them up."

"But wouldn't that make you feel better?" Ramiro added.

"I wish it would, but it would actually make me feel worse," I said, putting my arm around him.

As the boys were about to leave, I asked, "So how many people know about this?"

"Just a couple of the guys."

I knew that "just a couple of the guys" probably meant all 150 of my students. This was too juicy to keep under wraps. When the students left, I called my dad to tell him about the latest escapade.

"Why do you have to tell your students everything, Erin? The less they know about your personal life, the better!"

"I know, Dad, but they were plotting to beat him after work, and if I didn't intervene, I'd be bailing kids out of juvie tonight."

"Be careful what you tell people. There were two of you in that marriage, remember?"

"Are you taking his side?"

"No, I'm not taking any sides. I just want you to go through this with a sense of dignity. I don't want you to do or say anything that you will regret later. Be the bigger person, Erin—don't mudsling, don't vilify, and don't play the victim. You're stronger than that."

CHAPTER 22

Writing in my diary was one of the ways I found strength. I thought if my students saw that everyone has a story—even their teacher—maybe the writing process could be cathartic for them too. I, like my students, realized that it would take more than just writing to feel better—but at least it was a start.

When reading Anne Frank's and Zlata Filipović's diaries, my students were struck by the similarities between these teenagers' lives and our own. They recognized the emotions, thoughts, and experiences Anne and Zlata described as teenagers growing up amid violence. My hope was that my students, who had struggled with violence, abuse, the loss of a family member, or even learning disabilities, would be able to write their own story and see that they were not alone.

Perhaps we could take a cue from both Anne Frank and Zlata and turn our own diaries, our own stories, into a class book. Visiting Miep and Zlata over the summer seemed to intensify my desire for my students to write what needed to be written.

"Writing will help validate your pain, and sharing it with your peers will help you realize that you are not alone in your struggles," I said when introducing our class project.

I knew my students had amazing stories to share, and they were excited about following in Anne and Zlata's footsteps. To my surprise, this was not an assignment that needed any spin. They got it. It was a logical extension of what we had done over the last two years.

But I quickly discovered that not everyone shared those same sentiments. One in particular was a new student, named Sue Ellen, who confided in me that she was terrified about our new writing project.

Sue Ellen transferred into my class her junior year under the encouragement of her best friends, who were actively involved in my class. She came to our chaotic classroom for lunch while she was a sophomore and was blown away by the sense of freedom and comfort my students seemed to share.

After hearing tales from her friends and witnessing the camaraderie firsthand, she petitioned to get into my class. She lost her brother to a deadly disease at the end of her sophomore year and was now craving a sense of family to fill the void. Because her own family was in disarray, she was drawn to Room 203, but the prospect of writing autobiographical material made her uncomfortable.

After she wrote a diary entry about her brother, I noticed she was hesitant to share it with me. I assumed she was reluctant to turn it in to me based on the sensitivity of her recent loss, so I delicately said, "It's okay, Sue Ellen, writing will help you deal with your pain."

"It's not that. I just don't want you to think I'm stupid," Sue Ellen said, looking down, trying to hide her shame.

"Sweetie, I would never think that," I said, putting my hand on her shoulder. "Why would you say that?"

"I can't write," she said, reluctantly handing me her paper. I glanced over it and noticed that several letters were backward and words were misspelled.

"Sue Ellen, are you dyslexic?" I asked.

She looked at me with a blank stare. "What does that mean?"

"You have a tendency to misplace your letters. I'll show you on the chalkboard. If I write cat, I write C-A-T, but if you write cat, you might write T-A-C."

"Is it a disease?" she asked as if I were an oncologist diagnosing a terminal illness.

"No, your brain just processes information differently. That's all."

"So I'm not stupid?"

"Of course not! Where would you get that idea?"

"My teacher last year made me feel stupid. In front of the whole class, he told me that he didn't expect me to do well."

I was appalled that any educator would put down a student to begin with, but to insinuate that they were "stupid" made me want to revoke their teaching credential.

"Another teacher told me I was 'lazy' and that I didn't put enough effort into my work," she added. "I swear I'm not lazy."

"I know, Sue Ellen. I noticed how much time you put into your journal entry about your brother. Don't worry; we'll work on this together."

Two other students pulled Sue Ellen aside after class and admitted that they, too, had dyslexia and suggested that they could all work together.

To protect students like Sue Ellen and create an environment where she felt safe, I decided to create an "honor code" that would set writing parameters, such as how to peer-edit without hurting someone's feelings.

Although I encouraged my students to write honestly and tell their stories without embellishment, writing serious subjects on paper was a bit scary. Since we had been together for so long, some students could identify their classmates' handwriting. Some wrote with slants, some tagged, and some even used pink pens as their signature trademark.

Although we occasionally visited the computer lab in the library, our visits were often a source of frustration. Since most of my students did not have computers in their homes, much of the time was spent listening to the librarian explaining the rules. Sessions would be over before the students even completed their first paragraph.

Their desire to type their stories seemed like a perfect opportunity to talk to John Tu about borrowing a couple of computers to type their class book.

When I asked John, he paused for a moment and then said, "Borrowing old computers would not be a good idea."

I thought I'd overstepped my boundaries and asked for too much. How audacious of me. I was ready to do a major mea culpa, when he asked, "How many desks do you have in your class?"

"Thirty-five."

"Do you have a computer?"

"No, I borrowed my husband's. He took it with him when he came to get his clothes. But I can always use the computer in the teachers' lounge."

"What if I were to give you thirty-six brand-new computers?"

"Give? Brand new?"

"Yes, give them to you."

I was dumbfounded. It was the height of the dot-com explosion, and suddenly John Tu's company had grown into a billion-dollar enterprise in less than a decade. John made a point of using his money to make a difference.

"Erin, I've come to admire your students and how far they've come. They deserve every chance they can get. This way, your students can not only write a book, but they can become more technologically savvy in the process," he said.

"I don't know what to say—this is more than I ever expected. I'll take very good care of them, I promise. I'll return them at the end of the year."

"Erin, what am I going to do with used computers? These are my gift to you. Go write that book of yours."

Once we got the computers, I implemented the honor code that would make the process of writing and peer-editing our book project less daunting. Each student signed the honor code stipulating that they would remain anonymous throughout the process. To protect their identity, they would be given a random number instead of his or her name, and the stories would be typed in the same font so that no one's handwriting could be recognized.

As a preemptive measure, I informed my students that I was a mandated reporter and would have to submit information to social services about child abuse or endangerment. If my students were to write anything salacious, I would have to report it to child protective services, but I would be sure to provide the students with professional counseling when writing their stories triggered difficult emotions.

Once the project was official and there was a computer at every student's desk, they dove into the project. No one was more excited than Sue Ellen. She quickly learned that the squiggly red line helped her every time she misspelled something. She wasn't a very good speller and her typing skills left something to be desired, but I noticed that Sue Ellen was one of the first to come to class in the morning and one of the last to leave in the evening.

The students began writing with reckless abandon and poured their hearts into the writing. Every day, someone would share their story with the class and the students would inevitably commiserate with the latest diary entry. Writing became liberating, as each student discovered they had a story and found comfort in the computer. Although they couldn't change the cast of characters, the computer became their confidant, their therapist, and their outlet, and many of them hoped that they could rewrite their endings.

Writing, reading, and editing personal stories began to consume the students. They came to class early, often worked on the computers at lunch, and at the end of the day, no one wanted to go home. So it struck me as odd when Henry started missing school and stopped turning in his assignments.

I had given the students a self-evaluation form as an attempt to assess their efforts. What I found was that the students were generally harder on themselves than I had the tendency to be. I always loathed grading, and I thought getting them to be introspective and self-reliant would help the process. I always found grading to be somewhat subjective anyway, but since it was a necessary evil, a self-evaluation would not only empower my students but it could serve as a litmus test.

When Henry did not turn in his self-evaluation, I confronted him. Henry was smart but easily affected by his unstable environment. When he was a freshman, he confided in me that his mother was diagnosed with lupus and often could not take care of herself or the adopted baby she was trying to raise. The baby had been born addicted to crack and would get the shakes every morning around 3 A.M. Henry often turned to the streets to help his mom buy formula. I was worried that he might have regressed.

When I confronted Henry about missing school and not turning in his evaluation, he reached into his backpack and pulled it out. Scrawled across the crumbled evaluation was a huge F. An F to me was like waving a red flag before a cantankerous bull in Pamplona. I went ballistic. Without thinking, I grabbed his shirt collar and said, "Henry, I need to talk to you in the hallway!"

As I stormed outside, he sheepishly followed me.

"What does this mean?" I said, manically waving his self-evaluation in the air.

"Ms. G, you told me to be self-reliant, so I was being honest. I thought you'd be proud of me since I didn't try to bullshit you."

"You know what this is?" I asked.

"It's an F," he said.

"No it's not. It's a fuck you, that's what this is. It's a fuck you, and a fuck me, and a fuck everyone who cares about you. So unless you can stand there, look me in the eyes, and tell me to fuck off, I'm not going to give you an F."

There was dead silence. Then Henry's eyes filled with tears. "I can't say that to you, Ms. G."

"Good, then you're not getting an F. Even if you have to stay here until eleven o'clock every single night, I will not let you fail."

CHAPTER 23

Luckily, talking tough to Henry was a risk that paid off. My outburst was pretty severe, and Henry could have reported me to the principal or he could have pushed me. Instead, he pushed himself. He began to stay after school later and then befriended some of the other students who were struggling in class. As Sue Ellen wrote about losing her brother to Leigh's disease, Henry wrote about losing his brother to the system.

Watching students like Henry cross color lines and academic barriers inspired me to show my students a documentary about a group of activists called *The Freedom Riders*. In the midst of racial segregation in the 1960s, these progressive men and women boarded buses, rode through the Deep South, and challenged the discriminatory laws of our country. The documentary was intended to get the students interested in literature, history, and important themes like tolerance, inclusion, and overcoming adversity, but it also validated the power of writing.

While we were watching the powerful documentary, an idea formed. If the Freedom Riders could "ride" buses to fight injustice, why couldn't we call ourselves the Freedom Writers and "write" to fight injustice too?

The idea seemed to gestate and take real form. The students loved the idea of having a name that gave them an identity they could be proud of.

After we ruminated on the name for a few days, Darrius recommended that "if the Freedom Riders started their journey in Washington, D.C., to grab people's attention, why don't we go to Washington, D.C., too?"

As usual, my efforts to empower my students and dare them to dream had spun out of control.

"What would we do in Washington?" I asked, trying to sway them, realizing that once an idea was left to linger in Room 203, others would grab hold and run with it.

"We can give our book to someone powerful," Henry suggested.

"Who would that powerful person be?" I asked incredulously.

"Maybe the President," Henry said.

"Nah, he won't listen to us," one of my cynical students said, "because too many of us *have* inhaled."

Several students laughed. Others continued to toss out names of famous people. The next day, Charlie asked, "What about the Secretary of Education? He was on CNN last night."

"You watch CNN, Charlie?"

"Not on purpose. But the battery to my remote control is out."

"Maybe we could send him letters, but I don't know how all one hundred and fifty of us could make it to D.C. It's a heck of a long way," I said.

"Can't we just take a bus like the Freedom Riders?"

"It's over three thousand miles, and I can only imagine being trapped on a bus with some of your stinky socks after the first day." Some of the students laughed.

"But if we can get all these great people to come to us, why can't we go to them?"

And thus the idea to travel to our nation's capital was hatched. Logistics like how we would get there, what we were going to do once we arrived, and whom we'd give our book to were formalities that my students simply overlooked. But the more I tried to ignore the idea, the more it made sense to me too.

What I had learned with Zlata's visit is that people like to donate to a cause—specifically, one where they can be closely involved. At the event we hosted for Zlata, it was a win-win scenario for everyone. Donors were invited to share in our special evening and got to see firsthand where their charitable donation went. And my students learned how impressive it was when so many people came together—parents, florists, photographers, even neighbors.

If my students were going to truly pay homage to the Freedom Riders, I needed to encourage them to keep up that same sense of purpose and determination. What they lacked in an economic base, they could make up with conviction. We didn't have to go to D.C. to follow in the footsteps of the Freedom Riders. All we had to do was pick up a pen.

On the sly, I poked around the Marriott corporate handbook and sent off a note to one of their vice presidents. I had planned a personal trip to New York over the holiday break, so I offered to take the train to Washington, D.C., to meet with the VP to see how much of a stretch this trip would be. When he agreed to meet with me, I knew I was tempting fate.

My idea was simple: If I could get one company to help us, it would create a domino effect. When my dad was able to get autographed baseballs from the Angels, it was easier for me to get certificates to Disneyland and the Hard Rock Café for Zlata's visit. If the Marriott would help us with the D.C. trip, then it might make it easier for me to solicit help from others.

Armed with photos, newspaper clippings, and sample journals, I met with Roger Conner from the Marriott to discuss my students. I had worked at the hotel for several years now, and we had hosted events at both the Newport Beach and Century City Marriott Hotels. We discussed what it would cost to accommodate that many students if I could find someone to underwrite our trip.

My offer was simple. Four students per room at my current employee discount rate, which was $39 a day, plus tax. My rationalization was that the hotel wouldn't lose any money, and he would change the lives of 150 students forever. We talked about the feasibility of roll-away beds, hotel etiquette, payment plans, corporate sponsorship, and availability. At the end of the meeting, he agreed that if I could find the money, he would not only guarantee that rate over Memorial Day weekend, but he would let us stay at their most prestigious property, the JW Marriott, just a few blocks from the White House.

I called my father from a pay phone after the meeting. Part of me was exhilarated, while the other part of me was terrified. I hadn't really thought out all the finer points yet, like how we were going to get there and how we were going to raise the money.

Surprisingly, my father sounded optimistic. Since Zlata's visit, he had been increasingly supportive.

"If you put your mind to it, Erin, I think you can pull it off."

"Would you be willing to chaperone?" I asked.

"I wouldn't miss it for the world. You better ask your boss for permission, though. Taking kids across the country involves a lot of risk."

I decided to meet with the superintendent before I broached the subject with my principal or the students. If he was not supportive, then I would not go any further. But as I laid out my case, I even surprised myself about how meaningful the trip would be. As juniors, it correlated with both their American literature and history courses, we would work together to create a class book, and we would invite chaperones who had supported the students since their freshman year.

At the end of my presentation, Dr. Cohn agreed to the merits of our trip and said he would support our efforts. Just as I was about to leave his office, he said, "Who do you plan to present your book to?"

"I don't know yet. Do you have any suggestions?"

"Why not give it to the Secretary of Education," he offered. "He's a friend of mine."

I smiled, thinking about Charlie spotting the Secretary on CNN. "Here's his contact information," he said, as he scribbled the info on a Post-it. "If you and your students can actually pull this off, count me in. I'll chaperone right along with your dad!"

I was amazed how bold I had been with Dr. Cohn and the VP of the Marriott, and yet I didn't even have the courage to have a conversation with my husband. We hadn't talked since he left, and when he came to retrieve his belongings, all I did was cry. The dichotomy between my professional confidence and my personal insecurity baffled me. I wish I could have fought to save my marriage with the same determination I had when I fought for my students. But it was too late. My husband had filed the divorce papers, moved in with his girlfriend, and was moving on with his life. I would have to do the same.

With the blessing of the Marriott and Dr. Cohn, I assembled all the Freedom Writers in the gymnasium at lunch one day to make an announcement. I told them that we had permission to go on the trip, but we could do it only if all 150 of us attended and we all raised the money together. Feeling sensitive to the economic plight of the majority of my students, I said we would have to raise money for a plane, hotel rooms, buses, and food. It was not impossible, but it would be a lot of hard work, and we didn't have much time.

The students came up with ingenious fund-raising ideas. To celebrate their diversity, they would host an event that showcased all of their talents. They would have a multicultural food fest, an art auction, and a concert all in one huge event. They would send out a press release, make invitations, design original artwork, probe their families to make their favorite family recipes, and hone their talent for the show. The excitement of their event was palpable. They were so passionate, so talented, and so united.

Tragically, a week before the concert, there was a shooting in Long Beach and another innocent teenager was killed. Many of the Freedom Writers knew him. He wasn't in a gang; he was just in the wrong place at the wrong time. Guillermo, my resident artist, wrote "Rest in Peace" on his desk that day. Rather than being upset with him for the graffiti, I asked him to stay after class. I had an idea.

"Guillermo, why don't you make a button with his name on it," I suggested, "and you can wear it when we go to D.C. That way you can honor his memory while we are there."

His eyes lit up.

"Since you are such an amazing artist, would you design a button that we can ask others to wear?"

"Ms. G, there's a lot of us who've lost somebody," he said.

"As a tribute, maybe we can see if people will want to buy a button in honor of lost loved ones and we can wear it on the trip. It's similar to what women do when they wear a pink ribbon during the breast cancer walk."

Everyone loved the button concept. It was so symbolic. Henry asked if we could also wear buttons of children who had lost their innocence. That touched a lot of students, because suddenly they could pay homage to friends who were abused or had been exposed to things no child should be exposed to.

We could make a button for a quarter and sell it for five dollars. The students were like traveling salesmen, going door to door, asking friends and relatives if they wanted to buy a button or sponsor a name. Renee Firestone bought a button for every member of her family that she lost in the

Holocaust. Several of the students' parents from Cambodia gave us lists of people who had been murdered in the genocide of the Killing Fields. Zlata provided a list of names as well.

Darrius approached me after school one day, and he looked really sullen. "I have a list, Ms. G, but I don't have any money to buy buttons."

"Let me see your list, Darrius."

He handed me the piece of paper and looked down at his feet. There were thirty-five names. My heart sank.

"Darrius, don't worry, we'll find the money for these buttons."

I invited everyone I knew to our concert and encouraged them to buy buttons, bid on the artwork, and eat lots of yummy homemade food. The concert went off without a hitch, the symbolism of the buttons surpassed our expectations, and by the end of the evening, we had raised enough money that the trip didn't seem so unrealistic anymore. We were well on our way.

A few days later, I received a note in the mail from John Tu. It read, "Your students are absolutely amazing. Whatever you can't raise, I'll cover. . . . Go book yourself a plane, and make us all proud!"

CHAPTER 24

T he morning of our departure to Washington, D.C., we packed four
hundred people—kids, parents, and chaperones—into the Bruin Den
for a breakfast send-off. I had invited a few dozen chaperones: The Dream
Team Moms; my parents; my neighbor, Polly; my divorce lawyer, Lonnie;
Gerda, a Holocaust survivor; and some of my colleagues from Wilson. Each
chaperone would be dedicated to a small group of students for the duration
of the trip. We had 188 people in all.

Between bagels, juice, and family photos, I went over the itinerary,
answered questions, and tried to create a sense of trust for the parents who
were left behind. For most of my students, this would be their first time leaving Southern California, first time boarding a plane, and the first time staying in a hotel. I told my students to keep mementos from the trip so that
their parents could live vicariously through their latest adventure.

Because of our group's size, we were able to charter an entire airplane.
Since my divorce, I had begun teaching evening courses at a local university,
and one of my college students offered the services of his father's travel
agency. On our behalf, his father called the airlines directly and managed to
get United Airlines to donate a plane at a nominal fee.

When our four buses pulled up to the curb at LAX, we were greeted by
flight attendants holding signs and balloons. The electronic board in the terminal read "Welcome Freedom Writers."

Our "welcome" was jolted, however, once we landed in D.C. and headed
to the hotel. From the back of the bus, Guillermo pointed and exclaimed,

"Look, there's a swastika!" Everyone on our bus craned their necks to see a swastika spray-painted on a freeway underpass.

"How could there be a swastika in our nation's capital?" Guillermo asked. He was obviously shaken.

The image affected us all. It was so out of context. Such an affront. Shockingly, we spotted several more swastikas as we headed past the first monument on the Mall. When we arrived at the hotel, Geraldo gasped. "Look, Ms. G, there's another one," he said, pointing across the street. It was emblazoned on a newspaper stand directly across the street on Pennsylvania Avenue.

The next morning, Geraldo, bleary-eyed from staying up all night, met me in the lobby before we headed to breakfast. He and Guillermo had gathered several of the former graffiti artists in his room after we checked into the hotel to create a Freedom Writers logo. He had drawn a globe with the words *Freedom Writers* circling the top and *Changing the World* hugging the bottom. This was their solution to the swastika.

He took his drawing to the concierge and asked her to make several copies. He also borrowed some masking tape from her. As we made our way from the hotel to the U.S. Holocaust Museum, every time we saw a swastika, Geraldo and his posse covered it with our new logo.

After an emotional day at the U.S. Holocaust Museum, we went to the Lincoln Monument. It began to drizzle, which seemed to add to the ambiance. Several Freedom Writers made makeshift rain gear out of plastic garbage bags.

Once we got to the top of the steps, overlooking the wading pool, Darrius said, "Ms. G, this is where it all happened, huh? The 'I Have a Dream Speech.'"

As he said that, I looked around at my 150 students and all the adults who had become a part of our family. "Yes, Darrius, this is where it happened," I said.

"I guess you could say that the Freedom Writers *are* that dream," he said.

And they were. These 150 students personified the "Dream." Within moments, Darrius began corralling all the Freedom Writers on the steps. He encouraged everyone to join hands and to repeat after him: "Freedom Writers Have a Dream, Freedom Writers Have a Dream." As we proceeded down the steps, chanting, I hoped that this would be the generation that would be judged by the content of their character and not the color of their skin.

When we got to the bottom of the steps, Darrius pulled me aside with a huge grin on his face. "Maybe we can go on a field trip to Anne's attic or Auschwitz next year," he said.

I didn't have the heart to tell Darrius that I would probably be teaching freshmen next year, so I just smiled and said, "Let's get through this field trip first."

The next evening, we hosted a dinner at our hotel for Richard Riley, the U.S. Secretary of Education. Prior to dinner, the Secret Service swept the room and took their posts. As the students had done when they met Zlata, they dressed in their finest outfits. I had to allow enough "getting ready" time in our schedule, because with four girls per room, they demanded a lot of time to primp for this special occasion.

When Secretary Riley walked into the ballroom, a few of my students began to giggle. I found it very disrespectful. Didn't they know he was a cabinet member and that at any moment they could be thrown out of the ballroom by the Secret Service? I leaned over to one of my students, Chris, and asked why people were laughing.

"Because he looks like Mr. Burns from *The Simpsons*."

As I gave the Secretary a closer look, I too had to hold back giggles. Chris then walked to the front of the room and asked everyone to stand up while he led us in the Flag Salute. He then said, "Put your right hand over our left heart." The entire room broke out in laughter, even the Secretary. Although Chris was in ROTC, he was used to twirling rifles, not speaking in front of crowds.

The Secretary's speech was what we all needed to hear. He told my students that "if they wanted to honor the victims of violence, to get a good education. That's the place to start." In his thick southern drawl, he continued to encourage my students to be the first in their families to go to college.

When Dupree, whose dreadlocks were halfway down his back, handed Secretary Riley a bound copy of our stories, everyone erupted in applause. And on cue, Henry, who had moments earlier read an original poem, led the room in a rendition of "Stand by Me."

As the Secretary was whisked away by the Secret Service, the students put on their buttons, joined hands, and made a circle in the ballroom. Darrius led us in a moment of silence to remember all the people whose names we were wearing. I was wearing the name of Zlata's friend Nina, who had been shot by snipers in Sarajevo. Sue Ellen was wearing a button in honor of her brother, Maria was wearing one for her cousin who had been shot when she was five, Tommy wore buttons representing both his friend and his cousin, and Henry wore one to honor his brother, who was serving a life sentence in prison. Each button had a story, and each student was a witness to their life.

We had decided that we were going to have a candlelight vigil and circle the Washington Monument wearing our buttons. I envisioned that the Monument would look like a candle all lit up at night and would be a symbolic tribute for my students. I had made the proper arrangements with the Parks and Recreation Department to get a permit to gather at the Monument.

Chris began to lead all of us out of the ballroom toward the Monument. He stood next to my brother, hoping to learn a little about being in the military and leading the troops. Chris encouraged everyone to continue holding hands as they proceeded through the hotel and into the streets of D.C. As we were walking hand in hand across the street, a disgruntled driver, who did not want to be held up by nearly two hundred people after the light had turned green, honked his horn, rolled down his car window, and screamed, "Hey, what do you think you're doing?"

"We're changing the world!"

CHAPTER 25

A s we approached the Monument, our faces grew somber. Polly and several of the chaperones who were activists in the sixties began singing songs synonymous with the Civil Rights Movement, like "We Shall Overcome." My students—ever the activists—joined in on the chorus until they were eventually drowned out by sirens. As the police sirens got closer, I began to get anxious. Several police wagons were headed directly toward us. My heart stopped. I had left the permit in the hotel.

My mind began to race. My students' parents had trusted me with their children, and suddenly we were going to get interrogated by the police. This was a fiasco, and I saw myself losing my job. I was scared and embarrassed. My students, on the other hand, thought it was fantastic. After watching the dramatic footage of John Lewis being hosed down by police as he crossed the bridge in Selma, Alabama, or being dragged off the bus by Klansmen during the Freedom Ride, several of them volunteered "to go in the paddy wagon."

"Ms. G, can I get arrested?" Darrius asked. "At least this time, it'll be for something I believe in."

"No, Darrius, no one's getting arrested!" I assured him.

I looked for Dr. Cohn to see if he could help bail us out. Dr. Cohn and Lonnie, the lawyer, smoothed everything out with the police. The officers left without arresting any of my students.

My students placed their buttons next to the Monument in a silent tribute. They might not have changed the world that night, but they certainly changed themselves.

On the flight home from D.C., I sat next to Keith. While a lot of the students fell asleep from days of sleep deprivation, he was still wide-eyed and full of wonderment. I was excited when he asked if he could show me his scrapbook that he had been assembling since we left Long Beach. I had been so neurotic about losing a student on the Metro, managing our petty cash, and making sure everyone stayed in their prospective rooms, that I missed out on a lot of the nuances, so I reveled in seeing the trip through his eyes.

Keith had not missed out on a single detail. As he flipped through each page of his scrapbook, I saw that it was neatly laid out with mementos from every moment of the trip. He had his ticket stubs, a napkin from United Airlines, bus schedules, a wrapper from the M&M's I passed out at the airport, his hotel key, and postcards from every monument. He had also taken off all the labels from the soap and lotions in his hotel room. He couldn't wait to show the book to his mother. "I want her to see everything that we did," he said.

Keith was very proud of his mother. Although she had been in a string of abusive relationships, Keith was always there to protect her. When he was a little boy, one of her boyfriends locked him in the trunk of a car and left him there for two days. The horror of having to go the bathroom in that darkened trunk sparked an obsession in Keith to be meticulous. When we had walked through the cattle car at the U.S. Holocaust Museum a few days prior, he had held the hand of a survivor. She told him about the horrors of being trapped in a darkened cattle car with no food, no water, and no place to go to the bathroom, and for a moment, I knew Keith understood.

Keith put the importance of the trip into perspective for me. He was a year older than my students, but I adopted him as an honorary Freedom Writer and made him my teacher's aide. He lingered outside of my room every morning and was always the last one to leave my classroom in the evening. On a few occasions, I offered to drop Keith off. He would always make excuses. On one particular evening when the buses had stopped running, I insisted. He was mortified. He and his mother lived downtown where a lot of drug deals go down. As I waited for him to make his way into his apartment complex, I was propositioned by a known drug dealer. Keith ran back to my car and screamed, "Leave her alone, she's my teacher." On my drive home, I decided that even though Keith was not one of my English students, I would invite him on the trip to Washington, D.C., with us. Looking at his scrapbook validated my decision to invite him.

When we returned to the campus the next morning, our enthusiasm was met with camera crews. Many of my students assumed that the cameras were there to interview them about their trip to D.C., but they weren't. The camera crews and journalists were there to question the student body about two senior honor students named Jeremy Stroymeyer and David Cash.

We quickly learned that while we were in D.C., Jeremy had lured a little African American girl named Shirece Iverson into a casino bathroom near Las Vegas. His best friend, David, entered the bathroom, climbed over the stall, and saw his best friend in the process of molesting this little girl. Afraid of getting caught, Jeremy suffocated the girl, cracked her neck, and left her in the stall to die, while his friend David stood by idly.

Cameras outside the casino bathroom caught the images of these two young men entering the ladies' restroom, and on the day that we returned to Wilson High, Jeremy had been apprehended by the authorities.

By the time the students walked into my class, they had been besieged by reporters for old yearbooks and anecdotes of Jeremy and David. The reporters' fixation on this insidious murder really disillusioned the Freedom Writers. Unfortunately, my students knew that if a reporter was given the opportunity to report about 150 diverse teens doing "something good" or two Caucasian teens doing "something bad"—the negative news inevitably trumped the positive.

"Come on, Ms. G; we all know that if it bleeds it leads," a Freedom Writer said with great authority.

"Yeah, we always get a bum rap in the media," Darrius said.

"Everyone knows that the media is opportunistic," said another.

"Everyone? Shouldn't we know better than to use such sweeping stereotypes as 'everyone'?" I said.

"They just want to exploit us," another said.

"They?" I asked, pushing a lesson.

"I had one reporter offer to buy my yearbook, and another asked if I had any pictures of Jeremy. If that's not exploitive, Ms. G, then tell me the definition of the word," one student said.

"In that situation, those two reporters were probably trying to exploit you. But you can't take the actions of a few and stereotype every single reporter," I said, trying to steer the debate in another direction. It was obvious that their opinion of the media starkly contrasted with what I'd come to know of it.

I'd grown up trusting the media. Revering it, actually. My family had the *L.A. Times* delivered to our doorstep every morning, we watched *60 Minutes* religiously every Sunday, and my parents listened to NPR as they drove me to and from soccer practice. I always thought that everyone's kitchen table was littered with newspapers.

Ironically, as this debate about the media was raging in my classroom, a similar one ensued around Polly Stanbridge's dinner table. She was telling her guests about our trip to D.C. and that she was appalled that feel-good stories like ours rarely made their way to the headlines. Polly felt especially passionate about this subject, and that's how I initially met her. She had read an article in Newport Beach's *Daily Pilot* several years earlier. She offered to help then, and had been helping ever since.

"My neighbor writes for the *L.A. Times*," one of her guests offered. "I'll see if she wants to do a story about those delightful students."

The description of those "delightful students" must have piqued the interest of someone, because a reporter called me to set up an interview. Her name was Nancy Wride and she wanted to see if there was really a story to tell.

My limited experience with newspapers had been a double-edged sword, considering that previously the responses I received ranged from congratulations to death threats. Not only had the article caused a commotion in my community, but some of my colleagues had resented the attention my former students and I received.

My initial instinct was to say no to being interviewed because the Freedom Writers were not going to be in my class their senior year and our story was coming to its natural end. But my dad talked me into calling the reporter back.

"You have to take the good with the bad, Erin. You got to meet Steven Spielberg because of that article, for crying out loud! Who knows what will happen this time."

Chapter 26

M s. G, how can they separate us after everything we've been through?" asked a disgruntled Freedom Writer when I told them that we were not going to be together their senior year.

Facing the prospect of separation, the Freedom Writers galvanized. In the spirit of D.C., staying together became their latest cause. In lieu of a candle-light vigil or button sale, they planned walk-outs, sit-ins, and petitions, until one of them suggested calling Dr. Cohn.

Since Dr. Cohn had traveled to D.C. with us and seen how closely knit the Freedom Writers had become, he went out on a limb to assure my students that I could continue teaching them their senior year. As he had earlier predicted, some of the English teachers were outraged. They saw his support of me as favoritism and began to grumble about me more overtly. Some teachers had the audacity to suggest that I was having an affair with Dr. Cohn in order to get the coveted senior schedule. Although their insinuations were outlandish and hurtful, I was willing to endure the gossip in order to stay with the Freedom Writers.

As the senior schedule was solidified—with me teaching my students for a fourth year—I anticipated amazing accomplishments from my students and prepared for more animosity from my colleagues.

Over the summer, Nancy Wride, the reporter from the *Los Angeles Times*, made an appointment to interview the Freedom Writers and me. She decided that she would write a compelling story about how 150 disparate students came together and forged a family. She wanted the headline to read "Truth Stronger Than Friction."

To get to the whole truth, though, I knew that the students had to embrace her and the process. I wanted the Freedom Writers, especially the most cynical, to ask her questions and be reassured that she would be as objective as possible. And since there was no sense of urgency to get the story into the newspaper, I wanted everyone to let down their barriers and bare their souls. Before she could interview them, she agreed to face the firing squad. I wanted both sides to get a sense of one another, like dogs sniffing a tree.

I had prepped Nancy about some of our media discussions, and so she talked candidly about how the media has the power to manipulate or liberate. She tied in lessons we'd learned from the Holocaust and how the press was turned into a propaganda machine. She told the Freedom Writers that Goebbels, Hitler's propaganda minister, remarked that "if you tell a lie often enough, people begin to believe it." But in the case of Bernstein and Woodward and the Watergate story, the press was seen as courageous. Since Nancy was forthright, direct, and didn't sugarcoat anything, the students embraced her and signed on for the story.

The more the students let her in, the more she fought to write a longer column.

"Erin," Nancy told me, "I went to the editor of the paper and I made a pitch to have this story run on a Sunday."

And true to her word, the story came out on a Sunday—smack dab on the cover of the *Los Angeles Times*. My Sunday ritual was to get up at 4:30 A.M., put on my polyester uniform, and open up the concierge lounge at the Marriott. I'd pick up the morning papers from the valet at 5:30 A.M., set up the continental breakfast, and open the doors by 6:00 A.M. We had a steady stream of regulars who would come in for flavored coffee and the Sunday newspaper. While the morning news show played in the background, I would try to grade a few essays between guests. On that particular morning, there would be no grading.

The first guest riffled through our stack of the *New York Times*, the *Orange County Register*, *USA Today*, and finally settled on the *L.A. Times*. He took one look at the paper and then looked at me. "Is this you?"

There it was. A photograph of me next to the byline "Truth Stronger Than Friction."

"Um, yeah . . . that's me," I said, biting my tongue. Part of me wanted to grab it out of his hands, but another part wanted to climb under the table. I watched him read it, and it seemed to take an excruciatingly long time.

What was in that article? I was dying to know. I looked at my watch, and even though it was only 6:07 A.M., I called my dad.

"Erin, do you have any idea what time it is?"

"I know, Dad, I'm sorry. But you've got to go get the *L.A. Times* and read it to me."

"Now? You want me to read you the whole thing?"

"No, not the whole thing. Just an article. Our article came out today and [I cupped my hand over the receiver and whispered] I'm at the Marriott. People in the lounge are reading it right now and they keep staring at me. I need to know what they are reading. Please, Dad?"

"Okay," he said, and I heard him put on his slippers and scuffle to the front door. I knew he was slightly annoyed, but I also knew that he would do it, especially since he was the one who talked me into doing the article in the first place. As he narrated and gave me a blow-by-blow description of what he was doing, "I'm opening the front door . . . ," I noticed the man who was reading the article wipe away a tear. He folded up the newspaper and walked over to me.

"Can I just shake your hand?" he said. "It's an honor to meet you."

"Thank you!"

And just at that moment, my dad squealed, "Baby, oh my goodness—there you are. Right there on the cover!"

As my father was reading aloud, he kept stopping and saying, "This is really good, Erin" or "Nancy knocked this one out of the park!" Whenever my father used a Babe Ruth reference, I knew he approved. When he got to the end of the article, he said, "Wow, she even included a box that has your contact information."

"Which one?" I suddenly panicked, remembering what it felt like to see my personal information in black-and-white in the *Daily Pilot* and subsequently receive angry phone calls.

"Relax. It's your school information. I think people are really going to respond to this."

And they did.

A few guests from the Marriott even started pulling out their checkbooks right there in the lounge and making donations on the spot. When I got home from work, my answering machine was full of messages from my friends. I even heard from some of my "couple friends," whom I hadn't spoken to since my separation. My closet was full of bridesmaid dresses and dyed-to-match shoes, but I was the only one of my friends who had gotten a divorce. Many of my friends thought divorce was contagious, like the flu, so they stayed away from me for the health of their marriage.

Although my divorce was now final, I wondered if my ex-husband had read the article. Since we hadn't spoken a single word since he left, I assumed I would never find out. To keep from slipping into martyrdom about my marriage, I thought about the Freedom Writers and how much they would love this article. There was a fabulous photo of the kids embracing, illustrating how much they'd come to love one another. At that moment, I decided to call Nancy.

"Can I buy a copy for all the students?" I asked Nancy.

"I'm one step ahead of you," she said. She had the *L.A. Times* bundle about two hundred copies for me and suggested that I swing by and pick them up for the students tomorrow.

On Monday, when the students read the article, all their cynicism about the media dissipated. Nancy Wride had done them justice.

When I got home from school on Monday evening, I expected to get a few more calls from my friends, but when I clicked on my answering machine, I discovered that my machine was full. I pressed the key, and the first message was "Hi, Erin, I am a producer for *Primetime Live* and Diane Sawyer asked me to call on her behalf . . . ," followed by another from Bryant Gumbel, and so on.

There was also a message from Nancy saying that the response to the article was unprecedented and to call her immediately.

Nancy told me that the paper had been inundated with calls and that I shouldn't be surprised if I got a lot of donations. I told her about the phenomenon at the Marriott where strangers were writing me checks. Then I told her about my answering machine.

"A few television shows called me. What should I do?"

Nancy told me that in the industry it's called "getting the get." Many shows want to do an exclusive story, "so make sure you pick people that you're comfortable with telling your story."

I called the producers back, and since it was late in New York, I got their answering machines. One producer picked up, though. She worked for Diane Sawyer. She told me that Diane was actually in L.A. that weekend with her husband, Mike Nichols, and that she'd read the story and loved it. Diane wanted to do the story herself, but she was committed to doing a piece about Princess Di. I couldn't believe I was actually having this conversation. All I had wanted to do was leave a message.

"Has anybody else called you?"

Without thinking, I blurted out all the other options. Suddenly, I could tell there was a tinge of competition. Ah, this must be "the get" that Nancy spoke about. I told her I would need to think about everything for a while and I'd get back to her.

A "while" lasted less than twelve hours. The next morning, one of my students yelled from the back of the room, where they had just installed phones, "Ms. G, someone named Connie Chung is on the phone for you."

I was in the midst of teaching poetic devices. I looked down and noticed that I had chalk all over me. I suddenly got self-conscious. I had no idea what I wanted to say and I didn't know anything about television negotiations.

I picked up the phone and nervously said, "Hello." All the students' eyes were glued to me.

Connie spared no time in going for the pitch. She wanted to "get the get."

"I want to tell your story, Erin. I really do. Diane told me that several people are interested, but I think I can tell it. I just got hired by ABC, and this will be one of my first stories."

She went on to tell me that as a woman from a minority who broke the glass ceiling, she understood how to tell our story to twenty million people.

Twenty million people? I froze. Even though she kept talking, I didn't hear anything else she said. I found myself interrupting her and saying, "You

Pickup By: July 25, 2018

DUNLAVEY

DUNLAVEY, ROBERT JAMES

31549003765707

Teach with your heart : lessons I learned from the Freedom Writers : a memoir

EMAIL

can do it. I trust you to tell our story. Can I call you back, though? I'm in the middle of a poetry lesson."

When I got off the phone, I felt sort of silly for brushing her off, but at the same time I thought that it would be important to try and act as normal as possible in front of my students, even though I wanted to do cartwheels down the center of the classroom.

Since Nancy really ingratiated herself with the Freedom Writers, I decided that we should take the same tack with the television crew. I had no idea how it would all work, so I called the *Primetime Live* producer back and asked her if she would mind coming to class and describing the whole process to my students. Since none of us knew what to expect, we had a lot of questions.

The producer was kind of amused by my ignorance and agreed to come meet the kids. She was going to bring with her the actual producer of the segment, Tracey Durning. Tracey was flying in from New York City to do the piece, so they'd come in a few days. I was told that TV news shows like *Primetime Live* do not pay their subjects; I was relieved to know that we weren't beholden to them because of financial compensation. We were hopeful that the "payoff" would be similar to what we had experienced with the *Times* when unsolicited donations arrived in our mailbox. Maybe we'd motivate a few more folks to help the Freedom Writers.

Several days later when the producers arrived to speak to my class, both sides drew a line in the sand. My students asked questions in rapid succession, while the savvy producers, all dressed in black, fired back.

"Will it take long?"

"No."

"Do we get paid?"

"No."

"Do we have any say in the story?"

"No."

"Should we trust you?"

"Yes."

"Why?"

"Because it's a damn good story."

At the end of this sparring session, I realized that Tracey Durning was a fighter. She, like Nancy Wride, had her work cut out for her, but she was ready for the challenge.

The real challenge began when we realized that even though we were seasoned viewers, we were naive subjects. Creating a segment for a network TV news show would be much more than a quick interview after school one day or on a Saturday afternoon.

This was going to be a commitment. A very serious commitment.

I got sucked into the vortex of a *Real World* marathon once, and my ex-husband said that "reality TV is an oxymoron." I remember thinking I should use that example when I teach poetic devices. What I always wondered was how people could act naturally while they had a microphone pack attached to their waist and a sound mic overhead. I would soon find out.

To film the twelve-minute ABC piece, it took several weeks and multiple locations. They filmed in the classroom, in the halls, in Long Beach, at the Marriott, and everywhere in between.

Toward the end of the process, some of the students started getting a little restless. It was tough taking a test with a zoom lens in your face or going to the bathroom with a microphone attached to your belt buckle.

"Ms. G, I thought this was supposed to be news," one of them said wearily.

"It is. They just want to be thorough," I said, trying to be optimistic.

"It feels like they're making a movie."

It *was* beginning to feel like a movie; they were creating a story arc, complete with a cast of characters. They had time lines, storyboards, heroes, and heroines.

I began to notice that certain students were being singled out and asked more questions, or the camera lingered on them a little longer. Two such students rose to the forefront. Maria was one of them.

At one point we were walking into a building and the cameraman didn't quite get the shot he was hoping for. He quietly pulled me aside and asked if we could reenter the building so he could get "the shot."

I obliged and asked the students to reenter the building. Suddenly, Niya burst into tears and said, "I don't like this, Ms. G, I feel like a puppet."

She was right. We weren't actors. We weren't reality TV stars. We were a group of students and a teacher trying to tell a story.

A couple days later, the producers asked Maria if they could shoot an interview at her home. She panicked. What would her neighbors think if a film crew showed up? What would the other Freedom Writers think? How would her family feel? It was too personal. She felt too vulnerable. She wasn't ready to expose her home life to the world. Her reaction reminded me of the differences in our lives. I was made painfully aware of that when I took my students to see the basketball documentary *Hoop Dreams*. While I thought the film was a work of genius, they thought it was too close to home.

"Why did you take us to see this film? It's too damn depressing. If I want to see that shit, all I have to do is go home. I want to be entertained when I go to the movies."

The students did not want America peeking into their living rooms. After all, they had not signed up for that kind of piece.

"No, we won't do that shot over again," I would say if they didn't get the right angle.

"No, you can't interview that teacher," I would say when they wanted to add a little controversy.

"No, you can't interview the students in their homes." I began to feel like a broken record; I repeatedly said "no" to many of their requests, but I was trying to protect my students and the school.

Since I had suddenly taken on this new tone, the producers didn't like it. The more they pushed, the more protective I got. Suddenly, I exploded. "What do you want? A cockroach? A rat? Graffiti? What?"

"We want reality."

"But they're not comfortable sharing their reality with America. We have to respect that. They're minors. And I feel like it's my role to protect them."

On the morning of the big interview with Connie Chung, I got a frantic call at the Marriott at 7:00.

"Erin, Henry doesn't want to do the interview." There was panic in the producer's voice. "What should we do?"

"I'll call Maria and see if she can track somebody down," I responded.

"Can she find Darrius?"

Darrius? Of course, they needed an African American male for their slant. It was implied, not stated—but I knew. Now it made sense why the producers and crew paid more attention to some students and not others, why they volunteered to drive some kids home after school or asked about their families. They needed "characters" that could visually tell a story. Now I understood why Henry didn't want to be interviewed by Connie Chung. He didn't want the other students to get mad at him for being singled out.

To the producers, Maria had experienced the most profound changes in her life, so they would highlight her as a vehicle to tell our story. On an intellectual level, I understood this—but on an emotional level, I wondered if the other 149 students would understand. Could identifying certain students by name still allow an audience to see the sum of its parts? Would the other students get jealous, upset, or feel marginalized in the process?

Thankfully, Maria was able to track down Darrius and their interviews went off without a hitch. But since the *Primetime* piece would not air until the spring, I tried to assume a sense of normalcy with my students and have them continue writing their stories.

CHAPTER 27

To the outside world, it would appear that many doors were opening for the Freedom Writers due to all the media attention, but inside the walls of our classroom, I feared some doors might be closing.

Since the *L.A. Times* and the filming of *Primetime Live* had focused on only a few students, I sensed a little damage control was in order. A photographer snapping pictures or a journalist scribbling notes on a pad can make even a professional weary, so I empathized with my students' insecurity about others interpreting our story. After all, we were rookies, and overnight we'd been thrust into the big leagues.

I could see the parallels between players from my dad's baseball teams and students in my own classroom. No matter how much a team practices or how many World Series wins they have together, fans crave a "star" or a team spokesperson. Pete Rose was the star when my dad worked for the Cincinnati Reds, and it was Rod Carew while he was with the Angels. The same is true in the game of life. Zlata Filipović went from being a child of war to a spokesperson for Sarajevo. She said it was difficult dodging bullets one day and reporters the next. Unfortunately, the media came into our classroom as well and selected their stars. Once they got their story, they moved to the next battleground, leaving some kids emotionally scarred in their wake.

Some of my students were jealous of the handpicked stars, some felt overlooked, and some began to withdraw. Our cocoon had been tampered with, and not everyone felt safe anymore.

I wanted to be a cohesive unit again and repair our safe haven. To rekindle the collegiality the students once shared, I had to validate that everyone was an integral member of our team. Despite their many differences—race, religion, and social status—they all had an important story to tell. By binding all of their stories together anonymously, no one would be overlooked and there would be no stars.

"We need to take the lessons we've learned from the media and now define ourselves," I said. "After all, I will forever be a 'twenty-three-year-old idealistic teacher from Newport Beach who wears polka dots and pearls' if I don't set the record straight." I told them that I was much more than an age or a preppy caricature, etched in print. I wasn't that one-dimensional. And neither were the Freedom Writers. "If I want to be more than the 'Breck girl' who wears Nordstrom separates, I've got to write my own story."

"Writing our own stories will give us the opportunity to leave a legacy," one of Freedom Writers said.

And with that, I sensed that my little pep talk had worked. Going forward, I did my best to shield them from the onslaught of media attention that was streaming in and concentrate on our writing project. We would continue to work on the book project that they had been honing since their junior year.

As the Freedom Writers continued to write and edit one another's diary entries, I decided to nominate them collectively for the Spirit of Anne Frank Award that I discovered in a *Scholastic* magazine. Although the award was intended for individual teenagers who combat "discrimination in their own communities," I decided that nominating them as a team would symbolize how well they worked as one. Originally, I planned to use the application as an example of how to apply for a college scholarship, but as I began to fill out all the paperwork, I became convinced that they could actually win based on how they had united to bring Miep and Zlata to Long Beach, and how they had worked hard to visit Washington, D.C. The nomination form said that those honored "are bridge builders and advocates for tolerance and mutual respect." As I watched them come together to edit and share their stories, they were the epitome of bridge builders and advocates for tolerance.

Before our winter break, I received a call from the Anne Frank Center, USA, saying that they "loved our application" but that the intended winner must receive the award in person. She assumed that since we were in California, there was no way that 150 students could claim the award in person. The director wanted to know if I could simply nominate one student on their behalf.

"No, we're a team," I blurted out. "If we win this award, I promise you we will all find a way to accept the award in person." I had no idea how I could get one student—let alone 150 students—to New York, but the concept of picking just one student would defeat the purpose of nominating them as a group.

The director said our nomination posed an exciting dilemma for them. She asked if I could come to New York City to talk to her about logistics. Without hesitating, I said, "Absolutely."

I immediately called my father and asked if he would buy me an airline ticket for Christmas. "Sure, it'll save me some time at the mall," he said. As soon as I reserved my ticket, I made a reservation at the Marriott Marquis in Times Square using my employee discount. My discount would save me nearly $200 a day, and it was moments like that that justified getting up at 4:30 in the morning every Sunday.

In the lobby of the Marriott, I ran into the former chef from my hotel, Chai.

"What in the world are you doing here?" Chai asked.

I told him how I'd nominated the students for the Spirit of Anne Frank Award on a whim and that now we might actually win.

"Well, if you do win, I'll make sure we take care of you at this Marriott in the same way we took care of you in Newport. After all, you're family."

Just as he'd calmed me down before my wedding and at the event we'd hosted for Zlata, Chai made me feel less anxious about my interview. When I met with the director of the Anne Frank Center, USA, I told her that I was confident that we could find a sponsor to come to New York. Since we had received so many offers to help following the *L.A. Times* article, I was sure we'd be able to solicit some help to get the students to New York.

"If we win, we can stay at the Marriott in Times Square."

"What a coincidence! That's where the award ceremony is going to be held."

"Maybe fate is on our side," I said. And then I heard my father's voice saying, "Be careful what you wish for . . ."

As I left the interview, I wondered how I could actually pull this off. Maybe the best solution was to win "honorable mention" or runner-up. That way the students would still feel validated without making things too complicated.

I went back to my hotel to look over the program for the award presentation. The event would be held in less than a month. They were also honoring Gerald Levin, the CEO of Time Warner. I remembered reading that he'd recently lost his son, Jonathan. The story had seemed to captivate the nation. His son was a teacher at Woodrow Wilson High School in the Bronx. Although the son never divulged who his father was to his students, somehow they found out. One day, a couple of students followed him to his apartment, tied him up, and tried to extort money from him. After they went to the ATM and could retrieve only $200, they returned to the apartment and murdered him.

Honoring a teacher's legacy posthumously made the award even more meaningful. Suddenly, winning "honorable mention" didn't seem good enough.

As I was reading over more information in the package, I looked out the window and saw the Bertelsmann Building, which housed Doubleday, across the street. Marvin Levy's wife, Carol, who was a book agent, pitched my students' book idea to them. I felt so small in that building and remember talking way too fast. They politely passed on the project, and looking back, I can't say I blame them.

I noticed in the award's package that one of the sponsors was Doubleday. The publicist I had met was actually on the Spirit of Anne Frank Award committee. Her name was Marly Rusoff. I remembered her being very motherly. She could tell I was nervous and offered me water when I began to break out in a sweat. I think she even offered me a cookie. Even though Doubleday passed on our book, she seemed genuinely interested in our project. At that moment, I decided to give her a call and let her know about all the exciting things that were happening with the Freedom Writers since I'd stammered and sweated in her office.

I called 411 and got Doubleday's number. When I called Doubleday and asked for Marly's office, I expected a secretary to give me the third degree and scribble my number on a yellow sticky note. Surprisingly, the secretary put me right through. I assumed that I would just leave a message, but Marly answered. I stammered again. I told Marly that I was across the street at the Marriott and that I was in New York for a couple of days to interview for the Spirit of Anne Frank Award.

"Erin, this is such exciting news. I remember really liking your project. Tell me what you've been up to since I last saw you."

Although I was nervous, I found myself explaining how we gave our story to the Secretary of Education, how the *L.A. Times* had recently done an article about us, and how *Primetime Live* was planning to air a segment on us in mid-April. Then I told her a random story about how Bob Newhart donated $500 to us but none of the Freedom Writers knew who he was. When I told her that one of the Freedom Writers said, "I think he's that old guy from Nick at Nite," Marly laughed. She thought my silly story was funny. "This sounds like exciting stuff. Why don't you drop by my office today and we'll see if Doubleday can take another look at your book proposal?"

Drop by? Today? With a book proposal? I didn't have a book proposal; all I had was a bunch of photographs and artifacts I'd taken to the Anne Frank Center for the show-and-tell. I quickly came up with an excuse that I had another meeting to go to. "Could I stop by tomorrow?" I asked.

"Sure, why don't you come by my office around 10 A.M.?"

It was four o'clock. I had eighteen hours. I felt like I was in college again and I'd have to pull an all-nighter. I called the concierge, located a Kinko's nearby, and spent the next seventeen hours glued to a computer. I typed, cut and pasted articles, and panicked.

As it got later and later in the night, I kept trying to rationalize what I was doing. Why should Doubleday be interested in a bunch of diary entries from teenagers? At 4 A.M. it hit me: They'd published Anne Frank's diary.

Maybe it was the *L.A. Times* article or the fact that ABC was completing a piece on us, or simply my audacity, but Marly suggested that "Doubleday should take a chance on you." She offered to give our proposal to an editor who might be interested in our project. At that moment, I noticed all the best-selling books by John Grisham lining her bookshelf. Doubleday was a serious publishing house. "Projects like yours rarely make their way out of a classroom," she said. She acknowledged that it was risky territory for such a pristine house, but she saw something in us that reminded her why she got in the book business to begin with. She said we would be known as "the little book that could."

My impetuous trip to New York paid off twofold. Not only did we get a foot in the door of a publishing house, but we ended up winning the award. The ABC producer thought that would be the perfect ending for our *Primetime Live* piece.

Once I returned to California, I had to figure out a way to get my students to New York. Luckily, I got an unsolicited call from GUESS? Inc. The owners had read the *L.A. Times* article, and since they were Jewish and had lost family members in the Holocaust, they wanted to know if there was a way for them to help us.

GUESS? donated forty-five airline tickets for a third of my class to attend the ceremony, and they outfitted the other two-thirds from head to toe in GUESS? gear.

Forty-five students competed in an essay contest to be eligible for the trip. While in New York, the students had the opportunity to see the Broadway revival of *The Diary of Anne Frank,* starring Natalie Portman. The Freedom Writers were given the award and a $1,000 scholarship from the actress Linda Lavin, who played beside Natalie as Mrs. Van Daam, on behalf of the Anne Frank Center, USA.

The tension at school reached a tipping point, though, when the Freedom Writers won the Spirit of Anne Frank Award. Unfortunately, several teachers took their disdain for me out on my students. When my students asked their teachers to sign their field-trip form to New York, some teachers refused. Others retaliated by plotting to administer tests while the students were in New York. Once the students returned, they were smugly told they had received an unexcused absence or there was "no makeup test." The students came to me horrified. Their grades were in jeopardy.

I immediately went to Dr. Cohn. Luckily, he was quick to react. He and the president of the school board, Karin Polacheck, had joined us in New York for the award ceremony. He felt these students should be hailed, not penalized. It was obvious to him that some of the teachers were trying to sabotage the students. He took immediate action and the students were able to make up their tests. But his allegiance alienated me even more from my colleagues.

But rather than lament my awkward relationship with some of the teachers, I concentrated on my students. That dedication paid off when I received a call that Doubleday had found an editor who was interested in working with my students to publish their book.

I had all of my students meet in the choral room. Once all 150 were assembled, I had them pick up plastic champagne glasses full of sparkling cider and I announced, "We have an official book deal. Our book is going to get published!"

There were screams, cheers, and even some tears.

"It's kind of ironic," Sue Ellen said, "because a lot of the other teachers here don't think we can even read or write and now we're going to be published authors."

CHAPTER 28

W ith the term "published author" came a huge responsibility. What would our book look like? Who would our audience be? Would our entries be censored?

I gave our new editor, Janet Hill, a copy of what we had given to the Secretary of Education. It was a bound copy of 150 anonymous diary entries with the title *An American Diary: Voices from an Undeclared War.*

After she read the diary entries we submitted, she called back and said, "Erin, I hate to tell you this, but this is a collection of horror stories. But there's a compelling story lurking inside."

She was right. Every student wrote about some type of adversity they had faced, but there was no literary arc. In the *L.A. Times* article, the audience got to see who the students were, where they came from, and the adversity they faced and how they collectively overcame it. Unfortunately, with 150 stories simply bound together, the reader didn't get to see how they triumphed together.

"I think the reader will want to know what happened in your classroom over the last four years," Janet said.

Since we were in the eye of the storm, none of us had ever considered that our story was actually a story. Janet said she thought what happened in Room 203 and beyond was an amazing journey, since amid tragedy, there was also real triumph. Janet wanted the reader to feel the highs and lows of each individual, but in the end know that these dynamic students were going to make it. Thus, the story had to begin with the first day of their freshman year and end with their graduation. She also encouraged us to rename the book *The Freedom Writers Diary* in honor of our namesake. It made sense. With the new name came more introspection.

To make the writing process more fun, I continued to concoct corny lessons like my *Freedom Writers Diary* recipe. I told my students that they were the "secret ingredient" and the directions were simple.

Pre-heat the oven to room temperature "203"
Add in 150 "raw" students
Simmer for four years
Mix in a "cause"
Throw in a pinch of adversity
Stir in some controversy
Add a dash of danger
Bring hope to a boil
Don't let cool . . . serve hot

To follow suit with my kitchen analogy, the editor's role was to "trim the fat" or "season the meat." Although the analogies were silly, the students began to edit one another's stories with more conviction.

Amid the writing and editing of the book, the *Primetime Live* segment aired on April 15, 1998—tax day. With all that was going on, I hadn't had the time to file my taxes yet. My friend volunteered to fill out my returns after work.

Since I had multiple jobs and was barely making ends meet, I just assumed that I'd get a tax rebate this time around. Since my divorce, I hadn't filed for the right withholdings and I found myself owing more money than usual.

I was depressed, and I mailed my taxes at 9 P.M. and then headed to my father's to watch the 10 P.M. airing of *Primetime Live*. I wanted to watch it with my dad and stepmom, since we had filmed it in their living room.

Several of my friends who lived in other time zones had already called my dad to tell him about the show, but I did not want to hear a word, especially since I was still reeling from doing my taxes.

Sam Donaldson opened the piece by saying, "A wise man said that a teacher can affect eternity. You never know where their influence will stop.

This story is about just such an unlikely hero." I looked at my dad, and he winked. During the next twelve minutes, I had my hands close to my face, in the same way I would during a horror flick. At the end of the segment, I found myself crying.

But I wasn't the only one. My dad was sobbing. Only to be interrupted by the telephone.

"Steve, this is Gibby." Gibby was one of my dad's macho friends who scouted for the Los Angeles Dodgers. "You didn't tell me this was going to be a tearjerker. I'm sitting here bawling like a baby."

And the phone kept ringing. And ringing. And ringing.

Studios, talk shows, old boyfriends . . . everyone seemed to embrace our story. Everyone, that is, except for my colleagues. Even though I begged the producers not to vilify the other teachers, many of them did not like the media attention. After it aired, I got nasty looks in the hall and a few curt notes in my office mailbox. I could only imagine what they were saying about me in the teachers' lounge.

Outside the confines of our school, it became apparent that *Primetime Live* had piqued people's interest in our story. I didn't want to become ubiquitous and sell our soul for fifteen minutes of fame, though. ABC proved to be a case where we gambled and won. They told a beautiful story. But what was daunting was that someone else's perception of us was completely out of our control. Whether they tweak it or exaggerate it, you are left picking up the pieces once they leave. Maybe now was a perfect time to step away from the table and assess our next move.

The next order of business was to decide what to do with all the calls and requests that we were receiving. I decided to use a risqué analogy to get their attention. I explained to them that our story was precious, like virginity (which made a lot of the students giggle). Then I went on to say that if we wanted to protect something that was precious, we shouldn't jump in the backseat of any car that comes our way. We should wait for our Prince Charming, who will honor and respect us. "Based on all the suitors that have come a-callin', what do you think we should do?" I said.

"We should wait for Oprah!"

Another said, "She's not a backseat kind of girl."

And with that, we decided we'd patiently wait for Oprah while embracing our book deal and impending graduation. We invited everyone who had a hand in the Freedom Writers' success to the upcoming graduation celebration to send them off.

Little did they know that they would be sending me off with them.

Feeling frustrated from the alienation I had experienced at Wilson, I contemplated accepting a new teaching position at California State University, Long Beach, that Dr. Cohn had recommended.

Although the idea was flattering, there was a part of me that was terrified.

"Erin, if you can replicate your methods, maybe more idealistic teachers like you won't quit. Do you have any idea what the attrition rate for teachers is in urban schools? It's staggering. Maybe you can convince a few more teachers to stay."

Teaching at a university would be entering a whole other league. I was afraid I wasn't qualified and my college students would find out that I was flying by the seat of my pants.

I knew if anyone could help me understand ascending into a new league, it would be my dad, since he'd worked in the "Big Leagues" since I was born.

In professional sports there is always a debate when someone should turn pro. Should they finish their college career or should they seize an opportunity? I had heard my dad debate this argument firsthand with my good friend from high school, Kevin. Kevin was an excellent baseball player and one of the fastest kids in America. My father had had his eye on Kevin since he was sixteen. As a senior in high school, he had the world at his fingertips. He could go to college on a baseball scholarship or he could turn pro. My dad sat at Kevin's kitchen table with his parents and offered Kevin a contract to play major league ball for the Angels. Kevin was a second-round draft pick, and although he could go to almost any college he wanted, he decided to sign at the age of seventeen.

A similar phenomenon was happening with one of my students, Sean Burroughs. He had been a star on the Long Beach Little League team as an eleven- and twelve-year-old, and he was now facing the Major League Baseball draft at seventeen. Although my dad wanted to draft Sean, he knew that by the time the Angels got their turn, Sean would already be drafted. He was bound to be picked early in the draft. There was no doubt that he would turn pro.

My dad vehemently believed that when you are given a wonderful opportunity, you have to take it. I knew he'd be biased from the get-go about my situation, but I needed to hear the pros and cons before I made my decision.

"Dad, Dr. Cohn said that the president of California State University, Long Beach, wants me to join their faculty and help teach teachers in the College of Education."

"After all the crap some of the teachers at your school have put you through in the last five years, I think you should go for it," he said. "They stick nasty notes in your mailbox, they've tried to penalize your students, and now they're accusing you of sleeping with your boss. I can go on and on. It's not a healthy environment for you."

"I know, but I'm scared."

"Change is scary. Don't you think your students are scared? You've encouraged them to see the world, to write a book, and now to go to college. You made it seem easy. We both know it wasn't easy. You've helped them get to the next level. Now it's your turn. Let Dr. Cohn help you get to the next level."

"But will I be selling out?"

"Selling out? What are you talking about? You're a teacher. Hell, you've even taught me a thing or two," he said. "So even if your environment or your students change, you'll always be a teacher."

CHAPTER 29

R oom 203 had been a safe haven for the Freedom Writers, and some of them viewed graduation as an eviction notice. After all the pomp and circumstance subsided, they would be "homeless."

Taking all the snapshots down from our walls and placing our mementos in boxes was like striking a set after a series finale. For ensemble shows like *Friends,* the cast of characters become a pseudo-family, just like we did, so I empathize with the actors once the curtain comes down. It's hard to say good-bye to people who've helped shape you, be it on a sound stage or in a classroom. What if you never get another gig as good?

So even though we swore we'd stay connected, we all began to fly in different directions. I assumed the healthiest thing I could do for the Freedom Writers was to encourage them to fly the coop. I hoped that their wings were strong enough. Most were—some were not.

Many of them felt a sense of loss, which helped fuel the idea of pursuing another field trip. But where we would go and when? The idea of going to Europe had actually been planted while we were on the steps of the Lincoln Memorial. But due to my paranoia about deterring sixteen- and seventeen-year-olds from danger, I didn't give Darrius's suggestion to "honor all the folks we've read about" much credence. Since we had emerged from both D.C. and New York City relatively unscathed, suddenly going to Anne Frank's attic seemed like the glue that could keep our virtual classroom together.

But taking a field trip to a foreign country wouldn't be easy, especially if we were no longer congregating in Room 203. If we were going to go to

Anne Frank's attic or Auschwitz, it would have to be the following summer, if at all.

Trying to hold on to my past with the Freedom Writers while forging my own future proved to be a balancing act that would define my career after leaving Wilson High. It was a challenge to stay connected while the Freedom Writers and I were dispersing to different colleges. While they were trying to find their way in college courses, I was trying to re-create my unorthodox methodology on future educators at California State University, Long Beach. Since I was donning the title "Distinguished Teacher in Residence," I didn't want to reveal that some of my best material had been scribbled on napkins at my favorite pizza joint or on the backs of envelopes. I felt like I had to work extra hard to fit in with my new colleagues, who had fancy degrees and appeared to be more knowledgeable than I was.

But what I lacked in theoretical training, I decided to make up for with my practical experience. I had just come out of the trenches, and I thought taking a practical approach might make a small difference in the lives of my new students. In the same way that I wanted the Freedom Writers to make writing relevant, I wanted these future teachers to embrace the relevancy of education. I didn't expect what happened in four years to transpire in sixty-five semester hours, but if I could model the most meaningful moments, then maybe the art of teaching would be brought to life for them in the same way Anne Frank's and Zlata's diaries were for the Freedom Writers.

It took time to adapt to the different demographics of my college classes. Most were filled with young women who had grown up in suburbia, like me. They eagerly took notes after everything I said. Nobody told me to "fuck off" and no one challenged me. I missed all the debates we used to have at Wilson, the rolling of the eyes, and even the bad attitudes. If I was going to survive, I would have to shake things up a bit. I would need to have Freedom Writers come to my rescue.

One of the textbooks on diversity that I'd been given by my dean had a bunch of case studies on different kids. It gave me an idea. Why not partner the Freedom Writers with my graduate students so their case studies could be about real people? It would be a win-win for everyone. The Freedom Writers would have a reason to show up for my class once a week and the sweet suburban girls could get a taste of reality.

The scenario worked out perfectly. The Freedom Writers volunteered to be guinea pigs, sharing personal anecdotes about gangs or learning disabilities, and after each class, we discussed our plans to travel to Europe.

Since we had a year to plan, unlike the month we had to pull off New York, I tried to do things in a much more structured manner. Rather than rely on John Tu, as I had in the past, I wanted to see if other company presidents could be our new sponsors. I wrote grants, set up meetings, and tried to find corporate partners. I was afraid of going to the well too many times with John Tu, so I decided to solicit help from other CEOs—but I never quite made it through their front doors. Their secretaries wanted professional grant proposals filled with statistics and data. Data had never been my strong point. I was better at telling stories or painting pictures. Without the statistics or the relationships, I never quite closed the deal.

But in the spring of 1999, two crises were "data" enough for me: Columbine and Kosovo. Intolerance on our soil and abroad seemed to be the perfect justification for our trip. We'd dub ourselves "Ambassadors of Tolerance" and show how people from disparate backgrounds could come together. It made sense to the Freedom Writers; it just didn't make sense to any of the gatekeepers to the CEOs.

With time passing, I decided that we would have to assess who was serious about going on this tentative trip. If we could pull off our "Ambassadors of Tolerance" trip, it would be a serious commitment. We had mapped out the trip, and it would be approximately twenty days. Now that the Freedom Writers were eighteen, many of the students were the primary breadwinners for their families. Taking twenty days off from work was not feasible for those who were sustaining their families. Some of the students were deeply engrossed in school and didn't think their summer school classes would accommodate the trip. Others were cynical and didn't think I could pull this one off.

As the year progressed, the number of students who were passionate about going on the proposed trip hovered around fifty. Those fifty were empowered and came up with all kinds of strict rules and regulations for the trip. Their guidelines were pretty stringent: They wanted everyone to do a formal application, to do hours of community service, to mentor elementary school kids, to be enrolled in college, and to take courses that would prepare us for the trip.

The summer quickly approached, and still no sponsors had stepped up to the plate. I realized I'd better start reserving airline tickets and hotel rooms or we'd be in serious trouble.

The Marriott Hotels came on board again with my employee discount, as they had in years past. This, in and of itself, would save thousands of dollars. We could take advantage of my employee discount in England, Poland, and the Netherlands. We'd have to find another hotel in Sarajevo, but at least the rooms were reserved—and they agreed to overlook the down payment.

When I called to book airline tickets, I asked, "What is the drop-dead date that we'd have to pay?" They gave me seven days.

With the "drop-dead date" in sight, I decided to meet with John Tu to get advice. Although we had gotten help on incidentals, and the Freedom Writers had done their part to raise money by selling Freedom Writers T-shirts, no corporation had agreed to underwrite the trip. Since I wasn't able to come up with a "return on their investment" or a marketing ploy that would put them on the cover of a newspaper, no company was willing to sponsor us. John had never wanted recognition or even statistics. He wanted the students to learn and be accountable for their actions. Now I felt that I had to be accountable for my actions and admit to John that I had failed.

"Why didn't you come to me earlier?" John asked.

"I wanted to prove to you that we could pull this one off without your help."

"Can you?"

"No."

"How many Freedom Writers are planning on going?"

"About fifty. I've tried to instill the notion that they have to work hard for what they want. And they have. But we just don't have enough money to cover all the expenses. I tried to get an airline to underwrite the flights, but it's too costly in the summer. Every college student in America must be backpacking their way through Europe."

"How much are you short?"

"About two hundred fifty thousand dollars."

Without hesitation, John Tu took out his checkbook and wrote a check for $250,000. "Here, now go on your trip!"

I stood there stunned. I hadn't come there to get rescued again, and suddenly I had a check for a quarter of a million dollars in my hand.

Why would he do this? How could he believe in us so much? Why aren't there more businessmen who give to charity without strings attached?

I left his office and drove straight to Bank of America. As I stood in the line, I kept staring at the check in disbelief. When I handed it to the teller, she took one look at me, then the check, and then called security. I'm sure she wasn't used to people like me cashing checks like that. With my teacher salary and my other jobs, I still lived paycheck to paycheck.

After a lengthy discussion and several suspicious looks, the manager came over and said, "With such a large amount, we'll have to put a fourteen-day hold on this check."

"Fourteen days . . . I can't wait fourteen days. I have to buy airline tickets today. Our flight leaves in a week."

"Well, unless you can arrange for a wire transfer directly to your account, you can't get the money," the bank manager said.

Embarrassingly, I had to call John and tell him that his check was too big and they were going to put a hold on it.

"Come see my accountant. He'll help take care of the transfer."

John's accountant scared me. I always assumed that he thought my ideas were frivolous. He never smiled, he spoke in curt sentences, and he made me feel like a little girl asking for a larger allowance. I always felt compelled to tell him that I did chores as a kid and that I had three extra jobs so he didn't think I was taking John's money and going on a shopping spree at South Coast Plaza. Once, I even blurted out, "I bought my first car from babysitting money." He couldn't care less. As far as he was concerned, the Freedom Writers and I were a financial liability on John.

I was ready to get scolded, but the accountant actually smiled. "Say hello to Zlata for me," he said cheerfully.

I forgot that I had given the accountant an autographed copy of *Zlata's Diary*. His kids were reading the book in school. Apparently, he didn't think this trip was frivolous after all. I invited him and John to our bon voyage ceremony. I didn't think he'd come, but I hoped that John would.

A few days before we were going to leave, we did a presentation at our local Barnes & Noble for our friends and families about all the countries we were planning to visit. Our itinerary was going to take us from Los Angeles, to London, to Poland, to the Netherlands, and then to Bosnia. With the recent Kosovo situation and all the Albanian refugees fleeing the Balkans, my dad and I had had a disagreement about our safety in Sarajevo. He thought it was too dangerous and that we'd be held hostage by rebel soldiers. I'd decided to change his itinerary and send him to Paris for his wedding anniversary, rather than have him continue on with us to Sarajevo. I thought the promise of Paris would appease him, but he was walking around Barnes & Noble with security printouts from the American Embassy stating that traveling to Bosnia-Herzegovina was unsafe.

"Dad, are you trying to create an insurrection here?"

"I just want the other parents to know what you're getting their kids into."

"Thanks, Dad. If there's a coup tonight, I'm blaming you!"

Surprisingly, the other parents didn't flinch. My dad's scare tactics backfired. The security printouts actually made the Freedom Writers feel more resolute. The thought of being held hostage heightened their interest.

When John Tu called to let me know that he was trying to find a parking spot, I told the students that our "mystery benefactor" was here and they needed to close their eyes. Since I could no longer dangle a grade over their heads, I told them early in the fall that "our benefactor" wanted them to earn this trip. Up until a few days earlier, there was no benefactor, but this mysterious entity became increasingly useful. It made them work harder to "earn" the trip. While their eyes were shut, John quietly walked to the front of the Barnes & Noble book-signing area and yelled, "Surprise!" They opened their eyes and some of them started crying. Of course, it had to be John Tu in the end, since he'd been with us from the beginning. With his blessing and a sworn moratorium on security warnings from my father, we were ready for our departure.

At the end of the evening, my father pulled me aside and said, "I can't believe you pulled this off."

"Quite frankly, Dad, I can't either!"

Since my brother, Chris, had been in the army, I asked him if he could be my partner on our tour. We would share a room and strategize how to navigate our way through Europe. The night before we left, Chris had asked me to make sure we had some cash on us.

"But Chris, carrying cash isn't safe. Shouldn't we only use traveler's checks?"

"You'll see. We may need to grease some palms in Bosnia."

Hmm? Something told me that this was not going to be like any other trip I'd taken, especially since we would be visiting areas that were synonymous with intolerance—Auschwitz and war-torn Sarajevo, not the typical tourist destinations. Although the students were very excited about this trip, there was a much more serious tone as we boarded the plane headed overseas.

CHAPTER 30

L ondon was going to be the bookends of our trip to help make the transition to Europe easier. Once we had our bearings and had seen a few sites, we headed to Warsaw, Poland. We were staying at the Marriott in the center of Warsaw, and you could still see some of the remnants of Communism. We had invited Mel Mermelstein to come with us as our tour guide. His book *By Bread Alone,* about his experience in Auschwitz, had been published in Poland, and our Polish liaison said she felt like she was meeting someone famous.

While we were in the dining area of the Marriott, three Mexican musicians started playing guitars. Ramon found out that it was my dad and stepmom's anniversary. Since the students called me Ms. G, they affectionately nicknamed my father Papa G. My father had been a little grumpy all day trying to corral the Freedom Writers, so Ramon devised a plan to cheer him up. He paid the guitarist some Polish money for a wonderful surprise. When the guitarists began serenading my father and stepmom, we surrounded them and formed a circle. Suddenly, Karen whisked my dad up and they began to dance. After watching Eddie Murphy's "Delirious," my dad always claimed that he had what Eddie Murphy called "white man's overbite," and subsequently, he couldn't dance. Well, he sort of did, but on this night, it didn't matter. They danced, and we cheered.

As we were heading to our hotel rooms, my dad pulled me aside and said, "If someone would have told me that I'd be dancing to mariachi music in the middle of Poland, I would have thought they were crazy. Thanks, honey, this is the best anniversary present anyone could have ever given me."

The good cheer subsided, though, as we boarded the bus to Chelmno, an extermination camp, the next morning. Overcast skies were fitting for the long, somber journey through the Polish countryside. It was hours outside of Warsaw, and several hours from Auschwitz, but it would give us a chance to see a different side of Poland.

On the way to the camp, Mel told us about how thousands of unsuspecting Jews were lured into a church, then placed in specially rigged trucks. While they were en route, the Jews were gassed and died of asphyxiation. Once they were dead, the trucks drove to an isolated forest and buried the bodies in mass graves. When we arrived, we were shocked to see that the church was still standing. Next to the church was a barren site that had once housed thousands of Jews.

There were shirtless men in shorts filling up wheelbarrows with dirt. They were sunburned and had long cigarettes hanging out of their mouths as they sifted through the soil. Because the camp was so far away from any major city, it was devoid of tourists. With the exception of the men with the wheelbarrows, we were the only people there. We walked down some makeshift stairs into dirt-filled trenches. Suddenly, my student Christina screamed, "Oh my God!" as she picked up a bone.

Some of the girls screamed and grabbed the arms of the boys. Another student found a tooth in the rubble. I felt nauseated. This was too much to bear.

"They've just begun to excavate this site," Mel said as he picked up a rusty spoon. "It's as if people want to pretend this never happened at all."

As we were about to get back on the bus, a little man walked out of his house to ask what we were doing. Mel began to speak to him in Polish. It got a little heated. Suddenly, the man's wife came out to scold her husband. She started yelling; all the while Mel kept prying him for answers.

"What are they saying?" I asked our Polish bus driver.

"This man has lived in this village his whole life. Your friend is asking him what he saw as a boy and why he continues to live here."

"Why is the wife so angry?" I asked.

"Apparently, this is her parents' home. She too has lived here her whole life. She keeps saying, 'That was in the past, so let it be!' but your friend doesn't want to 'let it be.' He wants to know how they are not haunted by the ghosts of innocent people who died here."

Mel was relentless. Suddenly, the woman waved her arms in the air and stormed into her house. She did not want to talk about the past, even though people were presently excavating human bones practically right outside her front door.

We got on the bus and eerily retraced the route that the gas trucks took years before. When the bus pulled over next to a dense forest, we all paused. This was the site of a mass grave. As we boarded the bus again, no one spoke.

After an hour of silence, I convinced Chris to start looking for a place to eat. We were in the middle of nowhere. When we saw a horse-drawn carriage go past us carrying hay, we realized we were probably not going to find a McDonald's.

Chris spotted a little two-bedroom house above a garage with a sign that said "Restaurant" in Polish. Chris asked the driver to pull over, and he and Mel jumped out. I noticed Chris had brought with him the bag of our American cash. Although the mom-and-pop restaurant had only a two-burner stove, they said they could call some of their neighbors for backup. If we were not in a hurry, they would feed us the best schnitzel we'd ever have.

And they were right. It took about three hours to serve everyone, but during that time, we were able to see another side of Poland—a place where a family of three invited more than fifty strangers into their home and into their lives. Some of the students ate inside, but the majority of us sat in their backyard on a picnic table or on the lawn. At the end of our meal, one of the students started tapping his Coke bottle, making a beat. Another started tapping his fork on the table. Another picked up a pipe scrubber that was next to the garden hose and started rubbing it against the water grate. Mel got in the action and started blowing on the rim of a larger glass decanter. Students started clapping, stomping, swaying, and singing. I was amazed at how resilient they were. I looked up at the balcony to see the husband and wife who owned the home hug their daughter. The husband was tapping his feet. The wife was teary-eyed.

After hugging the Polish family good-bye and taking lots of photographs, we began the long journey to Auschwitz.

We didn't arrive at our hotel until late that night. The Globe Hotel was adjacent to railroad tracks that led to Auschwitz.

"These are the same railroad tracks that I rode on in a crammed cattle car," Mel said. He was only a boy then, but I could tell his mind was wandering back.

While we were standing in the lobby, Mel said, "Well, I'm off to stay the night in the old commandant's quarters in the camp. Would any of you care to join me?" Mel had befriended the docents at Auschwitz, since he'd been going there for decades. Each trip, he would take an artifact home with him to Huntington Beach. He owned a palette shop, and he had created his own museum on the property to honor the memory of the millions who had lost their lives.

In good conscience, I could not let the kids go spend the night with him. In fact, we had received a letter from a woman after the *L.A. Times* article stating that her parents had taken her to Auschwitz when she was just a teenager. At that time, Poland was still under Communist rule and there were not many hotels available, so her parents decided to stay at Auschwitz, and to this day, she still has nightmares about her evening at the concentration camp.

"No, Mel. I think it's best that they stay here."

"Are you sure?"

"Yes!"

"Well, then, I'd like to ask some of the students for a favor."

"Sure, Mel. They'll do anything for you."

"I'd like to ask them to sing a song at the Wailing Wall tomorrow. I think it would be a beautiful tribute." He was so touched by their camaraderie after Chelmno that he wanted to bring some of that spirit to Auschwitz. Mel described how the Wailing Wall was where a lot of Jews were lined up and executed. Visitors now put flowers there in commemoration of those who were slaughtered.

"I'm sure the Freedom Writers would be honored."

Mel pulled aside some of the students, and they all agreed. They asked him if they could add some poetry to the old spiritual "Wade in the Water."

I was a little shaken up from the day at Chelmno and the prospect of Freedom Writers being lured to the commandant's quarters at Auschwitz, but I tried to lie down and get some sleep. A doorman knocked on my door and handed me a message. It was from Janet Hill, our editor in New York. I had given her our itinerary along with our completed manuscript a few days before we left.

I called her collect from a pay phone in the lobby and she said, "I have good news for you! I've finished editing the book, and we're moving ahead!"

"Wow, Janet. Tomorrow we're going to Auschwitz, so it feels a little symbolic to me."

I couldn't sleep that night between the news from Janet and the sounds of trains going past our hotel. I could only imagine what it was like for Mel to hear the same noises while staying at the commandant's quarters. The next morning, as we met in the breakfast room of the hotel, it turned out that everyone had had a hard time sleeping. I made the announcement that our editor was sending the book to production today.

"It's more than just a coincidence, don't you think?" one of the Freedom Writers said.

"I think you're right."

At that moment, Mel said, "It's time. The bus is ready." We all took a deep breath and headed to Auschwitz. When we arrived, Mel had us walk under the infamous sign "Arbeit Macht Frei"—"Work Makes You Free." We felt an eerie chill. Having Mel lead our tour was incredibly emotional. Although he was like a grandfather to all of us, suddenly he was a mere teenager again, reliving what happened to him and his family. As he spoke, I was fixated on the tattoo on his arm. For more than fifty years, his ID number had been a painful reminder of his experience there. He was seventeen years old when he was deported to Auschwitz. He showed us how he was stripped of jewelry, glasses, hair, and most tragically, his dignity.

He pointed out the spot where he last saw his father. He explained that his father had told his sons, "We must separate. We must stay apart. Because if one of you makes it, you must tell the world what they did to us."

As the sole survivor of his family, Mel kept true to his promise.

He took us to the Wailing Wall and the Freedom Writers began to sing their tribute. They had taken Mel's request very seriously and stayed up all night writing poetry that would overlay "Wade in the Water." As they sang, others listened, simply mesmerized. The Freedom Writers touched the wall, laid flowers beside it, and had a moment of silence for all those who had been slain.

As we were taking a break for lunch outside the camp, Henry came up to me with a perfect red Gerber daisy. He'd purchased it from the gift shop. "This is for you, Ms. G. It reminds me of the little girl from *Schindler's List* who wore the red coat. It reminds me of all the little kids like Mel who passed through these gates."

I was so touched. "Henry, why don't you give the flower to Mel instead?"

Henry walked over to Mel and handed him the flower and explained its symbolism. Mel got teary eyed and gave Henry a hug. With his arm around Henry, we made our way to Birkenau, the camp adjacent to Auschwitz. Mel arranged for all the students to join hands and walk in a single file on the railroad tracks. We formed a human train and walked through the gates where thousands of cattle cars had once traveled. Mel pointed out which direction he went and which direction his family was sent under the supervision of Dr. Mengele, the "Angel of Death." His mother and sisters were sent in the opposite direction. They were immediately gassed and burned in a crematorium.

After lighting candles at the crematorium where his mother and his sisters had perished, he left behind the red Gerber daisy.

As we were leaving, one of my students pointed in the air and gasped.

"Look, Ms. G. There's a rainbow."

It was odd to see any kind of color in a place that I always associated with black and white. All the movies I'd seen about Auschwitz were dreary, and I always associated Auschwitz with rain and snow. It was odd that the sun was peeking through the clouds and that there were actually grass and flowers sprouting up. I imagined the camp to be desolate and barren. And even though it was a summer day, I just assumed there'd be no sunlight. Mel told us that he never saw the sun while he was at the camp, due to all the smoke bellowing from the crematoriums. Maybe the rainbow, just like the news about our book, was another one of those indescribable coincidences.

As we boarded a plane headed for Amsterdam the next day, it struck me how easy it was for us to leave. I couldn't imagine what it felt like for Mel, to be trapped inside a camp and know that the world had forgotten him. The

Freedom Writers swore to him that they would continue to share his story for decades to come. We would never forget.

When we landed in Amsterdam, John Tu's friend Paul Stribos was waiting for us. Paul and his family had graciously agreed to help plan our itinerary in the Netherlands. Besides a visit to Anne Frank's attic, he arranged for us to go to the seaside and to visit The Hague, where we would attend a war tribunal and hear about the atrocities committed in Bosnia.

Our first venture was to visit The Hague. Having seen the effects of genocide in Poland, hearing tales about it in Bosnia was an eerie precursor to our trip to Sarajevo. The tribunal hearing of a Bosnian war criminal who had massacred innocent Muslim men in ethnic cleansing camps reminded us of Zlata's father and how he was spared his life.

After the hearing, Paul took us to a seaside village for dinner. I learned early on in the trip that traveling in a pack of fifty nineteen-year-olds made for an instant party wherever we went. To blow off steam from the tribunal hearing, all fifty of my students took over a tiny little dance floor in the restaurant and began to dance. Within moments, I was dragged onto the dance floor too. Any inhibition I had about being a bad dancer was lost in translation. Suddenly, I felt a tap on my shoulder. It was my dad. He had a scowl on his face.

"It's time to go."

And it was. . . .

It was time for him to go. This trip had been a bit too intense for him, and the highs and lows we were experiencing on a daily basis were beginning to wear on him. Tomorrow he would fly to Paris with my stepmother, Karen. It's hard to match the stamina of a nineteen-year-old, and so after two weeks, he was beat.

The next morning, I found myself incredibly emotional. It was August 4—the day that Anne Frank had been captured. I couldn't stop crying. Not only were we in Amsterdam on such a symbolic day, but as I looked around, I saw how loving my students were to one another. They held each other's hands as they walked up the stairs into the annex, they put their arms around one another as they peered through the window, and they hugged each other as we watched the video about Miep Gies at the end of the tour.

As we went through the secret annex, my students made a real connection with Anne. Although they had read her book and seen the Broadway play that reenacts Anne's story, nothing compared to actually being in the annex. The Freedom Writers touched her artifacts, peered out the same windows, and listened intently for the sounds of the bell tower.

When we finished the tour, a tall Dutch woman approached us and asked if she could interview us. She was a journalist for a Dutch newspaper. Paul had contacted the Anne Frank Museum to see if Miep could personally give us a tour, but shortly before we came, she suffered a stroke. Although she couldn't join us, she sent some well-wishers on her behalf—one of which was this inquisitive journalist.

The journalist gathered a group of us outside the museum, near a canal, and began to ask questions. Maria became our spokesperson. When the journalist asked Maria to explain why we were all so emotional, she said, "If your life is always in a cage, and someone opened the door, your wings are not used to flying. My life, my environment, was that cage. I was in a gang until I was fifteen years old, and when I got out of the gang, I didn't know what to do. Ms. G, she taught me what to do with those wings. That's why it's so emotional when I saw her cry [in the annex], because I used to hate her, and the Freedom Writers, and now we're all standing in those same little rooms that Anne once stood in."

The journalist was very affected and said our story would be in the paper the very next day. The next morning, as we were about to board the plane for Sarajevo, one of my students spotted a photo of us on the cover of the Dutch newspaper. We couldn't decipher a single word printed in the paper other than the word "ghetto"—which Henry pointed out "must be the same in every language."

As we looked out the window of the plane in Sarajevo, we noticed the airport was still in shambles from the war. As we taxied down the makeshift runway, there were bombed-out planes littering the airport. Some of the buildings surrounding the airport had been severely bombed and were lying in ruins.

"It looks like the whole city is crying," Darrius said as we saw rows of rubble.

As we entered the terminal, we were taken aback by soldiers carrying machine guns. When they randomly began to frisk Freedom Writers and scrutinize the contents of their suitcases, panic set in. We didn't have an interpreter and had no idea what they were muttering about.

Although we were all a bit somber from the devastation of the recent war, Chris withdrew the most. It was as if he, like Mel before him, was having flashbacks. Since Chris had done reconnaissance in Bosnia at the height of the Bosnian war, it was bringing back a lot of memories that he'd suppressed since he was back in the States. Now they were crashing over him. We got off the plane and were greeted by soldiers with machine guns. I was glad that my father was in Paris at this point, because he would have said, "I told you so."

As we made the drive from the dilapidated airport to the Holiday Inn in Sarajevo, Chris narrated some of the atrocities he'd seen several years earlier in his battle fatigues. Some of the buildings looked like Swiss cheese, and the remnants of war were still evident.

The hotel we stayed at was where Christiane Amanpour and all the other CNN correspondents had reported from during the height of the war. I remember seeing Christiane wearing her flak jacket outside the Holiday Inn, reporting on the latest bombing at a bread line or a sniper picking off a child on their way to get water.

When we checked into our rooms, there were still remnants of bullet holes. In fact, that became a badge of honor for many of the Freedom Writers. "How many bullet holes do you have in your room?" they would ask one another.

After we were all settled, Zlata met us in the lobby. She agreed to show us all the sights that she had written about in her book: the post office that was bombed, the National Gallery, even her apartment.

As we were standing next to her apartment, you could see a park across the street. "Is that where Nina died?" Sonia asked, remembering the diary entry in Zlata's book that talked about her best friend being shot. It was. Zlata pointed to the hills and said that snipers used to hide there and would shoot at innocent children below. She said people began to "zigzag" when they walked anywhere in an attempt to throw off the sniper's aim. But as the war progressed, the people grew weary. With the weariness came defiance. She said people began to ask, "What if I'm running away from a shell? But then again, maybe I'm running toward another. So if it's my fate to die, I'll die. And the people stopped running. Stopped zigzagging."

Zlata's interpretation of the war reminded me of how the Freedom Writers interpreted gang life in such a matter-of-fact way. War had an uncanny way of anesthetizing people.

We took a day trip to Mostar, one of the cities hardest hit during the Bosnian war. It was a five-hour bus ride. Along the way, we stopped twice to use restrooms. There were no toilets or plumbing at the rest stops—there was just a hole in the ground. When we got to Mostar, I sensed that something was wrong, but I couldn't quite put a finger on it. Itinerary? Check. Passport? Check. Emergency cash? Check. I went through a list of things I could have forgotten. Could we possibly be missing a student?

After counting noses, it was made official that we were minus one. I had the Dream Team Moms count the Freedom Writers again and again, and we continued to come up one short. Ian? Oh my God. I felt awful. Where the hell was Ian?

"Ian was on the bus, wasn't he?" I asked frantically.

"Yeah, he was the first one on this morning," said his roommate.

"Did we leave him at the rest stop?" I asked in desperation.

He must be so scared, and I was so helpless. After all, we were in the middle of nowhere.

I pictured the worst. I pictured him wandering about town and getting lost. I even envisioned soldiers in olive-colored uniforms detaining Ian and holding him at gunpoint.

Being so far from home, we were bound to incur unexpected bumps in the road, but never in my wildest dreams did I think we would accidentally leave a Freedom Writer behind in a foreign country.

When I finally found a phone, I phoned the Holiday Inn. It turned out that Ian was there. Moments before we headed to Mostar, Ian had gotten off the bus to retrieve his hat, but by the time he returned to the bus, the bus had departed, leaving Ian behind.

"Oh my goodness, Ian. I was so worried about you. Are you okay?"

"Don't worry, Ms. G. I just took a nap and wrote some postcards to my folks."

"Okay, Ian, we'll be back in six hours, so please don't go anywhere," I begged.

With Zlata's help, we held a town hall meeting at the University of Sarajevo to discuss the war with Croats, Muslims, and Serbs. The students were still processing the horrors they had witnessed. They reminded me of my students years before. When asked about the prospect of tolerance, one of the students from Sarajevo said, "It's a bit difficult to walk up to a person who's been shooting at you and say, 'Okay nothing has happened.'" He had witnessed atrocities that struck a chord with my students. They too had been shot at, and they too had to make the conscious decision to forgive. As if on cue, Maria stood up and said, "You don't have to forget the war, but you have to learn to forgive." Maria had learned to forgive, and she was hopeful that others could follow her lead.

Because of the crises in Kosovo, soldiers had commandeered all flights out of Sarajevo for military convoys. A few days before we left the United States and headed to Europe, we were told that we could fly into Sarajevo but we couldn't fly out. In order to leave Bosnia, we had to rent a bus that would take us from Sarajevo to Croatia. It would take between twelve and fourteen hours. All the Sarajevo teens from the town hall came to our hotel the morning of our departure to wish us farewell. We felt like we had made a small difference.

As we were driving to Croatia, we had to go through several Serbian checkpoints. At each checkpoint, soldiers would come aboard our bus, yell and scream about these passports from Guatemala, or El Salvador, or Cambodia, and then Chris would quietly take some of the cash out of the green duffel bag and discreetly hand it to them. After they would leave the bus, I would see him wipe away his sweat. Although John Tu's accountant told me to keep receipts for everything we did, I hoped he'd understand why this part of the trip could not be documented. There was clearly no paper trail or receipts for this part of the journey.

When we landed at LAX airport, a bit haggard from our nineteen-day journey, there was breaking news on the airport TV. A white supremacist had opened fire with a semiautomatic weapon at a Jewish Community Center in a Los Angeles suburb and shot and wounded innocent children. As we watched the tragic images on the airport TV, we were jarred back to reality. Our vacation was over.

"Some kind of 'welcome home,'" Darrius said sarcastically.

CHAPTER 31

After nineteen days on the road with the Freedom Writers, I desperately craved stability. The kind of stability you get from being home. But after living out of a suitcase for three weeks, it was hard to return to a new apartment that was still in shambles. With my divorce final, I moved to an apartment in Long Beach, but it was more of a closet than a home.

I had stayed in my apartment in Newport Beach until the Freedom Writers graduated, and when I decided to change jobs, I also decided to move. One of the Dream Team Moms helped me find a one-bedroom apartment in Long Beach. It reminded me of a seventies ski lodge. Even though I'd been there for nearly a year, most of my mementos were still in boxes. I put all of the stuff from my marriage in a storage unit. When I forgot to pay the bill, they auctioned everything off. I suppose it was subconscious. What was I going to do with a boxed wedding dress and old IKEA furniture? I should have just donated everything to Goodwill to begin with. Now that it was gone, I'd be spared combing through old love letters and photos when I was feeling down.

My new minimalist lifestyle was a little too extreme, though. My walls were bare and my refrigerator had only condiments in it. I never had company either, a stark contrast to my previous place, where I was known to entertain often. I realized I was simply using this apartment as a place to rest my head. My dad had lived a similar existence when my parents first got divorced. He left his "dream house" behind the gates and moved into a shabby apartment overlooking the 10 Freeway. I remember eating my first Salisbury steak TV dinner there and sipping Shasta black-cherry soda right out of the can, while listening to cars whiz by below. When he eventually bought a three-bedroom house with a pool, we knew he had snapped out of his funk. Now it was time for me to get out of my funk.

Since I couldn't afford to buy a home, I decided to rent a home where I could entertain again. Luckily, one of my graduate students approached me and said, "Do you want to rent the most amazing home in Long Beach? It overlooks the ocean."

I had driven on Ocean Boulevard for years, with its amazing historic homes. Suddenly, I had an opportunity to rent the third story of a gorgeous home on this historic street. I'd called to see if it was available before we went to Europe, but in the chaos of the trip, I didn't follow up. I assumed they'd rented it immediately. I assumed wrong.

As it turned out, the landlord's daughter had been a Distinguished Scholar at Wilson High, and her mother, Sandy Noonan, had followed the Freedom Writers story. Sandy decided that they wouldn't rent it to anyone except me. Sandy would soon find out how chaotic my life was when her enormous home became the new Freedom Writers headquarters. Room 203 would be replaced by the house overlooking the ocean.

I had barely moved in when Doubleday sent me the book launch schedule. With trips to Chicago, Atlanta, New York, Washington, D.C., and San Francisco, I would once again be living out of a suitcase.

A few days prior to the book's coming out, I got a call from Congressman Patrick Kennedy's office. He was going to be in Los Angeles for an event and wanted to see if we could meet. Our editor had sent his office a copy of our manuscript because of his involvement with the International War Tribunal. Since he had helped with the selection of the chief judge at The Hague, I assumed that he wanted to commend us for braving the security warning and going to Bosnia. Although I was flattered, I was noncommittal. I knew that the impending book tour would be exhausting—even more exhausting than Europe.

We were going to get the books a couple days early, so I asked Doubleday to ship them to my father's house on Saturday. He graciously offered to host a book kickoff party. We could swim, sign books, and share our European photos.

One of the agreements I made with Doubleday was that I would do anything to help promote the book as long as the proceeds went to help further the Freedom Writers' education.

"When are you going to stop giving away the farm, Erin?" my dad asked.

"I wasn't planning to even be in the book, Dad. I submitted 'a collection of horror stories,' remember? If the book does well, they can use the money to pay for their college tuition. Anyway, thanks for letting the Freedom Writers come to your home. It means a lot to them."

It meant a lot to him too, although he'd never admit it. My father must have gotten the dancing bug from Poland, though, because I saw him later that evening in the kitchen clumsily trying to dance the Macarena with Maria.

On Sunday morning, I received a call from a congressional aide telling me where to pick up my credential to meet the congressman. I was no longer working weekend shifts at the Marriott, so I was thrilled that I didn't have to get up at 4:30 in the morning on weekends anymore. I was still in my pj's and drinking coffee with my dad and my brother, so the concept of driving to downtown L.A. to shake the hand of a stranger didn't seem too appealing.

"You should go, Erin. He's kind of a big deal," my brother said. He had just interned in Washington, D.C., and done some advance work with Vice President Gore. He had been bitten by the political bug. "I'll go with you!"

With everything that was on my plate, I just didn't feel motivated.

"Chris," I said, "I don't feel like it."

"Come on. Maybe Patrick Kennedy can help your cause."

After a little cajoling, I agreed to go.

When we got to the Bonaventure Hotel, I noticed that everyone was twice my age and wearing dark suits. In my fire-engine-red dress, I felt a little conspicuous. I was the only woman in the room, and I didn't even know what Patrick looked like.

"Look for someone with moppy hair," Chris said. "All the Kennedys look alike."

I ended up standing next to someone near the cheese platter, and I began to tell him how I lugged around ten pounds of Gouda cheese all through Sarajevo, contemplating giving it to the soldiers at each checkpoint. The man laughed and kept egging me on. I assumed he didn't know anyone either, so he was trying to blend in with the cheese as well.

"What is that pin you're wearing?" I asked.

"It's my membership pin."

"Are you a member of the Boy Scouts?" I asked.

"No, I'm a member of Congress. Erin, I'm Patrick Kennedy."

"Oh, I'm such an idiot. I'm sorry. I'm just glad I didn't say something offensive. I have a tendency to do that. In fact, I said 'fuck' once in front of Steven Spielberg and have spent the last five years regretting it."

He looked at me and smiled and then pulled out a document from his pocket that was all about me.

"Hey, what is that? A cheat sheet? What does that say about me?"

"Wouldn't you like to know?"

"Oh my God! Does it say anything incriminating?"

"No, it's just your press release from Doubleday."

"That's a relief. Well, I brought you a little present." I handed him our book and a homemade VHS copy of the *Primetime Live* special. "Please don't turn me in for copyright infringement. I had my dad make you a copy this morning. He thought you'd like it. It made him cry. But I wasn't supposed to tell you that. He's kind of macho."

"Will you sign my book?"

Since we had just gotten the books yesterday, I didn't know what to write. I wasn't used to autographing. All the students went around the house signing it like a yearbook. I needed to be profound and make amends for my cheese and "fuck" stories. When in doubt, I could borrow a line from one of my students. They were much wittier than I was.

> *Dear Patrick,*
> *When diverse worlds*
> *Come together . . .*
> *Beauty is inevitable!*
> *To the beauty that awaits us . . .*

After I signed it, I stared at the word "inevitable" for what felt like five minutes. I realized that without the red scraggly line underneath a misspelled word on the computer screen, I never knew if I spelled something right or not. How embarrassing would it be if I misspelled something in the first book I signed? I wanted to scribble different versions of "inevitable" on a napkin, sort of a process of elimination, but then he'd really think I was posing as an English teacher.

"Let me see what you wrote?"

It was the moment of reckoning. If I did misspell it, would he tell me? It was an interesting dilemma. After all, I sometimes don't tell people when they have a poppy seed stuck in their teeth, to avoid an embarrassing moment.

"Ah, that's sweet."

"Did I spell *inevitable* correctly?"

"Aren't you an English teacher?"

"I am, but I'm sort of nervous."

"You? Nervous?"

"Yeah, I fake it well."

"You should be a politician."

"I've got enough on my plate with a hundred and fifty Freedom Writers to worry about. It's like herding cats. I actually left a student behind in Sarajevo. It wasn't until five hours and two rest stops later that I realized he was missing."

"No, honestly, you should think of running. Your district is a hotly contested seat."

"How do you know?"

"I'm the chairman of the Congressional Campaign Committee and I recruit candidates to run for Congress."

"Are you trying to recruit me?"

"That's why I wanted to meet you in the first place. Ergo, the cheat sheet," he said, waving it in front of me with a grin.

"Hey, what's on that, anyway? Does it mention that my personal life is a mess and that the only thing in my fridge is ketchup? Or that I forgot to pay my storage bill and they auctioned off all my stuff?" Suddenly, I felt compelled to point out all my non-congressional-worthy flaws.

"You should seriously consider running, Erin. You'd be an excellent candidate."

"Thank you, but I'm starting a book tour tomorrow, and I just moved, and my life is out of control. Listen, I'd better let you go back to kissing babies."

"Would you like to have dinner with me?"

"No, I promised my dad that we'd have dinner tonight. He hosted the

Freedom Writers at his house last night and there's enough food to feed the Bosnian army. Do you want to come over and have some leftovers?"

"I better stay here, but it sounds tempting!"

I left, but in the pit of my stomach I knew that was not going to be the last time I'd see him.

Later that night, Patrick called me at my dad's house and I was surprised. "How'd you get this number? Did you have the Secret Service track me down?"

"You gave it to me. Remember?"

"Oh yeah. But I didn't think you'd actually call."

He said he'd like to see me again and would I at least contemplate running. "I'll be in D.C. in a couple weeks for the book tour, so maybe we can talk about it then," I said, and then got off the phone.

"Dad, Patrick Kennedy wants me to run for Congress."

"Absolutely not! You'd get crucified. Your skin is not thick enough. Besides, you've got a book to promote."

Something about my dad's demeanor made me feel indignant. It seemed oddly familiar. He didn't want me to be a teacher, either. Each time he challenged me, I became more defiant. Sort of an "I'll show you" attitude. Even though I had no political aspirations, I certainly didn't like being told I couldn't do something. But I had too much on my mind to challenge my father.

Our book *The Freedom Writers Diary* was published the next day, and our local Barnes & Noble cohosted an event at our university theater. About a dozen Freedom Writers read passages to a teary-eyed audience of several hundred supporters. To all of our surprise, the book had not been censored. It was raw, gritty, and peppered with profanity. Shockingly, Doubleday left the "f" word in—fourteen times, to be exact.

We celebrated at a local greasy spoon diner until 3 A.M., then I had to head to the airport to catch a 5 A.M. flight. I had won the Teacher of the Year Award from the California Credential Analysts and Counselors Association and was to receive the award in Sacramento first thing in the morning.

I was asked to give a speech to six hundred people. I'd never taken a speech class in college, so I had to wing it. After I received the award, I was totally overcome with emotion. I began to tell the story about meeting Miep Gies and going to Anne Frank's attic on August 4, and then I stopped. I felt like I was going to fall apart. Maybe it was because I hadn't slept the night before. Maybe it was because I was nervous. Or maybe it was because I was finally being validated by people in my own profession.

When I was finished with my speech, I got a standing ovation. I was overwhelmed. I was just excited that I hadn't made a fool out of myself.

I was escorted to the book line, and I was even more nervous looking at how many people wanted to get their book signed by me. I was still shaking from my speech, and I just hoped nobody noticed I was sweating. Trying to gain my composure, I pulled out a purple pen from my purse and tried to think of what to write. I wanted to write something special for every single person. After a few minutes, the Barnes & Noble manager said, "Erin, there are probably six hundred people in line, and at the rate you're going, they'll be here until Saturday. Can't you simply sign your name, or we'll never get out of here."

I learned how to sign more quickly, but I never wanted to lose that connection. I remember what it felt like to have my book signed by Zlata and by Miep. I never wanted to make it feel like an assembly line.

But soon the days became an assembly line. There were morning shows, radio shows, bookstores, and town halls. Each time I got in front of a group of people with my students, I wanted to set them up to hit it out of the park. I caught myself crying at each venue, while marveling at the Freedom Writers' self-confidence, poise, and determination to share their story.

A few days into the tour, I got a call from Congressman Dick Gephardt. When I called him back, I didn't know how to address him.

"Call me Dick."

He was like a father figure to Patrick Kennedy and had heard Patrick wax poetically about a teacher in Long Beach. Dick had noticed that I would be in Washington, D.C., on the book tour and wondered if I would be willing to address members of Congress about the state of affairs in education.

"I would be honored, but can I bring my students with me? We're doing the book tour together, and it really is their story."

"Absolutely!"

In retrospect, I should have taken his offer more seriously, but I was functioning on such little sleep that it didn't hit me until 4 P.M. on the day that Sonia, Maria, Henry, and I were supposed to present to Congress. We had just flown in from a whirlwind trip to New York and had only had about three hours of sleep the night before. My voice was raspy and we were looking a little disheveled when our sponsor asked if we'd like to go get freshened up.

"You have about ten minutes."

We rushed upstairs, and I quickly went for my red power suit. I ripped my last pair of nylons as I was pulling them on.

"Sonia, do you have any clear nail polish so I can fix the run in my stockings?"

"Sure, let me put it on the spot." She dabbed it on, but it clung more to my leg than to the nylons.

I put on my skirt, and somehow it seemed much shorter than when I had bought it.

"Sonia, do I look like Ally McBeal?" I asked her.

"Um, no, not really," she lied. She knew we only had three minutes left.

We rushed to the car, still putting on our makeup, when Henry asked from the front seat, "What are we supposed to talk about when we get to Congress?"

At our previous book appearances, we had been like a jazz ensemble. We finished each other's sentences, we set one another up with clever anecdotes, and we rescued one another from flailing. I told Sonia she should talk about Auschwitz, Henry about Sarajevo, and Maria about Anne Frank. Those topics were code words for weaving a personal story around our destinations, but they all seemed to get it. "And I'll bat cleanup," I said.

When we got to the Congressional Office Building, it was surreal. We had been there years earlier when the Freedom Writers visited Washington in high school, but now we were being whisked upstairs by Secret Service. We had badges and looked so official. We were led into Dick Gephardt's office and told he would be coming shortly with a surprise. I looked down and could see that the run in my nylons was slowly creeping toward my knee. I fidgeted with my skirt and knew it was too short, and I wondered why I hadn't worn pants. Henry looked shell-shocked, Sonia looked anxious, and Maria seemed cool as a cucumber. I felt like my bladder was going to explode.

When Dick Gephardt walked in, he looked more like one of my dad's golf buddies than one of the most important men in America. He gave each one of us a hug and told us that he had listened to us on NPR that afternoon. The disc jockey asked us if we'd ever met an original Freedom Rider before. We had not, we said, but their story had inspired us to stand up for our convictions. Mentioning the Freedom Riders gave us the opportunity to tell why our name was so meaningful. Dick said, "I have a surprise for you," and then he left the room momentarily, only to reenter with a distinguished gentleman. "May I introduce to you my colleague, Congressman John Lewis? He is an original Freedom Rider."

Sonia, Maria, and I burst into tears. I noticed Henry swallow and blink back a few tears too. I had seen his teenage face so many times, crossing that bridge in Selma or sitting on a bus during the Freedom Ride. His face was etched in my mind. Now, four decades later, he was a representative from Atlanta, Georgia.

I felt like we were meeting a rock star. We couldn't ask questions fast enough.

We were interrupted by a knock at the door and Dick's assistant saying, "It's time."

We walked down the hall, and Mr. Lewis grabbed my hand. "Don't be nervous. I'll be right here."

When we walked into the room, I noticed lots of faces from C-SPAN. I wished my brother was with me, since he was such a political junkie.

Dick put on the bootleg tape of our *Primetime Live* segment that I had given Patrick, and for a moment I worried that ABC would bust into the room right then and there and arrest me for showing the unauthorized copy. When the video was over, a lot of members of Congress were crying. Even Mr. Lewis. He winked, and with that, our jazz ensemble began to play.

When we were done, Maria announced that she would be the "first Latina Secretary of Education" and everyone let out a scream. They rose to their feet, they hugged us, and in the midst of everything, I felt a tug on my sleeve and I saw our escort for the book tour mouthing, "We have to go. We're late for the next event." We had to go clear across town to tape a segment for C-SPAN's Book TV and apparently a bomb threat was holding up crosstown traffic.

As we were leaving, Patrick came up to us and said, "Sorry, I missed it. How'd it go?"

"I don't know. I was so scared that I thought I was going to throw up."

"Judging by their reaction, I'm sure you did well."

Apparently, we did so well that the following day Dick Gephardt invited me to his office to run for Congress. I don't know if it was peer pressure, sleep deprivation, or sheer flattery, but I impulsively agreed.

CHAPTER 32

The prospect of running for Congress didn't sink in right away. I still had a few more weeks of travel ahead of me to promote the book, a taping of an *Oprah* segment that was slated to air on Martin Luther King's birthday, and a live appearance on Rosie O'Donnell's show.

Maria and I appeared on Rosie's show the first week of December, and by the time we went to commercial break, all three of us were wiping away tears. Rosie took Maria by the hand and thanked her for reminding her of why she did her show. When one of her producers told her that I had been approached to run for Congress, she agreed to support my candidacy.

True to her word, a couple days later, four days shy of the congressional filing deadline, Rosie in her opening monologue announced that "the teacher I had on my show a few days ago will be running for Congress." Rosie was so excited about my running that she even sent me my first campaign contribution. There was no turning back.

To officially kick off my campaign, I decided to do what I had always done—host an event at the Bruin Den, a site familiar to the Freedom Writers and me. Based on our history there, it seemed like a good symbolic location to commence my candidacy.

The Freedom Writers got to the Bruin Den early to help decorate. They began to make signs out of butcher paper, just like the ones from the past that welcomed Miep or like the ones that declared "Washington or Bust." Since I always encouraged my students' artistic ability, I never dictated how or what was put on a sign. But today, their artistic license would be challenged.

I had just hired a new campaign manager, who had moved to Long Beach from Washington, D.C., days earlier. My congressional district contained Long Beach and a few other surrounding cities. He watched disapprovingly as some of the Freedom Writers wrote slogans like "Vote for Ms. G." He intervened and things got a little messy. Suddenly, a stranger was barking orders at them to use more traditional slogans, like "Erin Gruwell Protects Social Security." Moments later, they were told that their signs "would scare the folks from D.C. because they looked like graffiti." Guillermo and our Picassos in training threw down the gauntlet. Even though he was bothered by having to include words like "Social Security" on his poster, he couldn't handle someone criticizing his handiwork. Maybe it was his tone, or the blond hair, or the fact that he insulted his artistic integrity, but Guillermo and his posse stormed out of the Bruin Den before I even got there, feeling "dissed" by Ms. G's "new handler."

Unfortunately, they would not be the only students disillusioned by politicos playing on their turf.

When I got to the Bruin Den, I found it hilarious that Freedom Writers were holding homemade signs supporting Social Security, especially since some of them didn't even have a Social Security card.

I was given a speech to read, but I decided to deviate and talk from the heart. Everyone in that room already knew me, and so to read them a bullet-point speech would have seemed disingenuous. I didn't want to come across robotic, so I simply talked about why I was running and how I needed everyone's help. As in the past, this was going to be a joint effort. It felt comforting to have all the usual suspects there—but I also noticed some of my boys conspicuously missing. It wasn't until much later that I learned that they had gotten their feelings hurt and did not want to be involved in a campaign that did not embrace them.

After my speech, we stood in a massive circle with plastic champagne glasses for a congressional toast. It felt more like a pep rally, and that we were all in this together. If we could win the Spirit of Anne Frank Award together and head off to New York City, why couldn't we all win an election together and head off to D.C.? I began to think of my campaign as a cause, and my students thought so too.

"This time we're not just writing a book, Ms. G, we're going to rewrite history," Darrius said.

After the kickoff was official, my brother volunteered to quit his job and help run my campaign. He had helped herd the cats in Europe, and now he would herd the lions.

We rented an office building above a doughnut shop down the street from Long Beach Community College, where a majority of the Freedom Writers attended. We thought it would be the perfect locale for volunteers to come and work around their school schedules. We rented all kinds of fancy office equipment and set up shop right before Christmas. Between the donut tab we'd established downstairs and the Internet access, my students started coming over to the congressional headquarters daily. They worked on their homework, talked about following in the footsteps of the Freedom Riders, and all the while rekindled the late nights we once shared in Room 203. They sustained themselves with donuts and lattes, and fully immersed themselves in Poli Sci 101.

I loved it, but unfortunately, my cranky campaign manager did not. He was used to sophisticated candidates who'd worked their way up from city council or state assembly, traditional campaigns with offices filled with men in dark suits and power ties, not kids wearing warm-up suits and tennis shoes.

Since I had no campaign history, I decided to seek the help of professionals. I wanted to be taken seriously, not patronized by the old boys' network. After all, there were only three months until the March 7 primary election. What I was doing was equivalent to spending the semester getting tutored and cramming for the final.

My first foray into politics came in eighth grade, when I decided to run for student body president of my middle school. My campaign manager was my friend Jessica, who convinced me to make campaign buttons in the shape of Ms. Pac Man. We spent hours at my kitchen table cutting up yellow construction paper and then gluing a red bow on them. Although Ms. Pac Man had nothing to do with politics, I figured embracing the latest pop phenomenon would help me win some votes. Besides Ms. Pac Man, I had no real slogan or campaign promises. On the day of the election, I coordinated my leg warmers with my laminated Ms. Pac Man button. Despite my cheesy campaign, I won.

Winning a middle school election triggered a few more campaigns and a few more silly slogans. I won a few and lost a few. While I was junior class president, I decided that I would run for student body president for my last hurrah in high school. I ended up losing to an anarchist sporting a Mohawk.

Even though my dad said, "Losing helps build character," I was still not convinced all these years later.

Ironically, I would be taking the anarchist's approach (sans the Mohawk) by running against professional politicians who had run (and lost) multiple elections. My competitors were disgruntled that I had decided to run "this late in the game." There were three of them, and with my name now on the ballot, they seemed united. Instead of taking their anger out on the opposing party, they streamlined their anger toward me.

Had I known it was going to get nasty, I would have never run. I'd learned my lesson from the anarchist. But I'd also been led to believe that the elected politicians in Washington were going to help "clear the field" for me. That was not the case. When each candidate received a call from a congressional member asking them to step down so I could run, they were indignant. What an insult—especially coming from the establishment. Being asked to step aside so I could run unopposed made them hunker down and prepare for a fight to the finish.

Instead of engaging in a fight, I decided to take the high road and try and win on my merit. But I soon discovered that politics is not always about merit.

I didn't know the jargon, I didn't know the rules, and I certainly didn't know how to raise money.

I quickly learned that running for office is about raising money. Lots and lots of money. I had no idea how to do that. Although I had raised money from people like John Tu in the past, I had always tried to make it a win-win scenario. A tax write-off, some publicity, or the opportunity to chaperone. With congressional money, there is no tax write-off or publicity. People give money because they believe in party politics.

I had never talked politics with people like John Tu—or anyone else, for that matter. I didn't even know where to start.

To help jump-start the process, some of the congressional fund-raisers from D.C. volunteered to come help train me on how to make a pitch. Although they were talented, many of them were only a couple years older than the Freedom Writers.

I was told that I should go through my Rolodex and call everyone I know. "You need to ask them for a thousand dollars."

"A thousand dollars? Are you serious?"

"Yes, that's how it's done. You're supposed to call them, ask for the money, and then bite your tongue while you wait for their response."

"I can't do that. Most of my friends don't have that kind of money. We're just starting out. Some are still in school, some are still paying off their student loans, and some just started making mortgage payments." I thought about my best friends from high school. They had gotten married and just started families. How could I pick up the phone and ask them for money when they were struggling to pay for child care? Even though they believed in me, I couldn't muster up the nerve to call them. "Some of my friends don't even know that I'm running."

"Then we'll start with those that do. We'll walk you through it."

But even after my training, I still couldn't do it.

I was told that I should go through my Rolodex and prioritize everyone in terms of income. High donors, middle donors, and low donors. What? They wanted me to classify my friends and family based on how much money they made. Most of my friends were worker bees like me—so putting a price tag on their heads went against everything I believed. "I can't do it. My friends don't have that kind of money," I said once again.

"Then let's practice on someone who will say yes."

The only person I knew who would say yes was my dad. Although he hadn't been very supportive of my decision to run, I knew he'd come through in a pinch. Besides, it was Christmastime, and that's usually when I hit him up for books, airline tickets, or one of my many other crazy schemes.

"Hi, Dad. I'm calling to see if you will contribute to my campaign."

"You're really going through with this? Erin, this is a really bad idea."

"Dad, can we not go through this again?" I whispered. I felt embarrassed because the big guns from Washington were eavesdropping. If this call was supposed to be a slam dunk, I was in for a very long game.

"Please? I need help getting started."

"Well, I'll give you five hundred bucks—but that's a stretch. We're in the middle of repaving our driveway, and we're way over budget."

Once I got him to commit, I was handed a scribbled note that said, "Ask him if he knows anyone else that would be interested in contributing to your campaign."

I winced. I already knew the answer. I'd been in this predicament before when I was a freshman in college. I saw a sign in the dorms that said, "You can make thousands in one week!" and when I called my dad to tell him I'd found a job to help pay for tuition, he said, "Be careful. Nothing's that easy." He was right. In order to make "thousands," I would have to schlep around the neighborhood like Willie Loman, demonstrating how a knife could cut a rope or how a pair of scissors could cut right through a penny. I started out with the homes where I used to babysit, since I was always roped into buying Girl Scout cookies from their kids. Most of them bought only a paring knife, and that was because they felt sorry for me. When I realized that I wasn't good at shaking down my dad's friends and I wasn't making "thousands" as a traveling salesman, I decided to bag groceries for the rest of the summer instead.

If I couldn't sell a set of knives, selling me would be a whole lot harder.

"Hey, Dad, do you know anyone who might be interested in helping my campaign?"

"I don't feel comfortable with you calling my friends. I really don't. I don't talk politics with them, and I don't want you to either. Besides, many of them are in the 'other' party."

The other party? I'd never thought of my friends, neighbors, or colleagues in terms of parties. Would I have to go through my address book and differentiate which party they were in? Party affiliation had never mattered before. The idea of identifying my friends along party lines was horrifying.

I decided to play it safe and call only people who had come to my kickoff. After my first day of fund-raising, I felt dirty, like I wanted to take a shower. I longed for a way out of this. I had left a lot of messages, spent some time catching up with old friends, and got an additional $25 dollars from my grandma. The folks from Washington were alarmed.

My brother sensed my fear and their frustration, and offered to host a fund-raiser at the law firm where he interned. Maybe calling strangers would be a lot less daunting than calling someone I had played soccer with in seventh grade.

As it turned out, the fund-raisers I hosted were much easier than picking up the phone and harassing my friends. I had no problems standing in front of a room full of strangers describing why I wanted to run. As long as I didn't have to ask them for money over the telephone, throwing small fund-raising parties seemed to be a temporary fix to my woes.

To help do things a bit differently, I solicited a congressional support team that was shamelessly idealistic. I recruited folks from presidential campaigns or other congressional races. Some worked in law firms, had just graduated from college, and some were tried-and-true union folks. Throughout the years, though, "politics as usual" had left them feeling disillusioned. Maybe my campaign could rekindle their passion.

But the more new people came in, the more the Freedom Writers were pushed out. Suddenly, they had to set up an appointment to talk to me while I was sequestered behind a closed office door. To get them out of the office, they were asked to go door-to-door with campaign literature. Even the donut tab was cut off without my knowledge.

A month into the campaign, we were supposed to be on *Oprah*. We had taped a five-minute segment in the early fall, but the producers had decided to show it on Martin Luther King's birthday as part of a compilation of stories that honored his memory. A few days before it was to air, I got a call from one of *Oprah*'s producers saying that she had received a nasty call from one of my opponents threatening to "sue Oprah" if she aired our piece. Since Oprah had just gotten out of a legal battle in Texas over a comment she had made about cows, her legal department didn't want to take any chances. They were going to pull our piece.

When I got off the phone, I was surrounded by several Freedom Writers. Our *Oprah* segment had absolutely nothing to do with my campaign. The piece was all about the Freedom Writers and our recent trip to Europe. But when one of my opponents overheard the Freedom Writers talking about being on her show, they got nervous that it gave me an unfair advantage with housewives and college students. They called Oprah's producers and claimed that they wanted equal airtime on her show.

"Can't we fight it?" one of my students asked. "We've already told every-one to watch it."

"I don't know. The producer said they didn't want to take any chances."

"Why are they doing this to us? I thought we were supposed to be the good guys?" Darrius said.

I knew that Darrius was referring to a comment that my brother had made in an attempt to convince the Freedom Writers to get involved in my election. When Darrius asked, "How do we know if we're a Democrat or a Republican?" Chris answered, "Because we're the good guys." Darrius then went on to ask, "But isn't that stereotyping? Ms. G always taught us not to stereotype."

"You're right, Darrius. We shouldn't stereotype. You can be whatever you want, honey," I reassured him.

But being "whatever you want" didn't mean that we had to become something we weren't. Although I was devastated by the *Oprah* loss, I didn't want to fight back. "We are the good guys, Darrius, and we'll just have to take this one for the team. We'll be on her show one of these days."

Even though I felt like I'd been sucker-punched, I didn't want the Freedom Writers to know how devastated I was. I didn't want them to know how scared I was, how insecure I was feeling, and how I had begun questioning my decision to run.

Just like the first few months with my students, I thought "what doesn't kill me will make me stronger." But I wasn't feeling strong. I wasn't used to reading negative editorials about me in print or being called nasty names in public.

"Ms. G, what's a carpetbagger?" a Freedom Writer asked one day.

"They use that term in politics to refer to someone who moves into a community to run for office."

"Why are they calling you that?"

"Well, I wasn't born and raised here, like some of the other candidates, so I guess it's a way of criticizing me."

"Why don't you fight back? Why don't you tell the papers all the negative stuff we know about your opponents?"

"I don't want to stoop to their level. I don't want to put out negative ads, or attack people's characters, or even dissect their past. I don't want to become something I'm not in order to win. I'd rather lose with my dignity intact than win by selling out."

"But they keep taking potshots at you. You gotta fight back, Ms. G."

"Didn't we learn anything from the Freedom Riders? They were attacked by vicious German shepherds, their bus was bombed, and the Klan stood waiting for them at every bus stop—but they never fought back. I guess I want to emulate them."

"But if you don't fight back, Ms. G, you may lose."

I had never contemplated losing before. Not really. I guess I assumed that up until now, most things that I had gone out on a limb for had come to fruition. I wondered what it would be like to lose—and to do so in such a public arena.

I didn't want to lose. I would simply try harder. I'd try to empower my team to believe that we were all running. We would canvass more streets and knock on more doors. We would register people to vote who had never voted before, we'd participate in parades, and we'd cover the city's landscape with positive signs.

Our new work ethic seemed to do the trick. We got endorsed by the party and by the papers, and we were doing well in the polls. We had a slew of volunteers on the streets, and we were heading into the last stages of the election leading in the polls.

The week before the election, the enthusiasm was contagious. I looked around our headquarters, which was littered with handouts, signs, and pizza boxes. I loved the camaraderie that came from seasoned pundits who were helping us create campaign literature and the "donut boys" we'd hired from downstairs to plaster our city with signs. Freedom Writers were on the phone speaking in Spanish, Khmer, and English, encouraging callers to get out to the polls. The Dream Team Moms had brought over baked goods, Mel Mermelstein was talking to folks from his synagogue, and even the folks from Washington were getting swept up in the magic.

"This is what democracy is supposed to look like," said a formidable fundraiser who'd been sent to help me. Even though I hadn't mastered the art of fund-raising, I had managed to excite my constituents.

"I think we have it in the bag," one of the Freedom Writers said.

"I sure hope so!"

I came into the office early the day before the election, and everyone looked pale. Something bad had happened, and they were trying to push me out the door.

"Stop handling me! What is going on?"

"One of your opponents paid for a phone ad that attacks you pretty bad."

My stomach sank. "How bad?"

"It's pretty ugly."

Apparently, one of my opponents took out a mortgage on their home to personally attack me. They had an old woman claim that her husband worked at Wilson with me and that I was a "terrible teacher" and that I used my students. The woman feigned tears at the end of her message and begged the listener to vote for "anyone but Erin Gruwell."

After listening to the message, I was paralyzed. A terrible teacher? Using my kids? Teaching my students was the only thing I have ever felt confident in. I wanted to tell everyone who received that message that I worked three jobs to pay for field trips, or that the money I got in the divorce settlement went toward school supplies, or that all the proceeds from the book were going to pay for the students' scholarships. How could I defend myself against such horrible accusations? I blew off the comments about my being too young, or too inexperienced, or sleeping with everyone in Washington. But attacking my profession and my relationship with my students was more painful than anything I'd ever experienced.

"Is it legal?" I asked, fighting back tears.

"Ah, it's shady. You see, with some of this new technology, the laws haven't quite caught up yet. Technically, if you attack somebody in print, the material has to contain the name of the organization that paid for it. It's dirty—really dirty."

"But how does it work? Who gets this message?"

"The machine is programmed to begin once an answering machine goes on. If a person were to actually pick up the telephone, the machine hangs up. It targets folks who are at work. So this message may be on thousands of answering machines across the district."

"We've got to fight back, Erin. The election is tomorrow," my brother said.

"Is there any way that we can do something similar but leave a positive message?"

"Polls show that negative ads are much more effective. They leave a lasting impression."

Someone suggested we go negative and another suggested that we should do something as long as it couldn't be traced back to me.

"You know—plausible deniability," someone in the room said.

"No, that's not ethical. I refuse to go negative. It may be political suicide, but I'd rather fight fair."

So they decided to take a chance, do a positive message, and max out my personal credit cards to pay for it in the process.

In a last-ditch effort, we decided to go on a motorcade throughout the district in hopes that our signs, enthusiastic Freedom Writers, and our cause would bring us victory.

While we were driving, Ryan Seacrest was on the L.A. radio station Star 98.7 talking about the importance of voting. One of my students called in to the station and then handed me the telephone. We were on the air live.

"You sound so young," Seacrest said.

"I am. I think I'm the youngest woman in America running for Congress."

"Really? Wow, are you hot?"

And with that question, I could see my campaign manager having apoplexy. But then I realized that he read the *Wall Street Journal* and listened to National Public Radio and he would not be caught dead listening to a Top 40 radio station the day of the election. I quickly changed the subject, threw in a few plugs about getting people out to vote and trying to change history. Ryan wished me luck and invited me to come on his show after I won the election.

When I got back to the office, our headquarters was abuzz. Someone from George Stephanopoulos's office had called, as had some of the major talk shows to set up an interview. Apparently, they thought I was going to win.

And for a brief moment, so did I.

But I didn't.

CHAPTER 33

When I lost by a slim margin, about six hundred votes, Sonia said, "Maybe you can contest it?"

But I didn't want to contest it. I didn't want to do anything. I was done.

Losing the election was psychologically devastating. It seemed like everyone I knew had a vested interest in my winning, and thus had a theory about what went wrong: "If only you'd started earlier" or "You should have been more aggressive." All the unsolicited opinions from my friends and family were bad enough, but when strangers began to weigh in, it was unbearable. I began to feel like a conspicuous "loser" everywhere I went. If I signed a check at the grocery store, the checker would say, "Too bad you lost." In the middle of my class, one of my students would say, "If only you'd won the election, you could have helped fix public education." I made myself miserable processing all the "what if"s and "should have"s.

The hardest part was shutting down the campaign office. One day, there were dozens of employees and volunteers, and the next, the office was empty. People I had employed no longer had jobs, Freedom Writer volunteers were displaced, and I was severely in debt.

Luckily, everyone who worked on my campaign was resilient. Since my staff was composed of type A overachievers, they were able to bounce back on their feet immediately. My campaign manager headed east to work on another campaign, another campaign staffer was snatched up by Al Gore, another went to graduate school in Cambridge, another fled to France to work in a law firm, my brother moved to San Francisco to work for the mayor, and I was left in Long Beach—alone.

Everyone who'd parachuted in for my campaign was gone, and I felt very vulnerable. Abandoned, really. While I wanted everyone to carry on with their lives, I also needed someone to help me pick up the pieces. But my pride got in the way. I had gotten all of us into this mess, and I was too ashamed to ask for help on how to get out of it.

While I was mourning my loss, a tragic incident happened to one of the Freedom Writers that made my sulking insignificant. Tony was beaten by four men and left for dead. While I was running, Tony was the poster child for Freedom Writer success. My old boss at National University was so impressed with the Freedom Writers while I was working there that he offered four of them jobs. Tony was such a conscientious worker that he was soon promoted to facilities manager. He made enough money to buy an old Camaro, subsidize his tuition at Orange Coast Community College, and help support his family. One evening, as he was jogging after a long day at school and work, four hoodlums brutally attacked him with baseball bats and a metal baton.

Hours later, the police discovered him lying in a pool of his own blood. Initially, they thought it had been another homicide. They shone a flashlight on him and nudged him with their nightsticks. When he was asked a question, he couldn't speak. His jaw had been severely dislocated and was hanging several inches lower than it should have. The paramedics took him to a local hospital, but when they discovered that he didn't have health insurance, they took him to another hospital to wire his jaw together. His face would have to be held together by a metal plate and several screws. The recovery was so difficult that he lost his job, his car was repossessed, and he had to drop out of school. Although he was desolate, he said to me, "Ms. G, what doesn't kill you will make you stronger."

It humbled me. I felt horrible for feeling like a martyr in light of Tony's circumstances. His fortitude was the impetus for me to go forward after my congressional loss.

The most pressing order of business was getting out of debt. The positive telephone message I ran on the day of the election to rebut the insidious attack on my character cost $20,000. I had no idea how I was going to pay a credit card that was half of my annual income.

When I called Patrick Kennedy for advice, he rather matter-of-factly said, "You should run again."

"Run again? Are you insane?"

"Everyone loses once. Clinton lost his first congressional bid, and so did George W. Bush. It comes with the territory."

But running again meant I could lose again. For sheer self-preservation, there had to be a better way.

I found one by happenstance. As it turned out, college professors were starting to use *The Freedom Writers Diary* in their courses. The first one to contact me was an education professor named Dr. Chuck Zartman from California State University, Chico. He called and asked if I would be willing to fly to his university and present to the College of Education. They would pay me a small honorarium. An honorarium? I never expected that someone would pay me to talk about the Freedom Writers. I talked about them all day for free. I figured I could use the honorarium to make the minimum payment on my credit card and keep the bill collectors at bay—for now, at least.

I took Maria with me for moral support.

Hearing Dr. Zartman read a passage from our book to a packed audience was surreal. He chose a diary entry about homelessness, and when he got to the end of the passage, he choked up.

I whispered to Maria, "I can't believe this."

"Neither can I."

The lights in the auditorium went off and he pressed the play button of the projector. Projected on the big screen was our *Primetime Live* segment. I wasn't used to seeing myself magnified like that. I noticed every wrinkle, every flaw. As I sat there scrutinizing my hair, I heard sniffles. The audience couldn't care less about my flaws. They were emotional, caught up in the storyline. When Maria and I walked onto the stage following the video, people gasped. It was as if we'd come to life right before their eyes. We started to share our story with them and found ourselves swept away by emotion.

Telling our story to different audiences seemed to sustain me, both financially and emotionally. Earning an honorarium was psychologically easier than dialing for dollars. The audience didn't care what my political affiliation was or what my views were on tort reform. There was no spin, no cynicism.

Our story had a way of moving different kinds of people for different reasons. One such person was the producer from our original *Oprah* segment. She had held on to our clip for nearly a year, and once the dust had settled from the election, she decided to air the segment in 2001 and asked us to join Oprah for a few minutes onstage. Our segment was a compilation of the Freedom Writers and me in high school, in Europe, and in college. The producer planned for me and two students to appear on Oprah's Martin Luther King Jr. special that showcased individuals who were living Dr. King's dream.

Using the interviews they had taped months earlier, Oprah's producer picked Henry and another Freedom Writer, Tiffony, to join me on the show. They flew us to Chicago and taped the segment a few days before Thanksgiving. The show was set to air on Monday of the Martin Luther King holiday weekend. My landlady, Sandy, was used to entertaining Freedom Writers by now, so she invited them over to watch the show in her living room.

Tiffony and I were nervous about how we'd appear on TV. The makeup artist flat-ironed our hair and put on more makeup than either of us was used to wearing.

When our segment came on, some of the Freedom Writers began to giggle. "You look petrified, Ms. G." And I did. I was clearly uncomfortable, and not ready for my close-up.

Regardless of my pained expression, Henry and Tiffony came across brilliantly; they even used words like "metamorphosis," from our days in the classroom playing vocabulary games such as Froot Loop Bingo. Watching them watch themselves on TV made me so proud. I saw my surrogate children blossom before my very eyes.

After watching the show and spending an afternoon with the Freedom Writers, I was glad that my days dabbling in politics were in the past. Or were they?

Being on the *Oprah* show must have sounded sexy, because it prompted pundits from my political past to reemerge. Without actually watching the show (and seeing me look like a deer in headlights), some politicos suggested that I throw my hat back in the ring. Since there is a congressional election every two years, why not run again? But my battle scars were still fresh and my support team was gone. I decided that I would continue teaching and give an occasional speech when asked.

A lot more people began to ask. And surprisingly, it wasn't just teachers. Kids. Parents. And soon, businessmen.

I got a call from an organization called the Million-Dollar Roundtable to be a keynote speaker at their international insurance meeting. Someone had told the conference committee that I had a unique message.

"How long have you been a professional speaker?" the director of communications asked me.

I wanted to laugh into the phone. I wasn't a professional speaker. I spoke to classes, student groups, and the occasional book club. He said they were interested in having me try out for their annual conference and wanted to know if I could send him a copy of my speech.

"Um, I don't have a speech."

"What do you mean you don't have a speech?"

"I've never written one. I try to understand the audience and then I tell a story that is relevant to them."

"Can you speak to businessmen?"

"I usually talk to kids or teachers. But I'd be willing to give it a try."

The committee flew me to Chicago to try out. While I was in the waiting room, I was really intimidated. There were several men in business suits who were motivational speakers "on the circuit." They each had their own shtick, and cool electrical equipment. I had no gadgets, and I felt like I was crashing someone's party. At any moment, the committee was going to discover that I was not a "professional" and get upset for wasting their money on my airline ticket.

When I walked into the room, it reminded me of the movie *Flashdance,* where Jennifer Beals, in her ripped sweatshirt and leg warmers, had to dance before a stodgy panel of elitists. There were a dozen white men seated at a long table before me. I was supposed to stand at the podium while they rated my performance. The podium scared me. I'd never used one before. I asked if I could stand in front of it.

"What about your notes?"

"Oh, I don't have any notes."

I could tell they were a little apprehensive.

I stepped in front of the podium and began to tell a story. I talked about my students and tried to weave in lessons about life, then found myself crying. When I was finished, there was a pregnant pause. A gray-haired man with wire-rimmed glasses took them off and dabbed his eyes with his handkerchief. The panel politely applauded and asked me to go to the waiting room while they discussed my performance.

At that moment, I wondered why I hadn't prepared a speech before I came, or even scribbled some notes while I was on the four-hour flight. Maybe they were insulted that I hadn't used more insurance terms in my speech, or maybe crying was completely inappropriate for this kind of crowd.

When they called me back into the room, I expected them to tell me that my message was not appropriate for the business world. The gentleman with the glasses started by saying, "Do you think you could deliver that exact speech again?"

"I hope so." Since I hadn't written it down and it wasn't taped, it was a long shot.

"Well, we'd like to ask you to speak on our opening night, following our loaded gun."

"Wow. That's an honor. Who is your loaded gun?"

"Rudy Giuliani."

I froze. How could I possibly follow someone like him? Without thinking it through, I asked, "May I bring a student with me?"

"Will your student be comfortable speaking in front of eight thousand people?"

Hell, I wasn't comfortable speaking in front of eight thousand people. But bringing a student would be my security blanket.

A few months went by, and I was still paying off my congressional debt through local speeches, when the insurance conference crept around. Henry and I were going to be flown to Nashville, Tennessee, and stay at the famous Opryland Hotel.

When we arrived, we were whisked off to rehearsal. I'd never rehearsed a speech before. We were escorted into a convention center and immediately saw eight thousand empty chairs, a dozen big screens, and a stage that rivaled that of the Academy Awards. The same men I had met in Chicago were seated in the front row.

"Do you have your speech for the TelePrompTer?" a man asked me. He was wearing a headset microphone.

"No. I don't need a TelePrompTer."

"Oh, so you've memorized it? Great. Well, we'll just set up the timer."

I didn't have the heart to tell the soundman that I hadn't memorized anything and that I was about to speak extemporaneously in front of eight thousand people. But I got up on the stage and floundered. Just like the time I was in the Doubleday office, I started to talk too fast. I could see the fear in their eyes. In a few short hours, there would be eight thousand bodies, predominantly men, filling these seats, and I was clearly not a "professional."

I got off the stage and said to the men seated in the front row, "I'm going to my room to practice." But I could see in their eyes that the seeds of doubt had already been planted. They were convinced that I was an amateur and that I was now a liability.

As I turned to leave, I said, "I promise I won't embarrass you."

CHAPTER 34

W hile I was in my hotel room, I paced and jotted words on a piece of hotel stationery. I was terrified of letting them down.

When the show started, it was like a Hollywood awards show. The MCs were wearing tuxes. There was music and a laser light show. I felt like an impostor. I didn't belong there.

As I was waiting backstage, Rudy Giuliani emerged with a huge entourage. He signed a few NYPD hats and a couple coffee-table books commemorating 9/11. Then he offered to take a picture with Henry and me. As he put his arm around me, I hoped that he couldn't feel the sweat on my back. With a frozen smile, he asked who we were.

"We're the speakers following you, Mr. Giuliani. You're a hard act to follow."

"Nah. Just think of me as the warm-up act."

And with that, he heard his name announced by the loudspeakers and he walked onto the stage in front of eight thousand cheering fans. At that moment, I wanted to tell the director of the show to pull the curtains closed after Mr. Giuliani finished and dismiss everyone for the evening.

Since there was no way to get ahold of the soundman, I turned to Henry and said, "Let's just go out there and make them cry."

And cry they did. Almost all eight thousand of them. After a roaring standing ovation, hundreds of insurance salesmen rushed the stage and asked to take my picture. "Teacher! Teacher!" I heard as they clicked their cameras.

"It's like Beatlemania," Henry said as businessmen were pulling at his coat sleeve and asking him to sign their program.

Our escort from the event frantically led Henry and me through the throngs of people. He was a large man from South Africa. He prophesied that our future would look different based solely on this single event. "Oh my goodness," he said, "if you could see what I see, you'd shit."

Because he had such a beautiful South African accent, it made the word "shit" sound more poetic. It reminded me of Freedom Writers trying to learn four-letter words in Polish, Dutch, and Serbo-Croatian.

"I just started speaking to get out of debt," I said.

"Well, that's about to change."

And he was right. The response from the event was overwhelming. Suddenly, I found myself speaking at venues all over the country. I began to follow folks like Barbara Bush and Archbishop Desmond Tutu.

I spoke about anecdotes that moved me and hoped that my stories would resonate with others. Although speaking to an audience was oddly liberating, I still found myself terrified before each event. Especially at small venues.

Up-close-and-personal presentations always reminded me of how I felt those first few days at Wilson High. Would people roll their eyes or yawn the way my students used to? At least at bigger events, a stage provided some distance, and people didn't have to see my leg shake or my lips quiver. So agreeing to speak in the living room of a successful businessman, Ric Kayne, made me more anxious than walking onto a lit stage.

I arrived at Mr. Kayne's house especially early, and he was surprised to see me before the waitstaff had even arrived. Since the event was being sponsored by his wife, he was attempting to escape to the golf course before all her girlfriends congregated in their living room.

"You were inches from a clean getaway, weren't you?" I said.

"You betcha," Ric replied.

"Why don't you stay?" I asked.

"I'm not into all of my wife's touchy-feely causes. Besides, I've got to practice for the Bob Hope Golf Classic."

His demeanor reminded me of my dad. Even though he was a bit gruff, I could sense that he was a lovable curmudgeon. Getting him to stay would be a big challenge, but I knew it would dramatically improve my speech. He was like the tough kid in the corner I always gravitated toward and wanted to win over. After much cajoling, he agreed to stay. As with the Giuliani presentation, I pulled out all the stops, and I was surprised that he was noticeably moved.

The next day, I got a phone call from his office. He wanted to set up a meeting. Unlike John Tu, who sat in a cubicle in the middle of all of his employees, Ric Kayne had a fancy corner office in a high-rise. As I walked down the hallway past money managers who all probably had MBAs, I felt increasingly anxious.

I sat in Mr. Kayne's office, noticing all his golf trophies, the replica of his private airplane, and the glamorous shots of his family, and felt really out of place. What could he possibly want from me? It reminded me of my meeting with Dick Gephardt and the boys on Capitol Hill. Without being prompted, I told Mr. Kayne that I had recently gotten some calls to make another congressional bid and I was actually contemplating it.

"You're not a politician," he said, sounding like my dad. "Besides, you will turn off half of the people before you even open your mouth."

I knew he was right, but I didn't want him to think I was a pushover. "But maybe an honest politician is what people crave!" To some, "honest politician" may seem like an oxymoron, but I still wanted to believe that the system was not completely tainted. I really didn't want to be patronized by political cronies again, but I also didn't want a stranger deciding my destiny.

"I was really impressed by what you did with those kids," he continued. "I was wondering if you could replicate your model on a national level."

I had thought about ways to spread the Freedom Writers story, especially after teachers asked me for advice in other states. I desperately wanted to give both teachers and students our blueprint, but I didn't have a vehicle to do so. I had practiced my techniques on my college students and they seemed to be working, but I was so overwhelmed after the election that I was just trying to keep from drowning.

"If you can replicate your 'secret sauce,' then I'd like to help you," he said.

Mr. Kayne was a venture capitalist and had apparently backed several start-up companies. He bailed businesses out of bankruptcy and helped people manage billion-dollar portfolios. It seemed odd to me that a man of his accomplishments would want to create a nonprofit organization that would help disseminate my teaching methods. He told me that he'd had learning disabilities as a child and always sympathized with children who didn't receive the help that he did, and that's why he wanted to help me bottle my secret sauce.

Although we talked in generalities about what the ingredients of this "secret sauce" were, I knew that if I was going to come up with a recipe, I couldn't do it alone. I'd have to run my business the way I ran my classroom—by empowering others. I'd have to gather up the Freedom Writers, and together maybe we could figure out what went into the sauce.

After several meetings with Mr. Kayne, he encouraged me to create a strategic plan. Since a strategic plan is nothing like a lesson plan, I asked a friend of mine who worked at a think tank, the Rand Corporation, to help me. We spent hours creating charts and graphs, but after I presented our plan to Ric, he looked disappointed. He didn't get it.

Although I was discouraged, I didn't want to give up. He was tough and sort of reminded me of Sharaud. I knew if I was going to reach him, I would have to do what I did with my students. With Sharaud, I had to become a rap aficionado and juxtapose Snoop to Shakespeare. If I was going to make any kind of headway with Mr. Kayne, I'd have to tap into his passion: golf. Although I knew little about birdies and mulligans, I figured my dad could give me a crash course.

After watching *Caddyshack* with my dad and channel-surfing through different PGA tournaments, I decided to throw out my strategic plan and make a goofy golf magazine. For my presentation, I would assume the identity of Tiger Woods and Mr. Kayne would be Nike.

Rather than creating a bland document with a bunch of numbers and statistics, my golf magazine would weave in education in the form of golf. I Photoshopped my head onto a female golfer wearing plaid pants for the cover, and the feature story was about the Kayne Classic. Since a golf course has eighteen holes, I included a PGA course where each hole represented one year in a child's education. I extended the education to include pre-K through college. I had letters to the editor, tips on how to shoot par, and even a phony picture of Ric hosting the Kayne Classic.

Just as I had with the Freedom Writers, I used props and dressed up in costume. I went to a thrift store and bought a green sports coat to look like

I'd won the Masters, and I asked a girlfriend to come with me as my caddy. We brought in a golf bag, tees, and everything else I could raid from my dad's garage.

I thought I was going to present my idea solely to him, but when I got to his office, he said, "I invited a friend to listen to your strategic plan."

I felt silly wearing a Nike golf hat and a green sports coat from a thrift store, rather than the usual suit I would wear to make a pitch, but I decided to dive into my presentation and stay in character. At the end of my presentation, Ric simply said, "You're a lunatic."

"I know. I did cornier stuff than this with my students. But do you 'get it' now?"

"So you are the Tiger Woods of teachers and you want me to be your Nike sponsor?"

"Yes! You got it!"

"Okay, what do you need, Tiger?"

I told him that I wanted to gather up some of the Freedom Writers to help me identify the ingredients of our "secret sauce." Under the auspices of a nonprofit, the Freedom Writers would become scholarship recipients instead of employees, and thus be my students again. Room 203 would be re-created at the university, and each student who participated could get college credit. While I was creating my golf magazine, I approached the president of my university, CSULB, Dr. Maxson, to see if I could create a Freedom Writer cohort on our campus. He thought it was a brilliant idea. If Mr. Kayne could provide their college tuition, then I could teach them the courses I had previously taught in the English Department and the College of Education.

Although Ric told me he'd sponsor about a dozen Freedom Writers, two dozen signed on. I decided that even if I had to personally subsidize their tuition, I didn't want to turn anyone away. With a range of students—from Sharaud, who had already earned his bachelor's degree, to Tony, who had just a few units at the community college—we would come together again just like we had years ago.

I enticed a friend to co-teach with me. I forewarned him that with the Freedom Writers, there were a lot of issues under the surface and before we could replicate Room 203, we might have to rehash some of the issues they'd been harboring.

We soon discovered that many of the Freedom Writers had floundered without the support of one another. Some had felt abandoned, while others felt like they'd failed. For many of them, it was difficult to make it in college without financial or emotional support from their families.

To make the cohort work, we would have to become a "family" all over again. We had always joked about being a pretty functional dysfunctional family, but since my congressional campaign had ended, the familial bond had seemed to dissipate. I was so consumed with my own dilemmas that I hadn't been there for the Freedom Writers. Now I would have to prove once again that I could be there for the Freedom Writers, and they'd have to help one another in college in the same way they had helped one another in high school.

Once I identified the first ingredient—family—the second was easy. I needed to create an environment that felt like a home in the same way Room 203 felt. We needed a place that could foster their creativity and make them feel safe. When my next-door neighbor in Long Beach decided to rent her home, it was serendipity. All the Freedom Writers loved this historic street, and the house was big enough for studying, collaborating, and even an occasional fund-raiser event. I approached her and told her I needed to find an environment that resembled a home. She said if I could get a cosigner for the lease, we'd have a deal. Ric agreed to cosign, and a portion of the rent would come from his financial commitment. With our second ingredient secured, it was time to work on the third—a purpose.

Our purpose was simple: to help other teachers become advocates for their struggling students. Once we identified all the factors of at-risk youth, we could come up with all the elements that worked for the Freedom Writers. To replicate our model, I taught the Freedom Writers how to speak to students, juvenile hall inmates, and even teachers; I taught them how to mentor middle and high school kids and how to motivate others to make a change in their community and follow in their footsteps.

After the first semester, I went back to the president of the university to see if we could extend this experiment into a full-fledged bachelor's degree program. For Freedom Writers who already had a BA, maybe they could get a master's. The president loved the idea, but I was forced to realize that Ric hadn't given me enough seed money to fund all the students, let alone their college degrees. We were able to use the royalties from *The Freedom Writers Diary* to help give Freedom Writers scholarships in the past, but this was going to be a much larger commitment than anticipated.

We had a place, a purpose, and now we needed help. Lots of it. If we were going to make a difference, I would ask everyone to help us—by joining our staff, being on a board, volunteering their time, or donating their financial or intellectual capital. With the 501c(3) status approved, our courses in session, a sparsely decorated home filled with computers, and a mission, I decided we should host an event to get some additional funding.

I had never been fond of dialing for dollars, but I called Patrick Kennedy and said I needed a thousand dollars and "one evening of your time." I tried to make him feel guilty for making me run in the first place, and luckily, he took the bait. I realized his presence would be the perfect catalyst to pull all the pieces together. Patrick would be the impetus to gather everyone together again.

I looked at the party list of everyone whom I had invited to my campaign "victory" party. Everyone had been there eating, celebrating, and dancing when the poll results had come in. I had to muster up the courage to go before a room full of enthusiastic supporters and tell them, "I've lost"— without falling apart on the dance floor. Their excitement had turned to pity, and I hadn't seen many of them since. Inviting them to an educational event would hopefully galvanize the troops—from the people who'd helped me while I was a teacher to those who'd supported me as a candidate.

Almost everyone came—and as I looked around the room, I realized once again how unique my Rolodex was. It was not like the old boys' network I'd witnessed before in the halls of Congress, or a homogeneous group like the ones I'd spoken to on the speakers' circuit. It was a room full of Republicans and Democrats, teachers and ex-delinquents, rich and poor, and every color under the rainbow.

At the party, I overheard someone asking Sonia, whom I had hired to work for our foundation, to describe what our mission was. Her answer said it all.

"We're changing the world by changing education!"

CHAPTER 35

Y our *Primetime Live* special is being used to train prison guards! Can you
believe it?" Tracey Durning said over the phone. Tracey, the producer
of the piece, always felt a unique sense of pride when the segment made its
way into a new venue.

"I'm coming to New York—why don't we meet for coffee?" I suggested. It
had been a while since I'd seen her, and it was always fun to catch up. I suggested a cozy café in SoHo called The Cupping Room.

"Oh, that's great. Dan and I live up the block. Can he join us? We just got
engaged."

I had met Dan Levine briefly while Tracey was filming our ABC segment,
so I was excited to see him. Since the Spirit of Anne Frank Award, I had discovered a real passion for New York and often fantasized about escaping
there after I lost the election. I looked forward to visiting one of my favorite
haunts and telling Tracey about my latest triumphs and tragedies.

While we were drinking lattes from saucers the size of cereal bowls, her
fiancé Dan asked, "So have you found anyone to make your movie yet?"

"No. We're not really looking. The Freedom Writers and I wanted to make
a documentary, but we are having trouble finding funding." Making a movie
had never been a priority for us. The Freedom Writers were afraid that it
would become another made-for-TV drama about the "Great White Hope."

I told Dan that I had met a few self-absorbed movie executives but I always
wanted to take a shower afterward, to rinse off all the saccharine. Some were
too slick; others were shamelessly narcissistic.

Although Dan was a movie producer, he did not share those traits. He was genuine and unaffected. He had recently worked on a film that he said was similar to our story. It was about an underdog taking on the system. "It's called *Erin Brockovich*. Have you heard of it?"

I hadn't. Since the election, I'd cut out luxuries like movies and manicures.

Dan waxed on about how good the movie was. One of the screenwriters who worked on the project, Richard LaGravenese, was "a genius." Since Richard had a reputation for writing strong female characters, leading ladies like Julia Roberts clamored to be in his movies. Dan was meeting with Richard on Monday morning and wondered if he could give him a copy of Tracey's *Primetime Live* and our book. Although I was apprehensive, I agreed.

I didn't want to get my hopes up. I was still kind of fragile. Suddenly, I was transferring all of my congressional angst onto an imaginary movie. What if Dan has an ulterior motive? What if making a movie turns out to be as painful as running for Congress? Making a movie is a risk, and I didn't want to get manipulated or exploited. Like D.C., Hollywood operates under its own set of rules.

Shortly after I returned to Long Beach, Dan called me and said, "Richard loves your story! He wants to meet you! Can you come back to New York?"

Since I didn't have much money, my travel plans were contingent on speaking invitations. Dick Gephardt had invited me to do an educational presentation at the Library of Congress, so I thought I could fly to D.C. for Dick's event and then take the train to New York.

I was nervous about meeting Richard. I wanted to manage my expectations. Since so many people I'd met in positions of power were charismatic, I didn't want to lose myself to another persuasive personality. I did not want to be impulsive, as I'd been when I was wooed into running for office. I told myself to play hard-to-get.

When I walked into his office, I took one look at him and my heart melted. He was an unassuming writer, not a movie mogul. He immediately hugged me and said, "Gosh, I was so nervous about meeting you."

I let my guard down. "Me too." So much for playing hard-to-get.

We walked to a restaurant a few blocks from his office. It felt more like a blind date than a movie pitch. We were sizing each other up and wanted to see if all the wonderful things that Dan had said about us, respectively, were true. I felt comfortable with him immediately. We seemed to have an easy and natural rapport. We began to talk about moments in film that affected us—like the little girl in *Schindler's List,* and the scene in *Shawshank Redemption* where the old man plots a crime just so he can go back to prison.

Richard believed in moments like that—a moment when people pause, or feel compelled to get a cup of coffee after a film to dissect the scene. He didn't seem "Hollywood" to me. In fact, he was born and raised in Brooklyn and his father was a cabdriver. When he told me about how he struggled to write his first screenplay, *The Fisher King,* I felt comforted. My father loved that film.

"Wasn't that film nominated for an Oscar?"

"Yeah, but . . ." Richard quickly changed the topic. He was clearly uncomfortable talking about himself. "Erin, who would you like to play you?"

"Play me? Wow, I've never really thought about that before." I was still struggling to reconcile my different worlds, so I couldn't picture an actress waltzing in to portray me.

"I would really like someone gritty. Someone like Hilary Swank in *Boys Don't Cry.*"

Then I felt weird. I don't like talking about myself either. I deflect. I self-deprecate. I give others the credit. So I turned the conversation around and started talking about the kids. After all, it was their story.

I told him about the infamous note depicting Sharaud, I talked about meeting Miep Gies, about standing on the steps on the Lincoln Memorial, and about egging on my dad to dance in Poland. As I told him stories, his eyes welled up. I could only imagine what a screenwriter sees. At that moment, I felt like I could hand over my baby to him and it would be okay. His intentions seemed pure. And for the first time in a long while, I wanted to trust someone again.

"I would be honored to tell your story, Erin. And I will try my hardest to do it justice."

I felt his sincerity, and without hesitation I said, "I trust you."

After we hugged good-bye, I immediately called my dad. "Dad, I found somebody to make our movie. He's an amazing writer and he 'gets it.'"

"Is Robert Redford or Jack Nicholson going to play me?"

"Dad, this is not about you. I need you to listen."

And he did. Every day. I would call my dad to talk about minutia, to talk about my fears, or to talk about my newfound happiness. My heart wasn't so heavy anymore. But he was still leery. When I called to tell him about the pitch to the producers, he said, "Make sure you get a good lawyer, honey," and after the meeting with the studio executives, he said, "Protect yourself, sweetheart. Remember, at the end of the day, you're a commodity to them."

My father wasn't the only one bursting my bubble. My agent, Carol, told me not to "lose my head." Her husband, Marvin Levy, had been in the business for forty years, and she knew that movies take a long time to make. Paraphrasing a line from the movie *All About Eve,* Carol suggested that I "buckle up because it was going to be a bumpy ride."

With Richard driving the movie, though, I felt safe. But heeding Carol's warning, I would put on my seat belt for good measure.

After a studio agreed to produce the film, Richard headed to L.A. to meet with me. I suggested that he spend the day with the students and me in Long Beach. He thought it was a fabulous idea. He was so excited to meet the students he'd seen on the video and imagined when he read the *Freedom Writers Diary.*

I invited Maria, Sonia, Tiffony, and Henry to come with me. Before I picked them all up, I went to the car wash to clean my messy Four Runner. When I went to the ATM machine, I couldn't retrieve any cash. I picked up the giddy Freedom Writers and we drove to Richard's hotel in Beverly Hills. When we got to the hotel, I realized we'd have to valet-park my car. "This is kind of embarrassing, but do any of you have any money?" I asked. Between us, we had enough to pay the valet charge and tip the driver a couple bucks. "I promise I'll pay you back next week."

"No worries, Ms. G. We've got you covered."

We walked into the foyer of the Four Seasons and felt conspicuously out of place. Richard greeted us holding our book; it was tattered, dog-eared, and nearly every line was highlighted. He wanted to have a meeting in the dining area first, before we headed to "our 'hood." When the waitress handed us the menus, we all looked around nervously.

None of us had any money. We all ordered water. Richard said, "Come on, this is on the studio. Order whatever you want."

"Well, in that case, I'll have Belgium waffles with a cappuccino," Henry said comfortably.

After breakfast, Richard agreed to scout all the different neighborhoods in Long Beach to get a better sense of where everyone lived. As we were leaving Beverly Hills, he asked if he could stop and buy a tape recorder. He didn't want to miss a single word. He also scribbled in a notebook every time someone said something profound.

We started our tour by taking him to the Carmelitos housing projects, where many of the Freedom Writers lived. Then we went down alleys, past mini-marts and graffiti-strewn apartment complexes.

"This is one of the most notorious drug corners in Long Beach," Henry said. Richard wrote it down furiously.

"There's a liquor store on every corner," he continued. More notes.

As I was turning down a dilapidated street, I noticed a police car pull up behind me. With four people in the backseat, I knew I was breaking the law. I started to sweat. My first instinct was to ditch him. I turned down a street and he followed me, then another and another. Then I panicked. I parked the car and jumped out.

"Ms. G, what are you doing? He probably thinks you're trying to score some crack."

I ran to the cop car and, with a guilty conscience, said, "I'm a teacher and these are my students. I know I have too many people in my car, but I'll make them wear their seat belts."

The police officer looked at me like I was insane. While I was talking to the officer, I could see that my students were all turning in their seats wondering what we were talking about. Richard looked very uncomfortable.

The police officer said, "This neighborhood is really dangerous. I suggest you leave."

"Thank you, Officer."

When I got back in the car, Henry told me I shouldn't have jumped out of the car like that. "You could have got clocked, Ms. G."

The rest of the tour paled in comparison. But Richard did get to meet my dad. Luckily, my dad was on his best behavior. I suspected that he had "casting" on his mind.

At the end of the day, we felt a sense of collaboration. The process felt more symbiotic than parasitic. The Freedom Writers liked how he listened to them and validated where they came from.

The rest would be a waiting game. Richard sequestered himself in New York to write the screenplay. I didn't envy his task of taking ten years and turning it into two hours.

Months later, when it was time to share the screenplay, he came back to California and we met in the restaurant of the Peninsula Hotel in Beverly Hills. The way he held the screenplay reminded me of how my student Khari apprehensively held his letter to Spielberg, so afraid of being judged. Richard had that same vulnerability. He asked if he could simply read it to me. Since I'd never read a screenplay before, I was kind of relieved. He had barely made it through the first page before I began to cry.

I cried off and on during the entire two hours that it took for him to walk me through about 120 pages. When he finished, he got up to go to the restroom. He was emotionally exhausted. An older lady sitting at a table adjacent to me noticed I was crying, and she came over to offer me Kleenex. I think she thought I was going through settlement papers with my husband and he was raking me over the coals.

"Are you okay, young lady?"

"I'm fine. I'm just a little overwhelmed. But thank you for the tissue."

After the reading, Richard told me about all the actresses who wanted the role. Actresses whom I admired, whom I had watched on the red carpet, and whom I read about in *People* magazine. It was too surreal.

"It's a long process, but I promise we'll pick the right person in the end."

The screenplay went through several more drafts, actresses came and went, and so did some studios, but Richard remained constant. He was determined to get the film made—even if it took a decade. To honor his commitment, the producers asked him to direct the film. Now all he needed was a leading lady.

CHAPTER 36

I always felt like a trapeze artist performing without a net when I first stepped in front of an audience. As I clutched the handheld microphone, I just hoped that none of the eager faces before me could sense my anxiety. Luckily, I had learned to mask my trepidation in front of an audience as a classroom teacher; it was an acquired skill that came in handy on the speakers' circuit.

While I was generally anxious before an audience, I marveled at Maria's ability to address any crowd. She was absolutely fearless. So when I was invited to be one of the kickoff speakers to approximately five thousand real estate brokers at the San Diego Convention Center, I asked Maria to accompany me. She was unbelievably poised and passionate, and I was hoping that through an act of osmosis her cool demeanor would rub off on me.

As Maria and I were preparing for our speech, I suggested that we use metaphors pertaining to homes to try and relate to all the real estate gurus. We both agreed that creating a home environment was one of the key elements in the Freedom Writers' success. I suggested that we contrast our individual home experiences to the ones we created in Room 203 and the new home office I was renting. Whereas I, like most of the audience, had lived in beautiful homes, Maria and my students had not. Most of them had lived in small apartments or government-subsidized housing projects. Tragically, some of them had lived in cars, in shelters, or even been homeless.

While Maria and I were trying to weave our story into as many home analogies as we could conjure up, the coordinator for the event popped her head into our little room and asked, "Would you mind sharing your green room? Someone's here to give away a prize, but he'll only be here for a few minutes."

"Of course. Who is it?" I asked.

"Hank Aaron."

My heart skipped a beat. I reached for my cell phone and immediately called my dad to tell him I was about to meet his all-time hero.

"Dad, you're never going to believe who's going to share our green room."

"You have a green room?"

"Well, it's not actually green. It's just a little room with some designer teas and a really fancy fruit plate. But that's beside the point. They just asked if Hank Aaron can share our room."

"Are you kidding? Who else is in the room with you?"

"I'm here with Maria. Do you want me to get something signed for you?"

"No. Why don't you talk shop with him instead?" I knew "talking shop" meant baseball stories. After all, I had heard them all of my life. I hoped I could pull it off and make my dad proud in the process.

When Hank walked in, he looked like a sweet grandfather in a suit rather than a star athlete rounding the bases. There was no entourage, no fanfare, and no baseball paraphernalia.

"Hi, Mr. Aaron. My name is Erin Gruwell, and my father likes to claim that he named me in your honor." I didn't want to tell him that my mom actually took the credit for picking my name, but I thought it was a good opener. I introduced Maria, and she handed him a copy of our book.

"Thank you, ladies. I have a long flight back to Atlanta tomorrow, so this will be perfect for the plane. What's it about?"

Suddenly, we found ourselves telling Mr. Aaron about our adventures, talking about racism and our fears and about making a movie. Throughout our story, he would interject what it felt like to be one of the first African American baseball players in the Major Leagues, how he had received death threats, and how his story had also been made into a movie.

When the event coordinator came to get him, we asked if we could give him a hug.

"Absolutely. I'd like to stay in touch with you," he said as he was about to head to the stage. I pulled out a piece of paper and jotted down my cell phone number.

When he left, I immediately called my dad.

"Well?"

"Dad, he was amazing. We talked about his baseball career, segregation, standing up for what you believe in, movies, and you."

"I'm glad I made the list," he said, chuckling.

"I feel like we connected."

"I'm sure you did. You have an uncanny way of connecting with people. I may know how to scout ballplayers, but you sure know how to scout people. You always see the best in them."

"Thanks, Dad."

"I'm proud of you. Anyway, if you're speaking on the same platform as Rudy Giuliani and Hank Aaron, I should probably come to one of your speeches to see what all the hype is about."

"Okay, Dad, the next time I do something local, I'll let you know."

"Now go out on that stage and hit a grand slam," he said.

Two days after the speech, my phone rang while I was in a meeting. I didn't recognize the area code. When I answered, I heard a booming voice say, "Erin, this is your buddy, Hank. I just finished your book and I loved it."

I scribbled on a notepad to Faye, the new director of my nonprofit, "It's Hank Aaron!"

"Who?" She motioned.

"Hank Aaron," I whispered.

"Who's that?"

"You don't know who Hank Aaron is?" I mouthed.

"No."

"Erin, are you still there?" Hank asked.

"Oh yes, I'm sorry. I can't believe you read the book, but I'm even more shocked that you called."

"Well, the next time you are in Atlanta, I'd like you to come visit."

"I would be honored to, Mr. Aaron."

As I hung up, Faye asked, "Who's Hank Aaron?"

"How could you not know who Hank Aaron is?" I asked. I guess being a tomboy all those years finally paid off.

Some time later, when my father finally came to see me address an audience, I was so nervous. The event was filled with hundreds of educators, so I knew they'd be a receptive crowd. My dad sat in the front row with his chest puffed out. He cried all the way through my speech and was the first one to leap to his feet when I was finished.

After the event, my dad took me to lunch.

"Now I can see why you're so busy. It's amazing how similar our lives really are, Erin. When I first began scouting for the Reds, I was gone for weeks at a time. Although it's difficult, you get to see our country. I hope you never take for granted the people, their food, and their hospitality," he said.

I tried to always appreciate wherever I went, even if it was a town in the middle of nowhere. A day before I headed off to a tiny town on the border of Canada, I got an uncharacteristically frantic call from my dad. His usual gruffness was gone and he left a message saying that he needed "his Erin fix." I called him back, and we had an intense conversation and he told me how proud he was of me.

"Make sure you call me and check in while you're away. I love you," he said before he got off the phone.

So while I was on a plane, getting ready for takeoff, I noticed I had a message from my dad's home telephone number. When I checked the message, it was from my stepmom, Karen. She was panic stricken.

"Erin, please call me. It's an emergency."

Even though I overheard the flight attendant say, "Turn off your cell phones and all electronic equipment," I decided to call anyway.

When Karen answered the phone, she immediately said, "Erin, your father had a heart attack."

Her words didn't register.

"He died on his way to the hospital," she continued. By this point, she was hysterical.

I was numb. I just spoke to him. I was supposed to call him when I landed to let him know I was all right. I looked up and saw the flight attendant making her way back to me. She began to yell at me to turn off my phone.

I was sitting in a puddle jumper that held about twenty people. The plane was about to taxi down the tarmac. The man sitting next to me was clearly uncomfortable, as he had overheard my frantic conversation with Karen.

"You have to turn off your phone," the flight attendant said again, waving her finger at me.

"But my father just died," I wailed.

"I'm sorry, but you still have to turn off your phone," she said callously.

I wanted to scream, jump off the plane, cause a commotion, but I didn't. I simply turned off my phone and began to sob.

The hour flight to Sault Sainte Marie felt like an eternity. I was claustrophobic and I began to hyperventilate. My friend Drew, who was traveling with me, kept saying, "Breathe, Erin. Breathe."

When we landed, I wanted to rush off the airplane and buy another ticket to go home. But when we walked into the tiny terminal, I saw a smiling teacher holding up a handmade sign saying, "Welcome, Erin Gruwell." She looked so eager. I rushed to the bathroom, hoping she wouldn't notice me. Drew went straight to the ticket counter to see if we could take the first flight out, but since Sault Sainte Marie was so small, there was only one flight a day. We would have to wait until the next afternoon to even try to get a flight. "What are our other choices?" Drew demanded at the ticket counter. He was desperate and clearly shaken.

"You can rent a car and drive to Toronto, but it will take you about eight hours to get there. And you'll need a passport." We didn't have our passports with us.

"Are there any other options?"

"You can drive to Detroit, but that'll take you about ten hours."

The woman with the sign was just standing there. When I came back from the bathroom, she said, "There'll be a thousand people tomorrow, and they're so excited to see you," without any knowledge of the news I had just received.

Drew looked at the lady and said, "We have to cancel her engagement— her father just died." The woman stood there speechless.

"I'm calling Faye," Drew said.

"You can't call Faye—she's getting married today."

He did anyway. Faye was marrying her French fiancé at a Beverly Hills courthouse at any moment. Her entire family had flown down for the wedding. I couldn't deal with the guilt of letting down a thousand people and wrecking somebody's wedding, so I called Karen for guidance.

"I don't know if I can make it out of here. And there's a teacher here who says there are a thousand people expecting to hear me speak tomorrow."

"Erin, you need to honor your commitments. That's what your father would have wanted."

At that moment, I put my arm around Drew and said, "It's okay, we'll stay." I couldn't process guilt and grief at the same time.

"No," Drew said adamantly. "We've got to get you out of here."

But I agreed to stay. In an odd way, I wanted to honor my dad by honoring my commitment.

I asked the woman if she'd cancel the book signing after the event, though. I didn't want to see or talk to anyone. As we were driving to my hotel, I sat in the backseat, numb. I looked out the window and saw a bald eagle. I'd never seen a bald eagle before. It seemed to follow our car all the way to my hotel.

When I got to the hotel, I felt helpless. I called Karen again.

"Karen," I said, "while I was on the way to the airport this morning I saw the most amazing field of sunflowers." Karen was silent for a few moments and said, "Honey, that's just around the time your dad died."

"You are your father's daughter. Now more than ever, make him proud."

In the morning, I was supposed to address a packed gymnasium of teachers. I was scheduled to speak for an hour and a half. "You don't have to talk that long if you don't want to," my event sponsor said. Drew glared at her. He was furious. He thought she was being insensitive.

"As soon as you're done, we'll get you out of here," Drew said.

I just nodded.

I sat on the front row of bleachers and kept wondering how I was going to make it through my speech. I hadn't slept all night, and I was dehydrated from crying.

When I walked onto the basketball court, I tried to suppress all my sadness and let a story momentarily sweep me away. I went to another place. I told them a story about Maria and how Anne Frank's diary changed her life.

I looked up at the clock on the gym wall and noticed I had only ten minutes left.

Then I thought about the bald eagle. I stopped. I just stood there. There was utter silence. I could feel my legs begin to buckle and a sense of sadness begin to consume me. I felt like I was drowning and I was going to take a thousand people down with me.

My voice cracked, and I said, "I'm sorry, but my father died yesterday." Then I burst into tears. I told them about losing my father, and how the eagle I'd seen yesterday reminded me of a passage in Anne's diary: "Sometimes I feel like a bird in a cage, and I wish I could fly away." It was now time for me to fly home.

On the flight home, I wrote a letter to my father in my journal. I wanted to remember details, and I was consumed with the urge to write everything down before I forgot.

After I got home, my shock was replaced by sadness. Faye offered to cancel my Monday-night class with the Freedom Writers. But I now needed them in the same way that they usually needed me. Although we generally met at the university, tonight we were going to meet in my living room. Faye set up chairs in a circle. The Freedom Writers sat in absolute silence until I came down the stairs. I couldn't hold back my tears. Neither could they.

Jessica broke the silence. "You know what I remember most about Papa G? He invited us to his home, and that was the first white home I'd ever been in. He treated us like we were his family."

And suddenly, they all began to share stories. Stories about him dancing in Poland, or holding their hands in D.C., or being the only "dad" they ever knew. I'd lost a father, and some of them felt they had too.

I decided that I would host his memorial service at my home. Even though my father had always said, "Don't take your job home with you," he changed his tune when he saw the beautiful house I was renting. He loved it so much that he actually offered to help me buy it, but my landlady had no plans to sell it. Since everyone I knew had been to the house for one party or another, I figured my dad would want people to gather in my home rather than at a funeral parlor.

I called the gathering a "celebration of life." And in lieu of flowers, I set up a scholarship in his honor. Since he was the best teacher I ever had, I would perpetuate his memory by helping other teachers.

I began to have an even greater appreciation for the personal pain my students had gone through, realizing that they didn't have a psychologist like I did to help me through the grieving process, or the editor of the paper to write an obituary honoring their loved one like I did, or even the resources to set up a scholarship or host a memorial service. What they had was inner strength and each other. I would try to emulate their strength, and I would need them to get me through this.

The Freedom Writers offered to help me with the service. Sonia made programs, Melvin and Tony set up five hundred chairs in the backyard, some helped the caterers, and others greeted guests as they lined up to pay their respects. My students sang, told stories, and shared lessons they'd learned from Papa G.

Shortly after the funeral, I got a call from an insurance agent telling me that I was the beneficiary of a check for a few thousand dollars. I immediately thought about donating all the money to my father's scholarship fund, but my stepmom talked me out of it.

"Honey, your father wanted you to have that money," she said. "Do something special with it. Something that will make you remember him."

I knew exactly what to do. On the six-month anniversary of his death, I flew to New York and went to Tiffany's. The string of pearls that he had given me for graduation had been lost on one of my flights. I had been wearing a knockoff set that I bought for twenty bucks. I decided that since my signature had become my string of pearls I would buy the most beautiful pearls in his honor.

While I was standing at the Tiffany counter, I told the saleswoman why I was there and she helped me find the perfect set—a string-of-pearls necklace and matching earrings. When I tried them on, I felt my father. I started to cry, and the saleswoman got a little teary too.

As I was leaving Tiffany's, my cell phone rang. It was a number that I didn't recognize.

"Hello?"

"Hi, Erin, this is your old friend, Hank Aaron. How are you doing?"

I was shocked. "Not well," I stammered. "My dad just passed away."

"Oh, honey, I'm sorry to hear that."

"Today is the six-month anniversary, and so I did something symbolic. I just bought a strand of pearls and earrings that I can wear every day to think of my dad."

As we talked, I thought about Maria and her belief in "signs." Just like that moment we were in Times Square and we saw the photo of Anne Frank, this unsolicited phone call caused me to stop and think. As soon as I got off the phone with him, I called Maria to tell her what had just happened, secretly hoping that she'd say it wasn't merely a coincidence.

"It's a sign, Ms. G," she said, rather authoritatively. "Papa G is letting you know that he is looking out for you in the same way you look out for us."

CHAPTER 37

A couple days before the 2005 Oscars, Hilary Swank called me on my cell phone to announce, "Erin, I got the role!"

I was stunned. I had suggested Hilary at my first meeting with Richard, but I never actually believed it would come to fruition. After all, she already had an Oscar, and had now been nominated for a second.

Carol had forewarned me that there were a lot of gender politics in Hollywood. Apparently, women have a tough time opening films. Movies with female leads are generally referred to as "chick flicks," and if the studios want men to go see them, only a few women are perceived to have enough box office cachet to open a film.

Although several high-profile names had been bandied about to play me, I felt like most of them were too blond or too glamorous. I wanted somebody with substance. I wanted Hilary. Now, with the success of *Million Dollar Baby*, she suddenly had the keys to the kingdom.

When Hilary called, I was standing in the lobby of the San Francisco Marriott about to address several thousand principals. The new U.S. Secretary of Education, Margaret Spellings, was going to open the National Principal Association Conference, and I was slated to follow her. With Hilary on the phone, how was I supposed to focus on my speech? Suddenly, I was coming apart at the seams. I wanted to ask her a million questions, but at the same time I didn't want to come across as too neurotic.

As we talked, I began to feel like I was talking to one of my girlfriends. She was so genuine, so grounded. We shared our mutual respect for each other and then she said, "I know this sounds silly, but I have to go get my dress fitted."

"Oh my God, the Academy Awards ceremony is in two days. I think you're going to win again."

"I don't think I'm going to win this time. I'm honored just to be nominated. But I want to thank you for fighting for me!"

"That's my nature. I always fight for things I believe in!"

As I was gushing about her taking home another trophy, she wished me luck with the principals. When I got off the phone, I wondered how I was going to hold it together when I wanted to go shout through the streets of San Francisco: "Hilary is doing our movie!" Talking to Hilary made me feel kind of sassy, and since I was following the Secretary of Education, I decided to push the envelope a bit.

Since the Secretary of Education read statistics from a TelePrompTer for a half an hour to principals already mired down in minutia and political mandates, my opening line was "I'm not going to stand before you and talk about data or statistics or political slogans. I am going to talk to you about teaching to a kid and not to a test." The audience went crazy. They leaped to their feet in a spontaneous ovation. Unfortunately, the Secretary had already been escorted out of the building by the Secret Service, but I hoped that she would get wind of my comments. At the end of my speech, I told them that Hilary Swank was going to play me in the Freedom Writers movie and I hoped she would help bring the passion back to our profession by reminding people how important it is to believe in all kids.

A few weeks after my speech and Hilary's triumphant night at the Oscars, when she won her second Academy Award, Richard invited me to New York to have dinner with Hilary and her husband. I was so nervous. I wondered what to wear for something like this. Black. Definitely. All black.

When Richard and I walked into the restaurant, Hilary and her husband were already seated. I looked at her and felt like I was looking in the mirror. She had dark hair that looked like it was still a bit wet from the shower, a strong jaw, and she wasn't wearing a drop of makeup. She looked gorgeous in her black turtleneck and blue jeans. We hugged each other and instantly began to cry.

I sat next to her and we kept looking at each other, smiling, crying, and even holding each other's hands. It didn't feel real—and yet I'd never felt more present. I felt like she understood me, understood the story, and understood that it was bigger than we were.

I expected her to pick at a plain green salad with dressing on the side, but she immediately dove into the bread and suggested we order appetizers. When the waiter came, I was pleasantly surprised that she ordered appetizers and an entrée, and suggested that she was going to save room for dessert. With each passing moment, my preconceived notions about Hollywood actresses went out the window. She was on time, she was down-to-earth, she ate dessert, and she was so humble.

"Just think, I don't have to die in this film!" she said, and we all laughed.

"And you get to wear makeup," I added.

At that moment, a bottle of champagne was sent to our table with a note from Richard's wife, Ann: "To the three fighters: One who fights the system, one who fights to get movies made, and one who is always a knockout. Figure out which one is which."

Ann was right. We had all fought battles. Some won, some lost. But we kept on fighting. And I was confident that the battle wasn't over. In some ways, maybe it was just the beginning.

We took turns telling stories about our lives. The parallels were uncanny. It had been an uphill battle for all of us. Family rifts, sibling rivalries, and the search for identity.

The more we shared, the more I felt validated that Hilary was the perfect choice to play me. While we had our similarities, we also had differences. She told me about living in a trailer park, and I told her about growing up in a gated community. While I had gone on to college, she had gotten her GED. Hilary felt that she could identify with both me and my students. And what impressed me more than anything else was her passion. I knew she would do our story justice.

At the end of dinner, we made plans to meet the next day at Richard's apartment to watch some videos of the Freedom Writers and learn more about each other.

I wanted to do cartwheels. Hilary was perfect. Absolutely perfect. I got back to my hotel and did what I always did when I had good news. I reached for my cell phone and pushed the speed dial to call my trusty confidant.

Suddenly, my happiness plummeted and I fell apart. In my moment of exaltation, my natural instinct was to share my excitement with my dad.

With every milestone I'd ever faced, I was always able to call my dad, the one person I wanted to share good news with—and now I couldn't.

CHAPTER 38

S tanding in front of the art deco theater, things looked different yet oddly familiar. It had been over a decade since I brought Sharaud and my students to the Lido Theater in Newport Beach to see *Schindler's List,* and now we were previewing our film *Freedom Writers,* starring Hilary Swank, in front of an audience of the Who's Who of Orange County.

The audience was filled with business people and their spouses; we were surrounded by a well-heeled crowd of movers and shakers, dressed in designer outfits and pin-striped suits. Thankfully, this time no one was grabbing their pearls, clutching their purses, or acting uncomfortable.

When I brought my students to this very theater years ago, nobody wanted to sit next to them, but tonight, not only did we pack the house, but these people came to honor the accomplishments of my amazing former students, the Freedom Writers, whose lives were going to unfold before them. Some were married, some had kids, but they were still the most functional dysfunctional family around.

The fraternity of Freedom Writers were there to answer all the questions of "Where are the Freedom Writers today?" And "Do you still see each other?" And "Is the story true?" They answered the questions with ease and such pride. Ironically, the community that at one point pushed us away was now the same community embracing us. I couldn't help but revel in how far we've all come.

Once the film wrapped, Paramount chose to release the film over Martin Luther King holiday weekend. The release date was rife with symbolism.

When I asked the studio if we could host an advance screening, they accepted. I chose Newport Beach because the roots of our story were there, and it felt like an appropriate homecoming.

I asked the studio if I could have two students help me introduce the film. I invited both Sharaud and Maria to address the crowd with me. Maria had been a consultant on the script and Sharaud played a school security guard in the film. The three of us had recently been traveling all over the United States addressing groups.

As I was about to thank everyone for coming this evening, I couldn't help but reflect on our odyssey. Suddenly I was overcome with emotion. So many unexpected things had happened to all of us. My father wasn't there to enjoy it, but at least there was an amazing actor who would immortalize him. My ex-husband and I had only talked once in nearly ten years, but now Patrick Dempsey was playing him. Maybe if my ex-husband had been Patrick Dempsey in real life, I would have never been a teacher in the first place. So, this was the one area where Hollywood could take some liberties for the sake of art.

But what was a sad reminder of art imitating life occurred prior to filming—Hilary and her husband separated. As she was falling deeper and deeper in love with her "Freedom Writers" she too knew what it was like to be alone. I couldn't help but think that it made portraying my divorce all the more real, all the more painful.

As I introduced Maria, the audience applauded. Gone were her days with the ankle bracelet and the plastered bangs, baggy pants, and bad attitude. She was now a college graduate who spent the majority of her time touring the country and fearlessly telling her story to the very people who once rejected her. She was wearing three-inch stilettos that made her just over five feet, a cocktail dress, and she had a French tip manicure. She was poised and elegant. As she picked up the microphone, she said, "We all yearn to find our rightful place in the world. At an early age I found mine. My place was with my people, my family, who mostly were second-generation gang members. My place was in my neighborhood, home to gangs, drugs, poverty, and hopelessness. The color of my skin, my history, and my last name never allowed me to forget my place. Growing up I only knew two things for sure: One, that the only rightful place I would ever have was the one I was born into, and two, that no matter what, I would have to fight every day of my life."

The audience was captivated. She had no notes, no TelePrompTer. She spoke extemporaneously, and her passion was penetrating. Maria recounted her life, touching on the fact that she had witnessed her cousin's murder, visited her father in prison, and watched her mother work three jobs her entire childhood. She added "all of my experiences growing up were a confirmation that I had to fight and a reminder of my place in the world."

The audience was thoroughly engrossed in what Maria was saying. They hung on every word. "My story can be found in the eyes of young people on any street corner of our country who are struggling and fighting. Some will drop out of high school, some will not see their eighteenth birthday, others will end up in prison, and some may become teenage parents. They all share a feeling that was once far too familiar for me, hopelessness."

As Maria said the word *hopelessness,* I couldn't help but marvel at the contrast between the young woman standing before them and the young girl I once taught. She was now a beacon of hope and a role model to so many.

She concluded her speech by saying, "As I stand before you, I am humbled, because I was supposed to be one of those statistics. Life taught me at a very early age to see the world for what it is, but the lessons I learned in Room 203 taught me to see the world for what it could be. My only hope today is that we can one day recognize our ability to serve others, and by doing so we will make a difference. Today is the day that our passion and our dream will be one. Because now without a doubt we know that we have the responsibility to grab a young kid by the hand and teach him or her how to find their rightful place in the world."

Maria thanked the audience; they leapt to their feet. Her humility reminded me of Miep. She was not there to simply tell her story. She was giving a voice to the voiceless.

Sharaud, who had stood beside Maria through her speech, was beaming. In my introduction I told the audience that Sharaud was now a teacher. He had chosen a career path that couldn't have been scripted by a Hollywood screenwriter. Sharaud had chosen to become a high school English teacher. He had just been hired to teach ninth-grade English at Polytechnic High School. He had been kicked out of Poly years before for bringing a gun to school. Now, in a marvelous twist of fate, the same principal who had expelled Sharaud from Washington Middle School was his principal at Poly.

A lot had changed for Sharaud in those years since high school. He stood tall and confident now, and he was no longer the defiant kid who challenged me or called me names. Sharaud, dressed in a suit and tie, took the microphone from Maria and effortlessly began to tell his story.

He was at ease in front of the crowd and commanded their respect. Every day he waltzed into a room and addressed an audience of the toughest teens Long Beach had to offer. Sharaud was now teaching all the teenagers in the district who were disciplinary transfers. Like him, these students had rap sheets and files filled with comments from principals and probation officers, and they had threatened teachers. Sharaud was as comfortable in front of those kids as he was before this affluent Newport Beach audience.

"Years ago, a troubled teen with no direction had the best and worst day of his life," he began, "when he was caught bringing a gun to Poly High School. Because I didn't fit in anywhere, I was an easy target and would get into fights every day. When I got tired of running, tired of my knuckles being swollen, tired of being an outcast, I armed myself with a gun so people wouldn't mess with me. But I went from wanting to defend myself to wanting to get revenge."

He went on to explain how his aggressive mentality could have gotten him killed or a life sentence. Sharaud said, "Getting caught with a gun at Poly turned out to be my salvation, because I was sent to Wilson High. My first day there was Ms. G's first day as well. Being in Ms. G's class allowed me to bridge the gap between my goals and my reality."

I couldn't help but think about how he was the catalyst for everything that happened. The note with the racist caricature of Sharaud triggered something in me that changed everything. That was the moment I realized I had to teach with my heart.

"Would you believe that the guy who once carried a pistol is now responsible for America's youth? I now teach English at Poly High School, the same school I was kicked out of. I'm blessed to be able to embrace the bad kids. It's truly a gift because I was once one of those kids. I consider it an accomplishment to serve as a role model for those who have no role models."

I thought about all the times I'd witnessed young people look up to him at speaking engagements, book signings, or talking to students at schools. Maybe through his example they'd come to the realization that they didn't have to hit a ball over a fence, slam-dunk a ball in a basket, or even be on MTV flashing their *bling bling* to make it. All these students had to do was look at Sharaud and say I look like him and I talk like him and someday I too can be like him.

"As a matter of fact," Sharaud continued, "I just got a student transferred into my class who shot a kid in the butt with a BB gun. He's fourteen, trying to get his life on track. I just hope that my students strive to be more than society expects of them. If I can help them find their vehicle for success, then I can go along for the ride."

Someone from the audience blurted out, "When did you change, Sharaud?" Sharaud smiled and said, "Change wasn't instant for me, but it was inevitable. I can't tell you when, but I know that it happened. I stand before you because it happened. It's amazing what you turn into when you have the right people helping you, giving you advice at the right time."

That seemed like the perfect segue to introduce the film. I said, "I hope you enjoy our story," and the three of us took our seats. As the lights dimmed, I leaned over to Sharaud and Maria and whispered, "Now it's your turn!"

ERIN GRUWELL, the Freedom Writers, and her nonprofit organization, The Freedom Writers Foundation, have received many awards, including the prestigious Spirit of Anne Frank Award, and have appeared on *The Oprah Winfrey Show*, *Primetime Live*, *Good Morning America*, and *The View*, to name a few. All 150 Freedom Writers went on to graduate from high school. Erin Gruwell is also a charismatic motivational speaker who spreads her dynamic message to students, teachers, and businesspeople around the world. She lives in Southern California.